JOINT APPLICATION DEVELOPMENT

Second Edition

JANE WOOD

DENISE SILVER

JOHN WILEY & SONS, INC.

NEW YORK • CHICHESTER • BRISBANE • TORONTO • SINGAPORE

Publisher: K. Schowalter
Editor: T. Hudson
Managing Editor: Robert S. Aronds
Editorial Production & Design: G&H SOHO, Inc.

Designations used by companies to distinguish their products are often claimed as trademarks. In all instances where John Wiley & Sons, Inc. is aware of a claim, the product names appear in initial capital or all capital letters. Readers, however, should contact the appropriate companies for more complete information regarding trademarks and registration.

The text is printed on acid-free paper.

This publication is designed to provide accurate and authoritative information in regard to the subject matter covered. It is sold with the understanding that the publisher is not engaged in rendering legal, accounting, or other professional service. If legal advice or other expert assistance is required, the services of a competent professional person should be sought.

Library of Congress Cataloging-in-Publication Data:

Wood, Jane, 1946–
    Joint application development / Jane Wood, Denise Silver. — 2nd ed.
        p.   cm.
    Includes bibliographical references and index.
    ISBN 0-471-04299-4 (paper : acid-free paper)
    1. System design—Methodology.   I. Silver, Denise.   II. Title.
QA76.9.S88W65   1995
004.2'1—dc20   94-33875
                                                           CIP

Printed in the United States of America
10 9 8 7 6 5 4 3

Excel is a registered trademark of the Microsoft Corp.
Excelerator is a registered trademark of Intersolv Inc.
FAST is a registered trademark of MG Rush Systems, Inc.
GroupSystems V is a registered trademark of the Ventana Corp.
Information Engineering Facility (IEF) is a registered trademark of Texas Instruments.
Information Engineering Workbench (IEW) is a registered trademark of KnowledgeWare, Inc.
Information Mapping is a registered trademark of Information Mapping, Inc.
JAD is a registered trademark of IBM Corp.
MeetingWorks for Windows is a registered trademark of Enterprise Solutions.
Microsoft is a registered trademark of the Microsoft Corp.
Post-it is a registered trademark of the 3M Corp.
Rapid Applications Development (RAD) is a registered trademark of James Martin.
The METHOD is a registered trademark of ATLIS Performance Resources, Inc.
VisionQuest is a registered trademark of Intellect Corp.
Windows is a registered trademark of the Microsoft Corp.
WordPerfect is a registered trademark of the WordPerfect Corp.

The Facilitators' Charter

A facilitator:

- *Guides without directing*

- *Brings about change without disruption*

- *Helps people self-discover new approaches and solutions to problems*

- *Knocks down walls which have been built between people, while preserving structure of value*

- *And above all appreciates people as people*

All this must be done without leaving any fingerprints.

—From a flipchart hanging on the wall at a Facilitator's Network meeting in Hartford, Connecticut

For
Allison and Jeremy
&
Michael and Sarah

"*A study of over 60 projects . . . showed that those projects that did not use JAD missed up to 35% of required functionality resulting in the need for up to 50% more code.*"

—Capers Jones

"*The successful use of JAD has pushed its use beyond traditional applications of the process. JAD is being used successfully for strategic systems and data planning, as well as for projects outside the IS community.*"

—General Electric

"*How do you design a system that users really want? . . . You can't. What you <u>can</u> do is help users design the systems they want.*"

—David Freedman

PREFACE

This book describes JAD™, a process that was originally developed for designing computer-based business systems. JAD (for Joint Application Development) centers on a three- to five-day workshop that brings together business area people (users) and IS (Information Systems) professionals. Under the direction of a facilitator, these people define anything from high-level strategic plans to detailed system specifications. The products of the workshop can include definitions of business processes, prototypes, data models, and so on.

The advantages of using JAD include a dramatic shortening of the time it takes to complete a project. Equally important, JAD improves the quality of the final product by focusing on the up-front portion of the development life cycle, thus reducing the likelihood of errors that are expensive to correct later on.

The first edition of this book appeared in 1989. At the time, JAD was just over 10 years old, and had not yet become widely known. No one else had yet published a book on the subject. We were introduced to the process in 1985, and in our travels to various conferences over the next few years, we met many people who wanted to know more about it. Most especially, they wanted specifics—a how-to guide. That's when we decided to write the first version of the book—a detailed, cookbook description that answered such questions as:

- What do you need to implement JAD in an organization?
- *Who* does what during each step of the process?
- What are the ingredients for a successful JAD?

Much has changed in the five years since the first edition. Many more companies are using JAD. Organizations of JAD facilitators have formed all over the United States and in Europe. But perhaps the most interesting change is that JAD isn't just for systems development anymore. People soon discovered that JAD techniques could be applied to almost *any* decision-making activity. So instead of "JAD sessions," many people began to hold "facilitated meetings."

Consequently, we have much material in this edition beyond "just JAD." If you master these techniques, you will be able to use them beyond computer systems topics. You will be able to lead facilitated meetings on just about any subject.

As in the first edition, this book guides you through the five phases of JAD. It includes coverage of CASE, visual aids, sample agendas, and lots of live JAD anecdotes. It describes the psychology of JAD and offers a variety of tools and techniques for dealing with the "people" aspects that can make the difference between a productive meeting and a rambling bull session that accomplishes nothing.

The research for this edition included a survey that we sent to several facilitators' groups in this country and in Europe. This has allowed us to glean a great deal of insight from these facilitators who have, in total, run thousands of facilitated sessions. We have included many of their ideas, tips, and war stories.

We also researched the growing literature on JAD. In this, we were considerably aided by the online and CD-ROM research tools that have proliferated in the libraries we used. Particularly helpful was the CD-ROM service called Computer Select, which gave us immediate access to the full text of articles. It saved hours of retrieving and copying from microforms or hard copy back issues. This research yielded an extensive bibliography.

The increased interest in JAD was evident during this library research. To find articles on JAD, we used to have to look under the "systems development" category. Recently a separate index entry was added for "JAD."

New in this edition are discussions of RAD, prototyping, participatory design, and a complete chapter on meetingware (also known as groupware). We added more coverage on group dynamics (and group dysfunction as well). We have described many techniques people use to promote creative thinking in their sessions. Finally, since many people told us they wanted to know more about how to market their services (that is, how to "sell" JAD within their own companies), we added a chapter on how to market facilitated services.

Perhaps you are skeptical because you have read other systems development books. You have plodded through turgid prose, been slowed by technical jargon, and found you cannot translate an academic process into something that works for you. This book is written for practical use. After reading it, you will know how to conduct all phases of JAD—from interviewing users, to running the sessions, to preparing the final document.

As you read this book, consider what our industry is up against—the real world of backlogs, time and budget constraints, and endless meetings about more projects to complete with fewer people. JAD will not rid the world of these realities. And the tens of billions of lines of Cobol code that are maintained today will still be there. But JAD does guarantee that you will get better results in a shorter time. Business needs will be clearly identified. Computer programs will require less maintenance later on. All this translates into quantifiable savings of time, money, and effort.

Jane Wood
Denise Silver

Philadelphia
January, 1995

ACKNOWLEDGMENTS

For you, the reader, acknowledgments are probably something to skim over quickly before getting into the real nitty gritty. But for us, this was an enjoyable part to write. We are delighted to acknowledge those who helped with this project.

First, we would like to thank the Provident Mutual Life Insurance Company. The company has been progressive enough to bring in a process such as JAD and supportive enough to provide the necessary resources to make it work.

For his many contributions to the book, we are once again indebted to Denise's husband, Bruce Schwartz. He did the grunt work for our research—combing the indexes, scanning the data bases, and retrieving most of the articles. He watched the kids, Allison and Jeremy, so that Denise could work with her co-author. He also read, edited, and critiqued the entire text, and rewrote some sections. Bruce is a firm believer in Rule 17 of *The Elements of Style* ("Omit needless words!"). Much of his contribution consists of words you will not read. And he is still master of the semicolon.

We deeply appreciate the help of Michael Kowalski for his creative concepts and numerous research contributions. This master of the metaphor suggested several communication techniques that helped bring elusive concepts to life. When challenged with a question, he was able to find the answer, along with supporting documentation from the most obscure sources.

For their help with our research, we thank the librarians at Drexel University, the University of Pennsylvania, and Rutgers University in Camden, New Jersey.

We thank everyone in the Facilitator's Network group for having us at their meetings in Hartford, Connecticut. Their sessions have been a great source of inspiration and comradery.

We thank Terri Hudson, our editor at John Wiley and Sons, Denise Brigham (for her information based on years of facilitation experience and for being our link to the Facilitators RoundTable group), Liz Davidson (for her valuable research), Dan Bartoes (for his helpful conversations including an afternoon conference call where we benefited from his extensive experience with JAD across the life cycle), Andrea Tannenbaum (for her comprehensive descriptions of her facilitation work), Sue Leonard (for being our link to the Midwest Facilitators' User Group), Lucy Hancock (for her contributions on creative techniques to use in group sessions), Alan Zemel (for his valuable expertise in the technical aspects of word processing), Mike Cavaliere (for his information about the evolution of JAD and other tidbits), Carol Sullivan (for being our link to IBM, the JAD originator), Paul Taylor (for overseas conversations on JAD and RAD, and for being our link to the European JAD User Group), Earl Brochu (for his prolific viewpoints on JAD and for sending us copies of his column in *Computing Canada*), Betty Johannessen (for her help in connection with the Facilitator's Network), Susan Burk (for her valuable comments on her facilitation work), Michael Kettelhut (for his informative articles about group dynamics and JAD), Plesman Publications Ltd. (for sending us back issues of *Computing Canada,* which we were unable to find in the stacks of our local libraries), Erran Carmel (for his comprehensive research on electronic meetings and participatory design), Marc Devlin (for being our link to the Southwest JAD Users Group), Sarah Major (for her help with some illustrations), Marc Garber (for use of his dining room table), Anna Schwartz (for the use of her apartment while she was in Florida), Elizabeth Taransky (for all her guidance), and Marvin and Claire Silver (who let us set up our writing retreat in their lovely Ventnor condo overlooking the bay).

We thank everyone who responded to our JAD survey. You will read many of their comments in this book. They gave us a global perspective!

Finally, we would like to thank the proprietors and waitresses of our favorite eateries in the Delaware Valley, where we spent hours at a time working on this project. These were Original Pizza, Gearo's Restaurant, the Windsor Diner, Au Bon Pain, and food courts everywhere. We owe a great deal to the endless cup of decaf.

We are fortunate to have had the help and support of all these people.

CONTENTS

PART ONE: IS JAD FOR YOU?   1

1. WHAT IS JAD?   3

    Where Did JAD Come From?   4
    How Systems Are Designed   4
    The Five Phases of JAD   7
    Using This Book   10
    About the Survey   13

2. WHY PEOPLE USE JAD   15

    Who Uses JAD?   16
    Trends Driving the Use of JAD   17
    How Are Companies Using JAD?   23
    A Few Short JAD Stories   24

3. JAD JARGON   29

    Joint Application *Design* or *Development*?   29
    A Process with Many Names   30
    JAD Leader or Facilitator?   31
    Business Process or Work Flow?   32
    What is Consensus, Really?   32
    The Word JAD   33

PART TWO: HOW TO DO A JAD   35

4. THE JAD TEAM AND HOW TO SELECT IT   37

    Executive Sponsor   38
    Facilitator   39
    Scribe   42
    Full-Time Participants   45

On-Call Participants   48
Observers   48

5. PHASE 1: JAD PROJECT DEFINITION   51

Open Issues and Assumptions   52
Getting the Management Perspective   53
Tips on Running Successful Interviews   56
The Management Definition Guide   61
Scheduling the Session   67

6. PHASE 2: RESEARCH   75

Getting Familiar with the Business   75
Documenting Data Requirements   77
Documenting Business Processes   78
Gathering Preliminary Information   89
The Session Agenda   91

7. PHASE 3: PREPARATION   95

The Working Document   95
Training the Scribe   99
Visual Aids   101
The Pre-Session Meeting   107
Setting Up the Meeting Room   109
How to Prevent PSS (Pre-Session Stress)   111
Checklists   113

8. PHASE 4: THE SESSION   117

Opening the Session   118
Assumptions   121
Data Requirements   121
Business Processes   123
Screens   126
Reports   138
Other Agenda Items   140
Open Issues   141
When Should the Scribe Take Notes?   143
Evaluating the Session   143
Closing the Session   144

9. PHASE 5: THE FINAL DOCUMENT 149

Producing the Final Document 149
Information Mapping 153
Editing 155
Assembling the Final Document 156
The Review Meeting 158
Approving the Document—The Final Okay 160
Changing Requirements after the Session 160

PART THREE: SESSION PSYCHOLOGY 163

10. JAD BUSTERS (OR HOW TO LEAD A GOOD JAD ASTRAY) 165

Compromise on Management Commitment 166
Skimp on the Participants 166
Spread Out the Sessions over Time 167
Ignore the People in the Trenches 167
Use An Untrained Facilitator 168
Abandon Your Own Authority 168
Stumble through High-Tech Tools 169
Muddle Them with Modeling 170
Talk Tekkie 170
Be Too Prepared 171
Take Too Long to Distribute the Final Document 171
In Summary 172
The Ten JAD Commandments 172

11. GROUP DYNAMICS 175

Group Dysfunction 175
Building Group Identity 179
Having the Right People in the Room 181
Preventing Scope Creep 183
Staying Flexible 184
When Should the Facilitator Interrupt? 185
Starting on Time 186
How to Handle Conflict 186
Chilling the Dominator 189
Encouraging Shy Users 190
Stifling Sidebar Conversations 190

12. THE FACILITATOR'S REPERTOIRE   193

 Communicate Well   193
 Separate the Idea from the Person   194
 Show a Natural Interest   194
 Listen Well   194
 Listen with the Eyes Too   195
 Maintain Control   195
 Empower the Group   196
 Handle Uncertainty   196
 Be Quick to Connect   196
 Focus on Business, Not Systems   197
 Keep the Role Clearly Defined   197
 Nurture the Innate Qualities   197

PART FOUR: TOOLS AND TECHNIQUES   199

13. PROMOTING CREATIVITY   201

 Creative Thinking Exercises   202
 Brainstorming   207
 Harvesting Ideas   210
 Nominal Group Technique with Post-it Notes   214
 Session Boosters   219
 Tips on Using These Techniques   221
 Using Humor   223

14. DECIDING BETWEEN ALTERNATIVES   227

 Six Steps to Group Decision   228
 Analyzing the Numbers   232

15. USING TOOLS IN THE SESSION   235

 Word Processors   237
 Scribe Forms   238
 CASE Tools   238
 Prototyping   251

16. MEETINGWARE   255

 What Is Meetingware?   255
 How Meetingware Can Help   257

Caveats and Cautions   260
When to Use Meetingware (And When Not To)   264
Meetingware Do's and Don'ts   266
Tips for Facilitators   267
How Companies are Using Meetingware   270
Some Statistics on Productivity   271
How to Justify Purchasing Meetingware   272

17. HANDLING LARGE PROJECTS   275

A Multiple JAD Marathon   276
Planning JADs   280
Jadding with Icosahedrons   281

PART FIVE: JAD AND BEYOND   283

18. JAD ACROSS THE LIFE CYCLE   285

Typical JAD Topics   285
Facilitating Across the Life Cycle   286
A JAD of Many Phases   295

19. BREAKING OUT OF THE LIFE CYCLE   303

Strategic Planning   304
Downsizing a Department   305
Defining a Corporate Policy   307
Prioritizing Projects   311

20. SON OF JAD: RELATED METHODOLOGIES   315

Rapid Application Development   315
Participatory Design   322
Empowering Groups   323

21. MARKETING YOUR SERVICES   327

Who Are You Selling To?   327
Know Thy Customer   329
Want to Buy A JAD?   331
Expanding Your Business   334
Benefits of Facilitated Sessions   336

PART SIX: IN CLOSING   341

22. JAD ANECDOTES   343

     A Review Meeting Does Not a JAD Make   343
     Mini-JADs and JAD-Lite   345
     A Good Agenda Goes Awry   345
     A Voice Response JAD   346
     Sleeper JADs   349

23. ASSURING JAD SUCCESS   355

     The Pilot Project   355
     Setting JAD Criteria   356
     Training Facilitators   357
     Facilitator User Groups   361
     How Do You Measure JAD Success?   363
     Charging Back Your Services   366
     Internal Consulting   367
     JAD Contracts   368
     The Evolution of JAD   369
     Conclusion   372

     Appendix A   Scribe Forms for the Management Definition Guide   375
     Appendix B   Scribe Forms for the JAD Session   385
     References   391
     Index   395

PART
1

IS JAD FOR YOU?

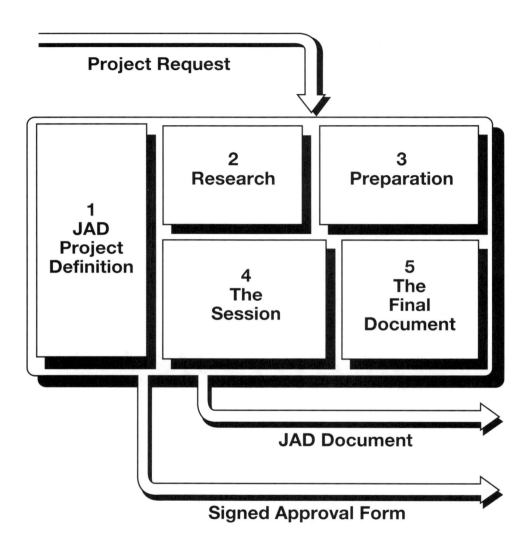

ONE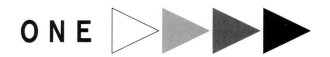

WHAT IS JAD?

Traditionally, JAD has been a joint venture between users and data processing professionals; thus the name *Joint Application Development*. In recent years, it has become a joint venture among any people who need to make decisions affecting multiple areas of an organization. It centers around a structured workshop (called a JAD session) where people come together to plan projects, design computer systems, or make business decisions. It involves a detailed agenda, visual aids, a facilitator who moderates the session, and a scribe who records the agreed-upon requirements. It culminates in a final document containing all the decisions made by the group.

In 1985, we brought JAD into our organization, the Provident Mutual Life Insurance Company. Nine years and more than 50 facilitated sessions later, we have enhanced JAD to include five distinct phases. We have used it for all kinds of projects including defining requirements for insurance applications, selecting software packages, and developing corporate policy. We have found it helpful for any kind of effort that involves decisions among people from more than one department.

For systems development projects, users prefer the JAD process because they become directly involved in the development effort. IS (Information Systems) people prefer it because the facilitator (whose main role is to work with end users) handles the tasks of coordinating and documenting the system requirements, as well as dealing with some of the delicate politics. This allows IS project managers and their staffs more time to concentrate directly on the nuts-and-bolts of systems development and programming.

WHERE DID JAD COME FROM?

In 1977, Chuck Morris and Tony Crawford of IBM conceived some innovative ways of getting users and IS to agree on requirements and design specifications. Their approach was loosely derived from another IBM methodology called Business Systems Planning. The first JAD sessions were held at IBM's offices in Raleigh, North Carolina.

> The folks in MIS were having trouble making up their minds, so IBM suggested sitting them down with representatives of the user community to talk about requirements. When these talks turned into orders, IBM realized they had a technique worth developing. (CASE Strategies 1989)

From this, JAD was born. In 1980, IBM Canada adopted and refined the process. Since then, it has been used by large and small companies around the world for all kinds of applications. There are insurance JADs, manufacturing JADs, and utility company JADs. There are JADs for strategic planning, defining requirements, estimating the costs of large-scale projects, and creating test plans. There are even JADs to plan other JADs.

People use various approaches to organize and run interactive design sessions. The process described in this book is based on IBM's original JAD.

Before looking at the five phases of JAD, let's explore how systems are traditionally designed.

HOW SYSTEMS ARE DESIGNED

Henry Ford was not the first to manufacture automobiles. The great innovation that he brought to industry was the assembly line—a method of *organizing* machinery, materials, and labor so that a car could be put together much faster and cheaper than ever before. The JAD process does something similar for computer systems development.

The goal in systems development is simply stated: Identify what the users really need and then set up a system or process that will provide it. Traditional methods for defining these needs have several built-in delay factors that get worse as more people become involved.

Traditional Systems Design

In most organizations, the systems development life cycle begins with the identification of a need, the assignment of a project leader and team, and often, the selection of a catchy acronym for the project. The leader pursues a series of separate meetings with the people who will use the system or be affected by it.

The leader continues these meetings over time. Often the key people involved are not so easy to reach. But eventually, having documented everything possible, the leader translates copious notes into a personal terminology. That's when it becomes apparent that the requirements from, say, Accounting, don't mesh with what the Sales department wants. So the leader calls Sales and finds out the contact there is in the field and will not be back until tomorrow. Next day the leader reaches Sales, gets the information, calls Accounting, and of course the person in Accounting is now out of the office, and so on.

When everyone is finally in agreement, alas, the leader discovers that even *more* people should have been consulted because their needs require something entirely different. In the end, everyone is reluctant to "sign off" on the specifications.

Other times, signing off comes easily. But when the system is delivered, it often has little to do with what the users really need:

> A user sign off is a powerless piece of paper when matched against the fury of top management. (Wetherbe 1991)

Slow communication and *long feedback time* is one reason the traditional process is so time-consuming. You can see why the communication problem grows worse as more people must be brought into consensus.

Other problems with traditional systems design methods can be described, in broad terms, as *psychological* and *political*. They result in such problems as:

- The *we-versus-they* gap that forms when users and IS remain sheltered in their own environments. As the gap widens, users begin to view their IS departments as a kind of electronic priesthood of technical enthusiasts who think they know exactly what the users want without even having to ask. The users see IS as an ivory tower of bits and bytes commanding users to "open your mouth, close your eyes, here comes another system surprise."

  > When the traditional systems analyst and potential end users first meet face to face, they come from widely different cultures. It is rather like a Victorian missionary first entering an African village. (Martin 1984)

- The *I've-changed-my-mind* gap that happens when meetings are spread over time. What users want this week can be substantially different from what they wanted last week. Such changes are only natural. But you do not want to spend your time documenting these ongoing changes in a series of separate meetings. You need to nail down the specifications all at once with everyone present, thereby getting group consensus at that point in time.

- The *tunnel-vision* gap when people designing systems assume that the people using a system are confined to one department only. When designing systems, people often involve only the department that made the original request. On the contrary, often the best information is gained from *outside* the department.

- The *separate-views* gap that exists when people work apart from one another. Separate meetings breed separate views of what the system should do. People have their own individual ideas of how the system should be designed. On the other hand, when everyone participates in the same session, a common view of the system is established.

For these reasons, the traditional ways simply don't work. For example, James C. Wetherbe, professor of Management Information Systems at the University of Minnesota, reported on a study of 76 data processing systems:

> Wetherbe noted with horror . . . that every single one of the 76 systems examined required revisions to even *approximate* management's requirements. (Freedman 1991)

Systems Design Using JAD

JAD centers around one structured workshop session. Everyone gets together in a room and talks it out. Everyone hears what the rest of the group has to say. There's no delay between question and answer and no "telephone tag" or waiting for memos to come back. This approach brings the following characteristics to the systems design process.

Commitment

Participants in the session are under a mandate from management to get the problem solved. Mandates alone cannot guarantee commitment, of course. But the participants' involvement in the design process gives them a vested interest in the final product. This is the source of true commitment. From the start, they are involved in building the application—so they want it to succeed. Everyone needed to make decisions is there in the same room. They define business processes, data models, and screens. They see the results on a whiteboard in front of them. They work together in an organized forum until everyone agrees, "Yes, that prototype works for us." No delays like, "Well, let's run it by Marketing," because Marketing is right there. All of it is done in three to five days. The participants emerge from the workshop with a product they have all agreed to. The responsibility is shared.

Group Cohesion

The *physical* and *social* settings of the workshop encourage bonds among participants that make them want to work together. They see each other in the same room every day, drinking coffee from the same pot. It doesn't take long to get to know each other. They are isolated from their normal work environments and, hence, from their "home-grown" ways of doing things. The resulting camaraderie is not unlike the group spirit that develops among people who sit on jury duty or find themselves lost at sea.

Productive Meetings

JAD eliminates many of the problems with traditional meetings. As you know, the business world is filled with meetings. They say managers spend between 30 percent and 70 percent of their time in meetings. Taking a conservative estimate of 10 hours of meetings per week, managers spend more than 20,000 hours of their lives in meetings. In this country alone, more than 20 million meetings are held daily. Most companies spend between 7 and 15 percent of their personnel budgets directly on meetings.

Yet meetings are not well regarded as a productive form of work. Sue Leonard (a facilitator at Amoco Oil Company) uses the quotes in Figure 1.1 to illustrate this point.

The fact is, the average meeting has no written agenda and its purpose is completed only half the time. You cannot entirely eliminate these meetings. (How could you possibly reengineer a business process without getting the people together?) But you can take the traditional grind out of these meetings. JAD turns meetings into workshops. These workshops are less frequent, more structured, and more productive. An agenda provides the structure. A facilitator directs the process. Visual aids clarify concepts being discussed. And the group dynamics, with constant feedback, stimulates creativity.

THE FIVE PHASES OF JAD

A favorite endeavor of anyone involved in defining a process is to divide it into phases. So it is with JAD. The process evolves from a definite start ("Help, we need a new system!") to a clear finish ("Here is the final product."). JAD has five phases. Each is covered in detail in Chapters 5 through 9. The following discussion illustrates these phases, using as an example a project where you have been hired to develop a special-purpose robot to prepare and serve meals in the corporate dining room. (Good help is so hard to find these days.) As you review the phases, notice how each one ties into the one that follows.

Figure 1.1

Phase 1: JAD Project Definition

This is where all projects begin. In the first phase of designing the robot, you (the facilitator of the JAD session) interview the managers from user departments (those who requested the robot) and IS (those who will build it). These meetings identify the robot's purpose (Will it do cooking, gardening, or back rubs?), scope (Who will use it and how often?), and objectives (How delicious must the food taste?). Functions are identified (Exactly what do you want from this robotic cook—Eggs Benedict every morning in bed or just a bagel on the run?). You list some basic assumptions (the robot should keep to a low-fat menu) and identify open issues (one person prefers that the menu include the finest Chablis, while the other wants the house wine). What you gather in these meetings is used to create a document called the *Management Definition Guide.*

In this phase, you also identify the JAD team and schedule the session. A successful session depends on having the right people in the room. They must be able to make binding decisions for their departments. In the robot example, all departments directly affected by the robot should be represented. Much of Chapter 4 tells how to select these people.

Phase 2: Research

This phase involves gathering more details about the user requirements. In the robot example, you meet with the actual people who will use it. You familiarize yourself with the existing business processes. (Do they already have a robot? What problems are they having with it? What enhancements do they need?) New business processes are defined. Proposed definitions are gathered for data elements, screens (this is a screen-driven robot system), and reports. Design issues are considered (How will the robot benedict the eggs, cacciatore the chicken, and bourguignon the boeuf? And what are all the physical motions required to flip a pancake?) Based on this research, an agenda is prepared listing what needs to be decided in the session.

Phase 3: Preparation

Everything you need for the session is made ready in this phase. You prepare visual aids and a *Working Document.* Flip charts and overhead transparencies, combined with some other interesting techniques, allow you to steer users through defining their requirements. The Working Document, which contains the proposed requirements gathered in Phase 2, is the basis for what will be covered in the session.

Phase 4: The Session

This is the heart of JAD—the actual workshop session. For a few days (anywhere from one to five days), you guide the team of robot designers in defining requirements using the Working Document as a guide. This includes defining business processes, data models, and perhaps building a prototype. Agreed-upon decisions are documented for the final document.

Phase 5: The Final Document

The information captured in the session is used to produce the *Final Document.* This comprehensive synthesis of robot requirements is compiled and distributed to the JAD team for their review. A review session is held with all the participants. Changes are discussed and noted, and key participants sign an approval form. The JAD process is now complete and program

No.	Phase	Resulting Output
1	JAD Project Definition	Management Definition Guide
2	Research	Data models Process models Preliminary information Session agenda
3	Preparation	Working Document Overheads, flip charts, magnetics
4	The Session	Scribe notes and scribe forms
5	The Final Document	JAD Document Signed approval form

Figure 1.2 The JAD phases.

specification can begin. Figure 1.2 shows the five JAD phases and their resulting output.

If the development effort does not involve the users in an organized approach such as described here, there is a good chance the final system will not meet their needs. In the case of the robot waiter, you could end up with a mentally unstable block of metal that rakes yards with a vacuum cleaner instead of basting birds with a brush. By proceeding through the JAD phases, however, you will end up with a state-of-the-art, twenty-first century roving robot that cooks delicious, delectable meals morning, noon, and night and (if it's in the specs) brings you your slippers at the end of a hard day's work.

USING THIS BOOK

You can use this book to determine if you want to try JAD in your organization. You can use it as a guide to manage JADs or as an instruction manual to guide you through each part of the process.

The best way for you to use the book depends on whether you are looking for the details or the overview. The information you are looking for probably falls within two basic categories that ask: Is JAD for you? or How do you run a JAD? The following sections describe the specific chapters that answer each of these questions.

Is JAD for You?

If you have overview questions like "Will JAD work for us?" or "How do we implement the process?", use this book to evaluate what you actually need to do JADs. You do *not* need to know such details as how to set up the room for the session (at least, not yet). You *do*, however, need to know what resources are required to make JADs happen and generally how the process works. Therefore, you should read:

- Chapter 2 (Why People Use JAD)—describes who uses JAD and the trends influencing people to use it.
- Chapter 4 (The JAD Team and How to Select It)—describes what people you need to run a JAD and how to select the JAD team.
- Chapter 18 (JAD Across the Life Cycle)—describes how to tailor sessions for different projects across the systems development life cycle. For example, you can customize the process for defining requirements, designing systems, or even reviewing code.
- Chapter 19 (Breaking Out of the Life Cycle)—discusses how to get beyond the life cycle and use JAD techniques for such projects as defining corporate policy and downsizing a department.
- Chapter 21 (Marketing Your Services)—tells how to sell your services to your potential customers.
- Chapter 23 (Assuring JAD Success)—covers selecting the pilot project, training the facilitator, how to charge for JAD services, and how to measure JAD success.

You can skip Chapters 5 through 9, which describe the details of the JAD phases. This way you can focus less on how the process works and more on what you need to make it happen.

How Do You Actually Run a JAD?

On the other hand, you may have already decided to use JAD. You want to know the details of how to make it work. In this case, you can benefit most from:

- Chapters 5 through 9—contain the recipe for running a JAD. They describe the five phases: JAD Project Definition, Research, Preparation, the Session, and the Final Document. These chapters present step-by-step descriptions of what to do for each of the five JAD phases, including:
  - How to determine the session agenda.
  - How to define business processes. A customized approach shows a

way to document these processes that you can use before, during, or totally independent of the JAD process.

- How to define data elements, screens, and reports.
- Steps that guide you comfortably through the terrain of an actual session.
- How to prepare visual aids.
- How to set up the meeting room. This shows the most effective table arrangement and describes what you need to prepare the room for the session.
- How to produce the final document. This includes preparing the document, tracking distribution, and getting approval.
- Samples of which memos to send to whom.

- Chapter 10 (JAD Busters)—covers pitfalls that are easy to fall into, and how to avoid them.
- Chapter 11 (Group Dynamics)—covers the people aspects of JADs, such as handling conflict, chilling the dominator, and encouraging shy users. This information applies to any forum where you need to guide people through a decision-making process.
- Chapter 12 (The Facilitator's Repertoire)—covers the characteristics of a successful facilitator.
- Chapters 13 to 17 (Tools and Techniques)—offers timesaving and quality-enhancing approaches to use throughout the phases. It covers such things as:

  - Using CASE tools and meetingware (sometimes called groupware) in the session.
  - Techniques for promoting creative thinking, brainstorming, and harvesting ideas.
  - Handling large projects

- Chapter 20 (Son of JAD: Related Methodologies)—discusses a few JAD derivatives such as RAD® and Participatory Design.
- Chapter 22 (JAD Anecdotes)—describes more real-world examples from other JAD projects .

A Note about "You"

Throughout the book, we refer to *you*. Let's define who this "you" is. You are the one managing the JAD project. You are the facilitator who prepares for and leads the session as well as the one who compiles the final document. In other words, although you will have people helping you throughout the phases, you are the one responsible for the JAD project from start to finish.

You, the reader, may not actually be this person facilitating the sessions. Perhaps you are a project manager, a programmer analyst, or the manager who will be hiring the JAD facilitator. In any case, you will understand the process best if you see it through the facilitator's eyes. Just remember, the "you" in this book is the facilitator.

ABOUT THE SURVEY

No two facilitators run a session exactly alike. Each adds a variety of techniques and styles to the session. That is why we wanted to tap into the experience and imagination of facilitators across the country.

Throughout the book, you'll see references to "a survey sent to several facilitator groups." To broaden our base of information for this second edition, we prepared a five-page questionnaire asking about many aspects of facilitation. We sent it to 750 members of various facilitator groups. For more about these groups, see Chapter 23 (Assuring JAD Success).

We asked questions about what kinds of projects people facilitate, what do they do in their sessions (for example, data modeling, defining project requirements, and so on), and do they charge back their time (and if so, how?). We asked how people document their sessions. Do they use flip charts, word processors, CASE tools, or electronic boards?

Based on the responses to the questionnaire, we made some tabulations that gave us a picture of the techniques and styles that have become commonplace among "practitioners." We also learned of a number of tools and techniques (such as ways to promote creative thinking and how to deal with difficult people) which we would like to pass on to you.

People responding to the survey came from all kinds of industries including banking, insurance, manufacturing, utilities, transportation, government, healthcare, and consulting. We even received a response from a facilitator at McDonald's®. (Can you imagine the data model for building a Big Mac®?)

We hope you enjoy the contributions of these diverse facilitators as much as we did.

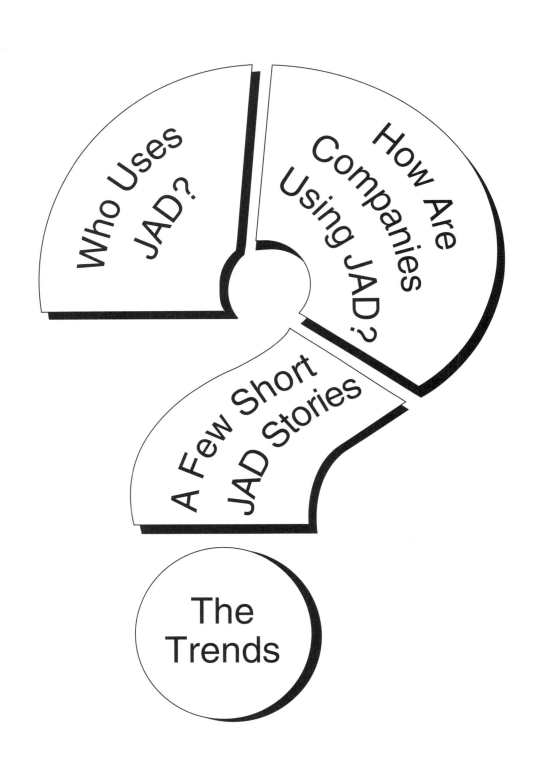

T W O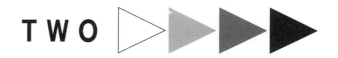

WHY PEOPLE USE JAD

There was a time when hardware was your grandfather's collection of nuts and bolts, and bytes were what you took out of peanut butter sandwiches. Now we have object-oriented data bases, client servers, code optimizers, code generators, and CASE tools all supported by sophisticated operating systems and complex hardware and telecommunications architectures. We invested in these state-of-the-art tools because we thought they might help us with the backlog of user requests that had burgeoned beyond our expectations. According to a 1992 survey of more than a thousand IBM and plug-compatible mainframe sites, the average backlog reported was 13.4 months. (Hosier 1992)

As each new productivity tool was installed, we saw new light at the end of the tunnel. But alas, as the adage goes, "Beware of the light at the end of the tunnel; it could be a train coming your way." And thus it was for us all—a train loaded with inflexible systems, tighter budgets, and constantly changing business needs. So we have gone in search of more productivity tools to solve our problems.

Another Vendor, Another Fancy Slide Show

Have you attended a product seminar lately? You know, the ones with coffee, muffins, white tablecloths, and friendly vendors with business cards. One thing you can always count on—three slides into the slick presentation, up comes the frame about the systems development life cycle and how we are spending too much time at the end of the cycle instead of at the beginning. Pie charts with percentages tell the story. Glib assertions back it up:

> More than 75% of all systems errors result from poor quality specifications. (Andrews 1991)

> Costs and time to change the design of a system *after* it is complete are 50 to 100 times higher than making those same changes *during* system design. (Wetherbe 1991)

> There's an awful lot of Cobol code out there—probably 50 billion lines—and it's been patched, repatched, and enhanced for 25 years. (Johnson 1990)

The vendors elaborate on this dilemma and tell us how we are not dealing with the problem. As the philosopher Eric Bush said, "Old computers go into museums. Old programs go into production." Because of aggressive target dates, tight budgets, and sketchy project requests, we are forced to throw our resources further and deeper into the development cycle. The vendors tell us we should spend 40 percent of our time in up-front analysis instead of an inordinate amount of time in coding and testing. In other words, we need error prevention now or we will face error detection and correction later on.

The vendors offer computer solutions. But we need people solutions too. How do we interview the users? How do we translate what they want into actual requirements? How do we handle the contradictory needs among the different departments that will use the new business processes?

JAD provides an answer to these questions. Unlike traditional vendor solutions, JAD is not a software package with an annual maintenance fee or a piece of hardware with a myriad of megabytes and a plethora of peripherals. JAD is a process that can be easily learned and practiced.

WHO USES JAD?

Since IBM's first session in 1977, JAD has been adopted by companies around the world. JAD success has been enjoyed by all sizes of companies from large, multinational institutions (like American Airlines, National Life of Canada, and Amoco Oil Company) to small businesses with no more than 50 people. How many of us use JAD? Here is an estimate:

> There have by now been well over ten thousand meetings labeled JAD (or one of its close cousins that have appeared in the marketplace). . . . We have found that most IS practitioners in large North American orga-

nizations have had some direct or indirect exposure to JAD. (Carmel et al. 1992)

At conferences four years ago, people would ask us about our work at Provident Mutual. When we told them we ran JAD sessions, they usually responded, "What's a JAD?" Nowadays, JAD rarely needs defining.

Companies have their eyes on the budget, downsizing, and the bottom line. They are looking to improve productivity with less expensive alternatives such as JAD, rather than investing in more costly hardware and software tools.

TRENDS DRIVING THE USE OF JAD

What trends have encouraged this movement toward JAD? From what does this growing need for facilitated sessions arise? Here are some trends that have inclined companies toward JAD.

Emerging Teams

The emphasis in corporate structure is shifting away from *hierarchy* and more toward *teams* of people. Groups are springing up in companies like never before.

> The best method line managers have found to effect the martini-like mingling (shaken, not stirred) of IS and users is teamwork. . . . Whatever their makeup, teams are the one unifying theme among companies trying to get users involved in software development. (O'Leary 1993)

In the last couple of years, our organization has formed the ISD Steering Committee, Technology Task Force, Training Task Force, Communications Task Force, and Product Implementation Committee, just to name a few. Certainly the responsibilities of these groups have been around for a long time, but they were assigned to particular departments or people. Now responsibility is often allocated to a diverse group of people rather than one specific place on the hierarchy chart.

Where does this diversity come from? Years ago, companies were typically very cohesive entities, comprised of a solid group of employees, situated in a fairly stable hierarchy, all working in the same building, serving one kind of customer. Now we have companies merging with other companies, opening up offices all over the world. Some companies are downsizing and sending out more work to other companies on a contract basis. This dissolving of company boundaries fosters the need for more task-oriented teams of people.

Focus on Quality and Productivity

Quality has been a hot topic for years now. Companies have quality awards, quality teams, and quality dinners. This movement has gained structure via the Baldrige Award, the Software Engineering Institute's process maturity model, and the ISO 9000 quality standard.

But what does "quality" mean in the applications development arena and how can we get some? To answer this question, Carey Project Organization, a consulting firm specializing in quality management and performance measurement, spent two years conducting two cooperative projects with industry. They researched 100 original sources and interviewed more than 400 IS professionals.

The most frequently cited success indicators for applications were:

- Timely delivery
- Achievement of project objectives
- Building positive communications and relationships with customers (Carey, 1991)

Many IS organizations are turning to JAD to accomplish these quality management objectives.

In the last few years, however, the quality focus has changed. People are becoming more interested in productivity than quality. IS departments are experiencing downsizing and, therefore, must do more work with less people. As Earl Brochu (JAD consultant) describes:

> At this time I think many clients with limited resources are mostly concerned with getting the job done. "Let's be productive today so there will be a tomorrow." They know quality costs in the short run. (Brochu 1994)

He backs this up with evidence that in the United States, the number of companies applying for the Baldrige Award has dropped off since 1991. Another recent survey in the United States indicates that:

> 42 percent of the DP organizations that favor improved software quality have no plans in place to achieve it. (Yourdon 1993)

However, whether the objective is to increase productivity or improve quality, teamwork can help. And JAD is teamwork.

Smarter Users

For years now, we've been hearing about "user sophistication" (which somehow elicits the image of a room full of snobbish businesspeople discussing abstract art). But it's true; users have become more knowledgeable and involved in the destiny of their systems. Consequently, they are more willing (in fact, sometimes outright demanding) to participate in developing their applications:

> The information system is now in perspective as a tool to help clients do their jobs, not something that belongs to IS. Users should not have to go to the "IS Oracle" to get their own information. (Edwards et al. 1993)

Users have taken on a stronger sense of ownership than ever before. Sometimes this stems from their increased understanding of their own systems. Other times, it is a reaction to their dissatisfaction with what IS has done (or not done) for them. In fact, many companies feel that their IS departments provide more hinderance than help. Users are not as tolerant to having IS hand them a hammer when they need a drill.

Shift from Technology to Business

The evolution of hardware and software has allowed users to relax somewhat on technology issues and give more attention to their actual business.

Consider PCs, for example. Remember when we all used the DOS operating system? To copy files from one directory to another, we needed to know the exact command and then type it correctly at the C> prompt. Now, in the wonderful world of Windows, we need only recall the menu selection of the function we need. We've migrated from having to *remember* the exact wording of commands to simply *recalling* where to access them.

If technology has an ego, it's probably mighty insecure right about now, because in certain business areas, the technology has improved to the point where users don't need to give it all the attention they used to. They are less concerned with such questions as: Do we have enough disk space? Can we do the project online realtime? And how will we download the data to the 52 agencies? They are free to concentrate more on questions like: How can we tie the data in Human Resources to Finance? How can managers get the information they need to make the right business decisions? This leads us to the next topic.

Focus on Business Process Reengineering

With emancipation from the burdens of technology and users focusing more on the business, a trend has developed toward business process reengineering (BPR). It has had a major effect on the content of facilitated sessions.

The term "reengineering" became popular in the summer of 1990 when Michael Hammer, management guru, generated interest in the topic with an article in the *Harvard Business Review*. Today, most companies are involved in some type of reengineering activity.

The BPR philosophy is best summed up by this advice:

> Don't just sit there doing what you've always done. Think about what you're doing, and how. Does it make business sense? If not, change the way you do it, or do something different. (Classe 1993)

Traditionally, we have defined the boundaries and scope of our projects in terms of computer systems and functions. We have talked more about *applications* than information. Here is a quote that echoes our old familiar ways of dealing with projects:

> Applications are kingdoms unto themselves; they do not talk to each other or add value to each other unless they were designed to do so. (Tozer 1992)

Now, we are just beginning to move towards defining projects in terms of *business activities*. In other words, we are looking more toward information needs and how they flow across functional business areas. We are becoming less constrained by the boundaries of the computer applications. These days, people talk less about *systems* and more about *information*. In fact, some facilitators don't even like to talk about "systems" in their sessions anymore. They strive to keep the focus on business processes:

> In [our] workshops, I don't allow the "s" word. The first person to say the word "system" gets smacked, or they have to pay a quarter.
>
> —Gary Rush
> (Edwards et al. 1993)

Rarely do companies have the time to sit back and re-examine their business. Or when they do, they focus on streamlining the existing business functions rather than rethinking how they can improve them. BPR gets companies to look at processes that cross functional areas and arrive at creative ways to do them better.

Facilitated sessions are ideal for BPR projects. In the session you can analyze and document the work flow and use brainstorming and other problem-solving techniques to determine how to improve the processes. The results of the session may or may not result in a system solution.

Tighter Budgets

People react differently to the increasing reality of declining resources and all the many byproducts of downsizing. Regarding JAD, some managers pull back from any kind of user involvement. With less staff to do the work, they feel "we just can't afford to give up the people for a three-day session." In these cases, tighter budgets can have a detrimental effect on facilitated sessions. Others, however, react to budget constraints with a heightened sense of the importance of user involvement in system design. "We can't waste time or money on a bad system, so we have to build it right the first time." This sentiment has moved many companies into JAD sessions.

Demand for Rapid Development

Today's business needs are volatile. Things change fast. More than ever, companies are forced to adjust rapidly to stay competitive in the marketplace. They cannot afford to bypass windows of opportunity just because IS can't deliver systems on time.

We now have Nintendo® toys for kids that enjoy more memory and processing speed than the largest mainframe computers of 20 years ago. Unfortunately, software improvements have not kept pace with these hardware developments. Certainly, there have been some improvements, but:

> Software development is still a craft rather than an engineering process. In addition, although we can develop software faster than in the past, it doesn't feel any faster because as quickly as we improve the development process and tools, we expand the scope of the systems we want to develop. The result is that it still seems to take two years to do almost anything, and the users still complain that it isn't what they (now) want! (Tozer 1992)

Departure from the Waterfall Life Cycle

The traditional process of systems development is based on what is called the "waterfall" model, where each life-cycle phase must be *totally* completed before the next one begins. Consequently, users cannot see the actual system until all phases are done, which for large projects can take years. Often, when the system is finally delivered, some functions are already obsolete.

Waterfall techniques worked just fine for the old, third-generation mainframe systems. Large-scale projects required a phased methodology for management to identify milestones, evaluate project status, and give (or not give) their approval to go on with the next phase. Now that we are involved with fourth-generation languages, prototyping, and multiplatform environments, we are beginning to move toward more flexible development approaches such as Rapid Application Development (RAD).

A Virtual Future?

Some say we are on the brink of a revolutionary change—and depending on how companies deal with this change, they will either fall in with the new way of business or fall out.

What people are talking about here is the change to the *virtual* corporation. As *Forbes* magazine describes:

> What does your company need to do to survive and thrive in the Information Age? It begins with a new kind of product. We call it a virtual product—*virtual* being an enduring term in the electronics industry to signify an entity or experience that perpetually adapts to the needs of the user. (Malone and Davidow 1992)

How exactly do companies "adapt to the needs of the user" and become virtual? First of all, when these pundits talk about "users," it is not in the sense we mean. They are not echoing our own sentiments about involving users in system design. They're taking it several steps further. They are talking about involving our *customers* and beefing up our relationships with the people we sell to, to the point of creating a co-destiny with them.

Today's corporate teams are just a precursor of things to come. The future will find teams forming not only across departments, but *across companies* too. Teams will extend to include our customers, and also our suppliers.

Because of competition, companies will be compelled to not only *meet* customer needs, but also to *anticipate* them. Customers will mingle with providers and suppliers will mingle with manufacturers, all in an effort to anticipate each other and stay virtual.

> Suppliers [will be] privy to the manufacturer's future product plans, market strategies, even financials—a degree of outside access that would dry the throats of most modern executives. (Malone and Davidow 1992)

Can this truly be our future? Will the norm evolve to have customers and suppliers in our JAD sessions? Imagine sessions that include the people who buy our insurance policies, automobiles, and electricity. Then imagine more sessions with those who supply us with whatever raw materials we use to do what we do. Perhaps "virtual" is where we are headed. When all this comes about, we will certainly need people who can manage the resulting diversity. Consequently, facilitated services will be all the more in demand.

After all, isn't that the facilitator's forte—to create consensus from a group of people with varied perspectives?

HOW ARE COMPANIES USING JAD?

The following examples show how companies are using JAD today:

- *Business process reengineering.* A bank decides to evaluate the work activities in its Human Resources department. The existing functions are labor-intensive, especially at certain times of the year. The four business functions (benefits, salary, staffing, and attendance) are performed independently by four separate people. A JAD is held to reengineer how work can be accomplished more productively and how automation might help.

- *Data modeling.* A company wants to define all the data required to operate its pharmaceutical business and make strategic and tactical decisions. A JAD is held to create entity relationship diagrams.

- *New systems design.* An insurance company decides to build an online system that allows the field force to view policy information from their offices across the country. A JAD is held to define the requirements.

- *Modifications to existing systems.* Due to growth at a manufacturing company, its accounting system no longer meets user needs. The company would like to modify the existing system instead of buying a new one. A JAD is held to define requirements.

- *Automating manual processes.* A medium-sized company with two small divisions has been growing, but still continues to manually track its training programs. A JAD is held to bring together the users in the home office and the two divisions to automate this process.

- *Conversions.* A hospital will be converting from one software package to another. The new package must be tailored to fit into the organization. A JAD is held to define all facets of the conversion.

- *Acquisitions.* An expanding enterprise acquires a subsidiary that will come under the umbrella of the parent company. A JAD is held to define the requirements for this consolidation.

JADs have also provided a forum for:

- Enterprise modeling
- Strategic planning
- Restructuring organizations
- Planning projects

- Prioritizing projects
- Selecting software packages
- Solving problems
- Resolving conflict
- Defining corporate policy
- And many other business activities

A FEW SHORT JAD STORIES

Here are a few "short stories" from satisfied users of JAD.

Equitable Financial Company

"Those who do not innovate lose market share and top sales people," says Frank J. Aiosa of Equitable Financial Company (a subsidiary of Equitable Life Assurance in New York). For this reason Equitable made plans to develop an integrated, PC-based information system for their agents. To determine requirements, they held a series of facilitated meetings with the field.

For each application, they formed a separate team of people from the home office and the field. Each team met in four high-level sessions to:

- Define basic requirements
- Develop a nonworking prototype
- Develop a working, completed prototype and a pilot strategy
- Determine whether the project was a "go" and then define the rollout strategy

In parallel, they held formal JAD sessions with a different group of people to define more specific business needs and, later on, the design. Aiosa says:

> Our experience with this project underscored the classic truism that a shared experience is the only worthwhile one. [We] brought together two heretofore diverse groups within the organization. This proved to be such an effective technique that we plan to use it in all subsequent phases of our long-range strategy. The agents we worked with became our cheerleaders in the field—and more importantly—our friends. We began the endeavor with a shared vision and mutual commitment. We ended it with a sense of pride. (Aiosa 1989)

Fidelity Investments

Fidelity's complex and diverse environment includes computer centers in Dallas, Cincinnati, and Salt Lake City. The company employs 7,500 people and manages 156 billion dollars. Recently, the company undertook a challenge: *to speed up development time.*

To do this, Fidelity Investments created a new development approach called Fidelity Advanced Systems Environment (FASE) 2000. It uses CASE, JAD, and prototyping. The JAD portion brings together users across many business units to develop mainframe, minicomputer, and PC applications. A key component is brainstorming.

Using this development approach, the company intends to cut system delivery time in half. The first project created a client-server accounting application, which "took just six months to develop—far less than standard 12- to 18-month development cycles. The same method is being used in more than 10 other programming projects." (Bozman 1992)

Rockwell Hanford

Rockwell Hanford (a former division of Rockwell International) needed to tie together their information systems, telecommunications, office automation, technical systems, computer-aided design and drafting, and robotics. The first step was to define requirements. They used WISDM, a facilitated approach once offered by Western Institute of Software Engineering in Bellevue, Washington.

Many people in the company were skeptical about using facilitated sessions. Their sentiments were along these lines:

> Aren't systems analysts supposed to go out and interview users, go through iterations for months, then eventually come up with a system? Doesn't it usually take more than a year to fully define requirements for major systems? Few believed that it could be done faster or better. (Corbin 1991)

As it turned out, the teams averaged only two and a half weeks to define their requirements. Then they went on to design their systems using more facilitated sessions.

National Life of Canada

In the late 1970s, National Life of Canada made a decision: They would become the fastest growing life insurance company in Canada. At that time, they were not so large, holding only the 53rd spot in the country. Furthermore, their automated systems that supported the field were behind the times. For example, their agency system was written in assembly language. National Life was going into the 1980s with a system designed in the 1960s. As they said, "responsive turnaround had become an oxymoron." (Jiwani and Coles 1993)

Also at this time, competition was growing—not just for selling products, but for attracting agents as well. An independent agent selling products from several companies might choose to sell an insurance policy from another company over National Life because of better incentives or a shorter time between commission payments.

What would get the company out of this antiquated automation dilemma? And how could they better compensate their agents to entice them to sell National Life's products? The answer: a new, integrated system called Flexible Agency System of Tomorrow (or FAST). And how would they develop this ambitious project? Of course, they would hold a series of JAD sessions involving people from the field, brokerage management staff, marketing administration, and the key IS people.

They parsed the project into phases: First they developed the brokerage delivery system, then the career agency compensation system, and finally the production reporting and management system. They described the sessions as "grueling, lengthy discussions, but highly successful." (Jiwani and Coles 1993)

The project paid off:

> We have seen more than a 30 percent reduction in user staff and operating expenses in the head office and in field offices, largely due to the success of this system. The programming staff necessary for maintenance has been reduced by 50 percent in comparison with the old agency system. (Jiwani and Coles 1993)

And regarding the role of JAD in the project:

> Throughout the development, we promoted the team's efforts and made all team members proud to be a part of something important. The effective working relationships and expanded knowledge between systems professionals and users will last a lifetime. The "ownership" assumed by both end users and systems people is 100 percent! (Jiwani and Coles 1993)

The closing of the story is that National Life of Canada did what they intended. They grew. They moved from the 53rd largest insurance company in Canada right up into the top 10 for new individual life business.

You can see that JAD has many applications. It can be used for almost any medium- to large-sized project.

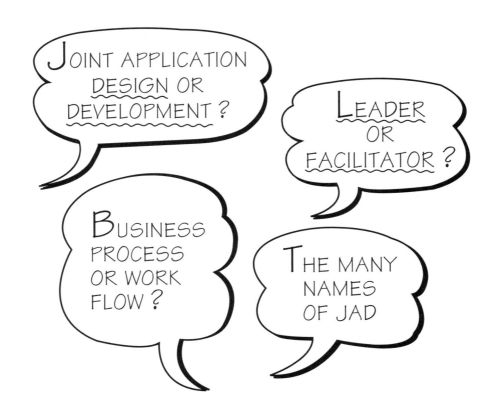

THREE

JAD JARGON

The computer industry loves buzzwords. We talk about vaporware, seamless integration, "gooey" interfaces, OO design, and legacy systems. While attending a conference on CASE, several of us enjoyed breakfast in the hotel cafe. As we fell into a rather animated discussion on the latest state-of-the-art whatever, we silently considered what this high-tech, acronym-laden conversation must sound like to the neighboring tables. A business breakfast is one thing. But you had better not talk like this at a cocktail party or you'll be standing by yourself muttering technical ditties to the pet parakeet.

Like the rest of the industry, JAD has spawned a language of its own. To acquaint you with it, we offer the following introduction to JAD jargon.

JOINT APPLICATION *DESIGN* OR *DEVELOPMENT?*

To begin with, there are differing opinions about what the acronym JAD really means. Some say that "JAD, an IBM trademark, has come to be used as a generic term, like Kleenex and Xerox." (Williamson 1991) A facilitator from a major airline company concurs: "To us, JAD is any group-facilitated process designed to identify strategy, define a process, or solve a problem." Also, a split has developed over what the "D" stands for. Some say Joint Application *Design*, while others say Joint Application *Development*. In a survey to several JAD user groups, we asked, "What does the 'D' in JAD stand for?" The responses were:

51 percent said "Development"

49 percent said "Design"

One joker said "Disaster"

Why are there different opinions? And which one is right? First, let's talk about how IBM sees it. When IBM originally used the JAD trademark, the "D" stood for "Design." Ask them today and they still say it stands for "Design":

> IBM considers the "D" to stand for Joint Application Design, with the use of "Design" being far beyond system design. "Design" in this case implies the design of a solution. Solutions, in this case, can be business or system related.

IBM has seen their technique applied across the entire systems development life cycle. And, as we shall describe in later chapters, JAD techniques are used in projects that have nothing to do with any part of the systems development life cycle.

We see that the term "Joint Application Design" is two-thirds insufficient much of the time, since both the "Design" and the "Application" parts are too limiting. The only part that always applies is the "Joint." It seems that the name JAD is following in the same footsteps as the name of its own creator. Originally, the "M" in the trademark IBM came from "Machines" in the corporate name International Business Machines. But as the company grew to offer much more than machines, the name IBM has also grown in its meaning. Perhaps that is where JAD stands as well.

As for us, we have gone over to the (slight) majority view—to the extent that we actually changed the title of this book from the first edition.

A PROCESS WITH MANY NAMES

A JAD by any other name is sometimes still a JAD. Here (in alphabetic order) are some of the names used to refer to facilitated sessions:

- Accelerated Design
- Facilitated Meetings
- Facilitated Sessions
- Facilitated Team Techniques
- Facilitated Work Sessions
- Facilitated Workshops
- FAST®
- Group Design

- Interactive Design
- Interactive JAD
- Joint Application Design
- Joint Application Development
- Joint Application Review
- Joint Requirements Planning
- Joint Sessions
- Modeling Sessions
- Team Analysis
- The Method®
- User Centered Design
- Workshops

So, if you don't want to call your sessions "JADs" (or any other name on this list), then you certainly can make up a new name!

JAD LEADER OR FACILITATOR?

Are you running a JAD session or are you facilitating a meeting? Are you the JAD leader, session leader, or facilitator? Are these just different ways to say the same thing or are we talking about distinctly different scenarios?

Technically, they are different. A "JAD session" involves some aspect of system design or, at least, development. Somewhere there's a computer involved. A "facilitated meeting," on the other hand, can address any subject. The only requirement is that it be led by a facilitator. For example, you could hold a session to sort out a department's project priorities, or to resolve a corporate controversy, or to decide whether to expand operations to Canada. None of these involve systems development, but all of them can absolutely benefit from JAD techniques. Therefore, they are facilitated sessions.

In the past few years, the use of JAD techniques has expanded to handle a broader range of challenges. When it goes beyond the arena of systems development, the purists refer to these workshops not as JAD sessions, but as facilitated sessions. So, if you're talking logic, it goes like this: A JAD session is always facilitated, but not all facilitated sessions are JADs. JAD is a subset of facilitation.

Now you may be wondering, what does it matter? Who cares what you call it, just get on with the session! Well, here is an example of how this evolution in JAD use (and consequently, in terminology) has manifested itself.

In the Hartford, Connecticut area (the insurance capital of the world), a group of people have been gathering bimonthly for years. Their common interest is JAD sessions and other facilitated endeavors. When we first had the pleasure of attending one of their meetings (in 1988), they called their group "JADLDRS," short for "JAD Leaders."

Years later, we found we were no longer receiving mail from this group. About the same time, however, we began getting meeting announcements from another group called the "Facilitators' Network"—same Hartford location, same types of agenda, but a different name. When we attended a meeting of this supposedly new group, we found out why they had changed their name. When we asked a long-time group member if she was a JAD leader, she replied, "No, I facilitate." The group members made a clear distinction between JADs and facilitated sessions. The old name, JADLDRS, limited their scope. They lamented that it did not include people who ran non-JAD sessions.

In this book, we talk about JADs. But keep in mind that all coverage on JAD leading, JAD sessions, and any other JAD-like manifestation, equally applies to facilitators and their sessions as well.

BUSINESS PROCESS OR WORK FLOW?

Years ago people talked about *work flow*. IBM's JAD had a component called "Work Flow Analysis." Facilitators said, "Let's analyze the accounting functions and define the department's work flow." Nowadays, with the business process reengineering movement, people talk less about functions and work flow and more about *business processes*.

Similarly, now that JAD is being used both in and out of the systems development life cycle, facilitators refer less to "users" (for IS projects) and more to the "business area people."

WHAT IS CONSENSUS, REALLY?

Consensus is a central element of the JAD process. In talking about various sessions, we might say, "We need to get group consensus on this issue," or we might ask the group, "Is there consensus here?" What exactly is consensus? Does it require every participant in the room to wholeheartedly concur with the decision? Or does it mean that some agree while others just reluctantly go along with it?

Opinions vary. Even Webster's dictionary acknowledges both possibilities. Here consensus is defined as "group solidarity in sentiment and belief." Who would question that interpretation? But the dictionary also offers various versions of consensus. First, it says consensus is "unanimity," then defines it as is "the judgment arrived at by *most* of those concerned."

Reprinted with special permission of King Features Syndicate

Relating to JAD sessions, we have all read articles that say, "You must get the approval of everyone in the session." Others take a more relaxed view:

> Consensus is agreeing to decisions that all parties will support, even though they may not approve personally. Therefore, consensus does not imply unanimity in the decision-making process. (Kettelhut 1993)

Our approach is to strive for the whole enchilada. We try to have everyone agree. In the real world, however, situations arise where although most people accept the decision, one or two do not. Nevertheless, they reluctantly go along with the group, realizing that there is no middle ground and that it works better this way for the majority involved. Sometimes such compromises are necessary. However, if the decision carries a flavor of dissatisfaction, where you see people relenting because they feel they have been unfairly overpowered by the group, then you do *not* have consensus. Open the discussion up again and aim for solidarity.

THE WORD JAD

Sometimes acronyms become words in themselves. The word "wimp," for example, was revived from the acronym for Weakly Interactive Massive Particles, a contribution from the world of particle physics. Once unleashed into common usage, it came to denote weakness in general ("he's a real wimp"). Next it mutated into a verb form (to "wimp out"). In the same way, when people work with the JAD process on a daily basis, the acronym JAD can start taking on many forms. Figure 3.1 shows how it has come to be used and abused in our organization.

For clarity's sake, we have tried to keep these variations to a minimum. In this book, you will find:

- JAD, the process (for example, is JAD for you?)
- JAD, the particular project (for example, the Fixed Assets JAD)
- JAD, the workshop (for example, the JAD session)

Now that we have covered the what, why, and when of JAD, let's look more closely at how the process works. The next part describes who is involved (the JAD roles) and takes you through each step of the five JAD phases.

The Word	*Part of Speech*	*Used in a Sentence*
JAD	Noun	*JAD* has worked well for us.
JAD	Adjective	We attended the *JAD* session.
JAD	Verb	To *JAD* or not to *JAD*. . .
Jadding	Present Participle	They've been *jadding* all day.
Jadded	Past participle	That project should definitely be *jadded*.
Jadable	Adjective	People will want to JAD anything that seems *jadable*.

Figure 3.1

HOW TO DO A JAD

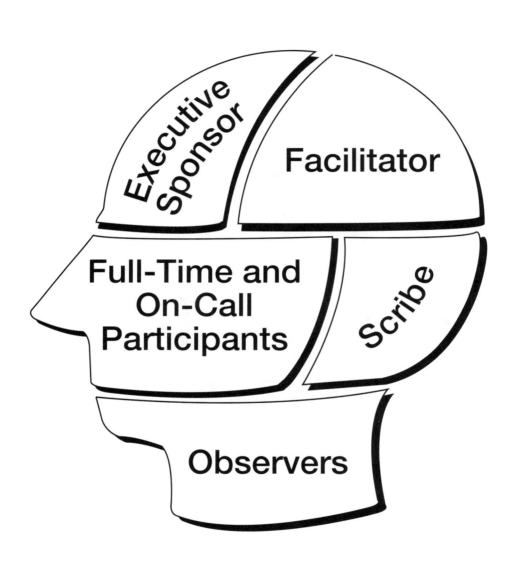

FOUR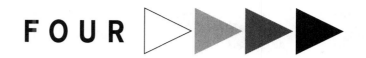

THE JAD TEAM AND HOW TO SELECT IT

The success of a JAD session depends largely on who is in the room for those three to five days of decision-making. The following describes the roles of the participants and who should fill them. These descriptions include what each role does before, during, and after the session.

These JAD roles are covered right up front, before getting into details about the JAD phases. However, you don't actually fill these roles right away. You generally select the facilitator and the executive sponsor during Phase 1 (JAD Project Definition). Then you select the other team members during Phase 2 (Research), *after* you have identified what you want the session to accomplish.

EXECUTIVE SPONSOR

This is the person who controls the project's funding, gives vision and direction, and empowers the people to make decisions. This is the person who is high enough in the organization to free up the calendars of the attendees. This is the person with senior-level authority to make decisions for all aspects of the project. For example, we ran a JAD to define user requirements for a new Fixed Assets system. This involved participants from Accounting, Finance, Budget and Cost, Tax Planning, Facilities Management, and Administrative Services. The Vice President and Controller was an excellent executive sponsor because most of the departments represented in the JAD reported to her.

The prime responsibility of the executive sponsor is to make the words "management commitment" a reality. This commitment should begin with the executive sponsor. After all, this person, who is responsible for all (or nearly all) the areas where the new business processes or system will be used, has a vested interest in the project's success.

What if the logical person to select for executive sponsor has a weak personality or has no influence in the organization? This kind of person will not help your project and will not give you the management commitment you need. In this case, select the person who has the *most* authority to make decisions for the project *and* has the right personality. It is better to have an executive sponsor who can make *some* decisions for the project than to have someone who has the formal authority, but will not make decisions at all.

Before the Session

The executive sponsor takes part in discussions with the JAD facilitator to define the purpose, scope, objectives, and overall strategic direction of the project.

To make the company's commitment known, the executive sponsor kicks off a preliminary meeting held the week before the JAD session. He briefly summarizes the project, its benefits, and its significance to the company. The executive sponsor also discusses his role in resolving open issues during the session.

During the Session

Whether the executive sponsor attends the session depends on his or her involvement in the project. If the session is for high-level decisions (such as strategic planning) or if the executive is involved in the day-to-day workings of a business area, he should attend. Usually, this is not the case, and he need not be there. The executive sponsor should, however, be accessible by phone throughout the session. There may be cases where an impasse is reached because two departments cannot agree. This requires a discussion with someone who can make decisions for both departments—the executive sponsor. Although we always plan for this contingency, we have only once made such a call during a session. Before the session, however, we often consult with the executive sponsor on issues that affect more than one department.

After the Session

The only remaining job for the executive sponsor is to sign off on the JAD "deliverables" (that is, the final work product) and to receive copies of the open-issue resolutions.

FACILITATOR

The key word that describes the facilitator is *impartial*. This person, who guides the team through the complete JAD process, should be objective, unbiased, and neutral. The facilitator should have no vested interest in the final product except that it works effectively, efficiently, and meets user needs.

To Whom Should the Facilitator Report?

For systems development projects, the facilitator ideally comes from neither the user area nor the programming department. For example:

- One approach is to use IBM's concept called the *Development Center,* where a separate staff is hired whose sole purpose is to implement tools and techniques, such as JAD, that increase productivity in the development group.
- Other companies place the JAD staff in a group entirely separate from IS—for example, in a group that focuses on quality within the organization.

All these reporting structures support impartiality. In smaller companies (and even in some larger ones), a liaison group between programming and user departments may not exist. Then the facilitator more likely comes from programming. In this case, maintaining impartiality is more difficult. The facilitator's primary role during a workshop is to lead the session rather than to represent IS views.

In our survey to several facilitator groups we asked, "To whom does your group report?" People responded:

89% report to IS

7% report to a user group

4% report to a group independent of IS or a user group

We began our JADs in 1985 using the first approach (reporting to the Information Services Department). Because our group, Business Systems Engineering (BSE), did not report through Applications Development (the programming area), we were able to maintain impartiality. In 1992, our BSE group moved to a newly created Business Systems Planning area. Consequently, our link (in the hierarchy) with IS was severed, increasing the potential for even greater impartiality. Nevertheless, our common location and our long-term alliances (some of our best friends are programmers) keep our ties with IS strong.

In any case, during the session, the facilitator is neither designer, analyst, nor project manager, but acts as a guide, moderating and steering the participants through what can be a rugged terrain of decision-making. The facilitator should have no stake in whether a policy number is 7 characters or 9 or whether the marketing plan focuses more on career agents or brokers. Those decisions are up to the users. The facilitator simply provides a forum in which the decisions can be made.

What Makes a Good Facilitator?

Chapter 12 describes in detail the characteristics of a good facilitator. Here, we briefly cover the qualifications to look for when hiring a facilitator.

Unlike most other JAD roles, which are assigned only for the duration of the project, the facilitator can be hired into a full-time position whose main responsibility is doing JADs and planning for them. When JADs are conducted less frequently, the facilitators can come temporarily from a traditional systems analyst or project manager position, *as long as they have had sufficient training and experience in facilitation.*

Some companies use outside consultants to lead sessions. Consultants usually bring everything needed for the session, but all for a rather significant fee. This is cost-effective if you plan to do only a few sessions per year, or are just getting started, or have a temporary shortage of facilitators.

When selecting a facilitator, you need someone with an energetic, outgoing personality who can:

• Organize on a project level

• Communicate well

- Lead groups
- Summarize discussions
- Steer groups away from tangents and unnecessary details
- Be sensitive to group dynamics and company politics

Facilitators involved in systems development projects should have a good understanding of data-processing concepts. Finding someone who is familiar with both structured analysis and data modeling is a definite plus. Knowing the business area being covered gives depth to the facilitator's effectiveness (relevant discussion can be more easily distinguished from extraneous digression). However, it is not essential that the facilitator know the business area in detail. In fact, too much knowledge can cause a facilitator to take sides in a role that should remain neutral.

Larry Konopka (of Advanced Computing Techniques in Glastonbury, Connecticut) says:

> Our facilitators are usually experienced in project planning, development methodologies, CASE tools, life cycles, and doing presentations.

At a facilitators' group meeting in Hartford, Connecticut, the attendees were asked "What do you like about being a facilitator?" The responses were interesting. Some said they were attracted to the power and the control. They had always enjoyed the process of turning a floundering meeting into a productive session. Others were more interested in being "part of the solution." Facilitating sessions allowed them to take on the role of "professional middleman" between users and IS. Others enjoyed learning about different parts of the company through the variety of session topics. And still others were hams at heart and felt facilitating offered a corporate stage for their talents.

Before the Session

The facilitator conducts interviews with the executive sponsor and with management from the related business areas. This is when the project purpose, scope, and objectives are identified to build the Management Definition Guide (described later in this chapter). Then, working with people in the business areas and IS, the facilitator gathers information on requirements (for example, prototype screens). This is compiled into a Working Document to use in the session (more about this document in Chapter 5). The facilitator also plans the agenda for the session and visual aids such as flip charts and overhead transparencies.

During the Session

The facilitator guides participants through the agenda, flags tangents, and keeps the session on track, while remaining impartial and aware. The facilitator is sensitive to what interests are being represented to ensure that no one area is dominating. This person determines when agreements are reached and prompts the scribe to document the decisions. When open issues arise, the facilitator writes them on a flip chart to review at the end of the session. And just before the participants reach their overload point, the facilitator calls a welcomed break.

After the Session

Once the session is over and agreements have been documented, the facilitator oversees the creation, review, and distribution of the final document. When appropriate, the facilitator leads the post-session review meeting.

JAD Support Person

This optional role helps when you run sessions for large projects with tight time constraints. The JAD support person helps prepare visual aids, the Working Document, and the final document.

SCRIBE

In the session, one person is designated to record all decisions. In a twentieth-century revival of a somewhat archaic word, this person is called the *scribe*. This role is critical to a successful session. Just as in the days of robed monks, quill pens, and illuminated manuscripts, scribing is an art. Unfortunately, the modern-day role is not so romantic. You might hear comments like, "I'm a programmer, not a scribe!" because people sometimes see it as grunt work, secretarial work, and definitely *not their kind of* work. But, on the contrary, scribing is a key role that can demand serious analytical skills.

Other names for the scribe role include design analyst, workshop analyst, JAD analyst, documenter, documentation specialist, and recorder. A facilitator from Belgium said they use the French word, *secrétaire*. And a facilitator from London, England uses the term, "workshop support person." Some companies are quite against the term "scribe"; as one manager from the midwest said, "We abhor the word 'scribe'!" They use "documenter" instead.

We prefer "scribe." It's short, descriptive and, precisely owing to its medieval origin, it carries a useful connotation. Scribes were usually religiously trained and one of their duties was to "faithfully record" what was said in their presence. So, too, is their duty in our modern usage.

By capturing all the decisions made in the session, the scribe maintains the "group memory." All these notes evolve into the final document. Some people use a series of forms to record these decisions. For example, to document a new data element, the scribe might use a form with space for the length, format (alphabetic, numeric, or alphanumeric), and a complete definition. In the same way, the scribe can use forms to capture open issues and assumptions.

What Makes a Good Scribe?

When selecting a scribe, you need to consider many aspects of the person's qualifications. After all, this person often acts as the facilitator's able assistant. You need someone who:

- Has a good working knowledge of the business area. That is, the person understands it enough to be able to capture decisions accurately.

- Has good analytical skills. (Programmer/analysts or supervisors from business areas often make excellent scribes.)

- Has expertise in the JAD documentation tool of choice (CASE tool or word processor).

- Can take notes well and extract from discussions. Sessions with clear prompts from the facilitator and preplanned scribe forms do not require as much synthesizing or interpreting. But if the session is not so predictable, you need someone who can extract and document.

- Has good technical writing skills. This is always "nice to have," and sometimes it is crucial. It is especially useful after the session when the scribe prepares the final document.

- Has clear handwriting (doctors need not apply).

Selecting the Scribe

To fill the scribe role, you can select someone from the project team (such as a programmer, analyst, or someone from the business area) or you can use someone from the JAD staff. For years, we preferred to select our scribes from the project team. But now we use scribes from the JAD staff.

In determining which approach is best for you, the question comes down to this: Should scribing be done by people with knowledge of the business area or by people from the JAD staff who are more familiar with the JAD process itself? There are advantages and disadvantages to each approach.

The "By-Project" Scribe

When scribes are selected by project, you have people who are familiar with the business area and can therefore follow the subtleties of the discussion. This familiarity makes their recording task more meaningful and thus, effective.

Another advantage is the positive by-product that comes from scribing. Because they must follow the discussion closely and word the decisions clearly, scribes naturally leave the session with a deeper understanding of the session outcome. Programmer/analyst scribes find this benefits their work whether they are coding or further defining specifications. Business area scribes gain by having a head start on how the new business processes will work.

The disadvantage of this approach is that whenever new scribes are selected, you must take the time to familiarize them with the required tools and the recording process. Also, when you select the scribes, you might not know enough about their abilities to be sure they can do the job well. At some point, you might end up with a scribe who knows the business but does not have the communications skills to record decisions effectively. Furthermore, even with competent scribes, you must deal with variations in style from one scribe to the next.

The "Staff" Scribe

The other alternative is to designate someone in your JAD group to be the ongoing scribe who records the decisions for every session. This way, you train the scribe only once. The staff scribe becomes familiar with the tools; in fact, the scribe perfects the task with each project, picking up tricks of the trade along the way.

Also, with a staff scribe, you are dealing with a known entity. There are no surprises about how that person performs. The style is consistent. Here is a comment from Larry Konopka (of Advanced Computing Techniques in Glastonbury, Connecticut) who not only prefers staff scribes, but scribes who also have experience facilitating sessions:

> We find better results if the scribe is another facilitator. That way, the scribe can anticipate the one leading the session, know what to look for, and spot things that the lead person misses.

There are disadvantages in using a staff scribe. Staff scribes cannot be familiar with every business area. Certainly their background gives them expertise in some areas, but they do not bring the in-depth business knowledge to each session that by-project scribes would.

Another disadvantage relates to staffing. You must keep someone in your group to do the scribing. Since the task is intermittent, you must have other responsibilities for that person. This may not be too much of a problem. The communications skills required for scribing are generic, so they can be applied to other tasks as well. (Technical writers usually make good scribes.) The degree of this potential problem depends on what your scribe's other duties are and how often this person can be pulled in to document a session.

So, the question of whether to use a "by-project" scribe or a "staff" scribe comes down to the question: Which has more value—the scribes' familiarity with the business area or their familiarity with the process of scribing? Time has led us to the latter. You need to evaluate which way works best for you.

Before the Session

The facilitator meets separately with the scribe to talk about the scribe's role in the session and to discuss which tools should be used to capture the required information.

During the Session

As the session progresses and decisions are made, the scribe does not need to determine when or what to write. The facilitator prompts the scribe on what to do. For details about the scribe's role in the session, see Chapter 8 (The Session).

After the Session

The scribe reviews notes with the facilitator and helps prepare the final document.

FULL-TIME PARTICIPANTS

Full-time participants include everyone involved in making decisions about the project. For example, in a systems development project, this includes the users (who know what they need) and the IS people (who know how these needs affect the computer environment).

Commitment is essential. Full-time participants are just that, *full-time*. Everyone must attend every day of the session. If a person returns having missed even one session day, you have the following problems:

- Half the group spends valuable time updating that person on what was missed while the other half becomes bogged down, bored, and frustrated because they "went through all that yesterday."

- Decisions will probably be revised (taking even more time) because that person's needs were not known, let alone considered.

JAD is a cumulative process, like learning algebra. You have to be there today to understand what happens tomorrow. And you cannot be the "lone ranger." You are dependent on what others contribute and they are dependent on you. One person's comment leads to another person's suggestion which leads to a final decision that works for everyone involved. Therefore, full-time participants must attend the entire session.

Who Are These JAD Participants?

JAD sessions include two types of participants: those that represent the long-range strategic and tactical direction of the business and those who must live with the project results on a daily basis. For success in the session, and ultimately with the final product, participants should be knowledgeable about the business area and willing to discuss their opinions, not argue them.

Business area people range from lead clerks to supervisors to upper management. Clerks and supervisors are concerned with how the new business processes will support their day-to-day work. (Are the screens easy to read? What are the default values? And how many keystrokes will it take to get from one screen to the next?) Management is concerned not only with ease-of-use, but also with what the system produces. (Do the reports give us the information we need? Are statistics provided to make management decisions?) At least some people at the session must have the authority to make decisions. The words "I'll have to check with my boss," should not be heard in a JAD session.

In systems development projects, IS participants range from programmers to data modelers to project managers responsible for the system being designed. They provide information on existing systems and technology. For example, they can make users aware of the benefits of local area networks and client-server technology. IS participants can determine the feasibility of design requests, estimate costs, and suggest other approaches when necessary. In other words, they add a reality check to some of those blue-sky ideas that can only be implemented with great difficulty and high cost. Also, their presence ensures that user needs are understood and can be translated into an effective system design.

When multiple company locations (for example, subsidiaries or divisions) are directly affected by the new or enhanced business processes, those locations should also be adequately represented.

All in all, you want the people empowered to make decisions, as well as some who will actually *use* the new business processes on a daily basis. A person's rank in the company should not give that person an advantage in the session. *All participants are equal.*

Determining who should attend sessions requires a balancing act. You want enough people to have full representation and decision power in all the areas that are directly affected. At the same time, you want to keep the session small enough to be productive. As every business person knows, beyond a certain number, the productivity of meetings is inversely proportional to the number of attendees. So try to find the balance between too many people and not enough. Seven to fifteen people is about right in most instances. More are required for large projects that affect multiple departments.

For systems development projects, a good ratio is five users to two IS people. Figure 4.1 shows a sample participant list for a typical session.

Title	JAD Role
Vice President, Corporate Control	Executive sponsor
Senior Business Systems Analyst	Facilitator
Programmer, Financial Systems	Scribe
Director, Finance	Team (User)
Supervisor, Finance	Team (User)
Data Entry Clerk, Finance	Team (User)
Director, Budget and Cost	Team (User)
Director, Tax Planning	Team (User)
Director, Purchasing	Team (User)
Director, Facilities Management	Team (User)
Project Manager, Financial Systems	Team (IS)
Senior Programmer/Analyst, Financial Systems	Team (IS)

Figure 4.1 List of session participants.

ON-CALL PARTICIPANTS

These people are affected by the project, but only in one particular area. In other words, most of the session is not relevant to these users. They should participate only when and if their expertise on a particular topic is required. For example, someone in the Law department might attend two hours on Wednesday when legal implications are covered. Or they might be consulted by phone. In either case, they need to be accessible on the session days when their expertise is needed, as determined by the agenda.

OBSERVERS

Sometimes people ask if they can sit in on a session. Perhaps they are training to become a facilitator or just want to know what this "JAD mania" is all about. They could be IS people who will participate in later phases of the project or business people who wish to gain an overall understanding of the project. Letting people observe your sessions can help in the marketing of your services later on. These observers will no doubt be impressed by the process and will convince others to use it.

Observers can receive memos and other information sent out before the session, but they should not become involved in any of the session decision-making. What level of participation should observers assume? Two approaches are touted:

- Allow them to answer questions, but nothing more.
- Muzzle them completely.

You need to use your own judgment. If an observer is sitting in the back of the room harboring within his head the very information you need to carry on with the issue at hand, then you would be remiss to stubbornly stick to the rules by forbidding him to speak. But if you continually allow observer comments, you may find certain observers (spurred on by the sound of their own voices) subtly crossing the line between offering information and selling opinions. Before you know it, your easy-to-manage 16-participant session has acquired four new characters, altering the group dynamics dramatically.

Another step some facilitators take is to not let observers sit together. For example, Terry John (of British Telecom) says:

> We find that sometimes observers get restless in the sessions because they cannot speak. For example, in one session, they began carrying on

conversations themselves. When we asked them to refrain from talking, they began sending notes back and forth, which became all the more distracting. So now we make a habit of seating observers apart from each other.

Whatever approach you take, speak with observers beforehand to make sure they understand their roles (or lack thereof).

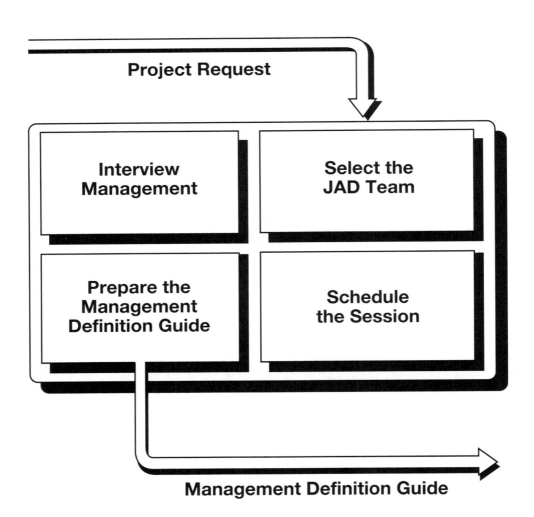

Project Request

Interview
Management

Select the
JAD Team

Prepare the
Management
Definition Guide

Schedule
the Session

Management Definition Guide

FIVE ▷ ▶ ▶ ▶

PHASE 1: JAD PROJECT DEFINITION

Where do projects come from?

- Some projects come from user requests. (The request form says, "We need this new enhancement to speed up processing and increase departmental operating efficiency.")

- Other projects are the result of market research. (The concluding paragraph of a consultant's rambling report says, "For your company to remain on the leading edge in today's marketplace, you must update your old system to keep pace with the new generation of emerging technology.")

- And still other projects originate from a senior management whim. (The VP says, "Well, I was talking with my counterparts in Boston. They are converting all 60 of their mainframe applications to PC LANs. We should do the same. I think this new initiative, which I've outlined here on the back of this place mat, is a dandy idea. See if you can do something with it.")

No matter what the source of the project, whether it be a whim or a fully researched, cost-justified, unequivocally proven, do-or-die initiative, the project ends up in your hands. Now you must take it through the following five JAD phases:

- JAD Project Definition (Phase 1)
- Research (Phase 2)
- Preparation (Phase 3)
- The Session (Phase 4)
- The Final Document (Phase 5)

This chapter covers Phase 1: JAD Project Definition. First, it discusses how open issues and assumptions are handled throughout the project. Then, it describes in detail how to interview management, produce the Management Definition Guide, and schedule the session.

OPEN ISSUES AND ASSUMPTIONS

Before we get into the actual steps of JAD, it is worthwhile to talk about two entities that are inherent to the process. Open issues and assumptions weave through all phases of JAD. They begin propagating as soon as the project begins. In early management interviews, for example, the executive sponsor raises a concern, which the facilitator notes as an *open issue*. At the same time, another manager introduces or "assumes" a basic business decision, which the facilitator documents as an *assumption*.

Open issues are unresolved questions about the business that can arise at any time during the JAD project. Following are examples of open issues:

- Will we centralize purchasing or let each business area develop its own purchasing policy?
- What type of training program is most suitable for the field and who is responsible for delivering it?
- What is the scope of the automated download? What frequency of the download will best support the field's prospecting and marketing needs?

Assumptions are basic decisions that the participants have agreed upon and must keep in mind during the session. These assumptions usually fall into categories. For example, they can be technical (such as assumptions about screen design, hardware environment, or data bases) or more business-oriented (such as assumptions about work flow or corporate policy). Following are some examples:

- Insurance agents can view policy information screens for their own clients only. Agency managers can view screens for all their agents.
- The various field sites will decide whether to use the new client file

system or keep the one they are using. However, we will support only one format for the monthly download of policy information.

- The Policy Form Tracking sheet will be printed on 3-part carbonless paper without preprinted numbers.

As the JAD Project Definition phase continues, some open issues are resolved while others remain open. And new assumptions arise. Whatever their status, all issues and assumptions are brought into the JAD session for discussion.

During the session, the group resolves some issues and identifies new ones. At the end of the session, the team reviews all remaining open issues. All those that can be resolved are documented as assumptions. Even with all participants present, however, some issues may require additional research or may be slightly outside the scope of the project so as not to justify spending session time on them. Such issues are assigned (by the group) to the appropriate people to resolve by a specific date. A coordinator is designated for issues assigned to more than one person. When the session is complete, all agreed-upon assumptions and unresolved open issues become part of the final document.

After the session, the project manager tracks the status of open issues and assures that they all are resolved on time.

GETTING THE MANAGEMENT PERSPECTIVE

Now, let the JAD process begin. The start of a JAD project really begins with the first high-level interview. Before you compile, analyze, and document detailed decisions, you need to identify what management wants from the project. These requirements can be gathered in management interviews. The information will be used to:

- Produce the Management Definition Guide. Written from a business perspective, this document includes the purpose, scope, and objectives of the project.
- Select the JAD team.
- Schedule the session.

Thorough, effective interviews not only assure that your session has the proper scope and objectives, but also give the executive sponsor a chance to modify the approach at the beginning of the project. Doug Lawson (from a major national insurance company) explains the consequences of an executive sponsor adjusting the objectives later on in the session:

> My worst experience was when an executive sponsor unexpectedly and radically changed the objective of a particular JAD without first telling

the facilitator or participants. The group and I attempted to adapt, in hope that weeks of preparation were not wasted, but results were less than optimal.

Since you are interested in a broad scope of the project (at this point), you should interview:

- The executive sponsor to glean the highest-level perspective of the project
- Business area managers who are directly responsible for the project

For example, you might interview the department manager who will manage the daily use of the processes.

Questions to Ask

The questions you ask management depend, of course, on the project. Here are some sample topics that you might want to cover in these interviews:

- How did this project originate? (This identifies the *purpose* of the project.) Look at this closely. You may find that aspects of the project that stimulated its creation have since been solved or redefined.
- What are the major problems you are having in this business area?
- What do you want to gain from this project? (This defines *objectives.*) For this question, people often reply that the project will "increase productivity." But what does this really mean? Further quantify this by asking such questions as, what are the expected decreases in costs, increases in business assets, or improvements in customer satisfaction?
- What are the consequences of *not* doing this project?
- Who will use the information and how often? Which other areas of the company are *directly* affected? What is the expected growth of business in the area? (This identifies *scope.*)
- Who are good contacts for these various impacted areas? For first-time JAD participants, summarize the JAD team roles. Explain that you are interested in selecting the best possible people to fill these roles. (These are possible candidates for your *participation list.*)
- Which areas of the company are *indirectly* affected by the project? For example, who will either give or get information? (This further identifies *scope* and possible *on-call participants.*)
- What existing computer systems are impacted? (This further identifies *scope.*)
- In general, what activities does your area do? (This identifies *business processes.*)

- What limitations should we consider? For example, what are the constraints in time, budget, or government regulations? (This identifies *constraints.*)

- What resources are required? For example, people, physical space, hardware, and communication needs. (This identifies *resource requirements.*)

- What are the requirements for data security?

- What general business decisions have been made about this project so far? (This identifies *assumptions,* which evolve throughout the project.)

- At this point, what unanswered questions do you have about this project? (This identifies *open issues,* which also evolve throughout the project.)

- We have tentatively scheduled the session for May 7 to 11. Will these dates work for you? Full participation of the JAD team is critical. Can you support us by committing the participants from your area to attend each day of the session?

- Are there any political issues that we should be aware of? For example, do you know of any working groups or specific people who are resistant to the changes this project will create? (Saving this kind of question until the end of the meeting, after you have developed rapport, will make the people more likely to discuss those sensitive issues you should know about.)

- Do you have any other comments or suggestions that might help us in preparing for the session?

If You Want to Use Forms

There are nine forms that can be used to capture the information required for the Management Definition Guide. Some people find that using these forms helps foster clarity on who supplies what information and in what format. Others find this approach too constraining. After running many JAD sessions, we rarely use the forms anymore. However, when preparing a Management Definition Guide for the first time, they can help.

If you are using forms, give them to everyone in the meeting. Explain exactly what information goes on each one to reinforce what you are looking for. Then give the people a day or two to gather the information and fill out the forms. Although the forms are a starting point for capturing the information, you need to go further.

The "Word Processing" section of Chapter 15 describes how to use these forms. Samples are shown in Appendix A.

TIPS ON RUNNING SUCCESSFUL INTERVIEWS

In both this JAD phase and the next, your focus is on gathering information through interviews. Asking the right questions is imperative.

> The roots of an unwanted system begin with . . . asking the wrong questions of business managers. (Freedman 1991)

There are many good books on the subject of interviewing, but most are written for journalists, lawyers, criminal investigators, or people interviewing job candidates. Here are some tips for ensuring successful interviews in the business world.

Know Your Objectives

Make sure you know exactly what you want to gain from an interview. Of course you want to get information, but what are you going to *do* with this information? Will you turn it into a chart or diagram to use in the session? Will it be the basis for a new agenda item? Will it make you realize other interviews you need to have? Or perhaps the purpose of the interview is to *give* (instead of get) information? The point is to know exactly what you want to gain from the interview.

Meet With the Right People

Who you meet with depends on your objectives and where you are in the project. For example, are you at the beginning of the project where you want general or strategic information? If so, talk with the executive sponsor and managers. They can summarize the current business flow, overall problems, and plans for the future. On the other hand, are you further along in the project where you want to know about the guts of the existing system and the details of the business? (For example, what happens to this filled-in piece of paper after you receive it? And what problems are you having with this particular screen?) Then, of course, you want to hear from the people in the trenches. Furthermore, you want to *watch* them work and see how their functions fit into the overall scheme of things. (More about this later.)

   How many people should attend an interview? Interviewing is different than decision-making. When making decisions, you need many people in the room to offer varying perspectives. But when interviewing, you can focus on one perspective. Usually, the more people in your interview, the more diluted your information will be. For one thing, people mold their answers to the other people present. Someone who uses a system every day and is intimately familiar with all its shortcomings and idiosyncracies might not be as free to expound on these deficiencies if his manager is sitting beside him (especially if he's up for a performance review next week). Likewise, the manager will not reveal information about future plans and possibilities (such as downsizing) that have not yet been shared with the staff person who is also sitting in the room.

Combining interviews with three or four people who have no reason to be inhibited by each other's presence may save time and can be effective (for example, people in the Accounting department who all perform the same tasks). But do not mix interviewees with different perspectives or you may lose valuable details.

Meet at Their Place

Where is the best place to hold your interview? In the comfort and familiarity of your own cozy cubicle? Wrong! You want to hold your interviews at their location. Remember who is reaping information from whom. Your interviewees are the ones who need access to materials for questions they did not anticipate. And they are the ones you want to make comfortable, so they feel more free with their information, especially when delving into controversial, politically sensitive subjects.

Holding the interview at their location also yields a beneficial by-product. Being in their environment, you can glean other pertinent details about the way they work. Perhaps other questions will arise. Maybe problems will surface that otherwise may not have entered the conversation. For example, let's say you notice a pile (in fact, a very large mound) of computer-generated reports. Furthermore, these reports look extremely fresh, as if they were never read. And you know by the size of the three piles that they could not have arrived all in the past day or two. So you inquire about this and your interviewee replies, "Yes, these reports arrive every Monday. We look at the totals for column 3, write them in our log, and then just keep them around in case we need them." Well then, you can add "investigate report distribution" to your list of items to address.

Although the interviewee's location is usually the best place to meet, you may find situations to the contrary. For example, from meeting with a particular supervisor before, you may know that her office is laden with distractions—people with incessant questions, phone calls that will "just be a minute," and so on. If you are interested in work flow, this chaotic interlude may be informative to you. But if your objectives are otherwise (such as inquiring about sensitive aspects of the project), you need to arrange a conference room away from the distractions.

In the extreme case, for example, you do not want to discuss how job positions will be realigned while the staff bustles through their activities in the work areas surrounding your interview. When you do meet in a conference room, however, try to arrange a room in their area. That way, you come to their turf, thus communicating from the start that you are interested in how their business runs. Also, if they need something from their desk, it's close by.

Indeed, an important aspect of every interview is to let them know that you are genuinely interested in how they do their work, what problems they are having, what solutions they envision, and how information can help in the solution. This encourages the trust that you must earn now and will need from them as the project continues.

What Questions Not to Ask

Most often, people begin an interview with such queries as, "What information do you need?" or "What functions do you want from the system?" What's wrong with this line of questioning? It's putting the cart before the horse or, in our case, putting the system before the problem. If people knew what kind of information they needed, they would have asked for it already.

> Systems analysts assume managers surely know what information they need. . . . The problem is that this technique is akin to a psychoanalyst talking to a patient lying on a couch and asking, "What type of therapy do you need?" (Wetherbe 1991)

Let's say you spend days preparing overhead transparencies of prototype reports. As you go through each report, you ask, "Do you need this one?" At this point, people are often uncertain of their needs (since their *problems* have not even been identified yet). So, being afraid to give up something they might need later, they naturally say, "Oh sure, we'll take one of those." The result: more of the same—too much paper and not enough of what they really need.

To prevent this repeating cycle, avoid beginning with questions about functions and information. Instead, focus on *problems* and *solutions* first, then look at what *information* they need to solve the problems. James C. Wetherbe (professor of Management Information Systems at the University of Minnesota) describes an example of this line of questioning (Freedman 1991) in Figure 5.1.

Managers are very clear about their problems and potential solutions. So focus your questioning that way, saving information needs until the end. This difference is subtle, but dramatic.

Get Ready for the Interview

Here is where you translate your objectives into a list of questions to ask. This list is no more than an overall guideline of what to cover and a reminder of what not to forget. It is by no means a comprehensive script.

1	Question	What *problems* create obstacles in your work?
	Answer	Being out of stock too often and allocating limited inventory to the wrong customer.
2	Question	What are good *solutions* to these problems?
	Answer	Better inventory management and letting the warehouse know the importance of customers and of specific orders.
3	Question	How can *information* help in any of these solutions?
	Answer	Systems could provide out-of-stock and below-minimum reporting, automatic reordering and electronic access to customer and order importance.

Figure 5.1

What you learn in the interview will prompt you to ask new questions that you might not even have considered at the start.

After creating this outline, review it to determine what your interviewees can bring to the meeting. For example, are there reports, screen samples, or documents that can help? Then give your interviewees a call with enough lead time to assemble these items.

Also, if any of the questions might require research, let the interviewees know so they have time to query staff members or otherwise dig for data.

Your Opening Lines

Your opening depends on how familiar you are with the people you are interviewing. If you have worked with them before, your opening comes naturally as you ride on the rapport you have established over the years. But if you are meeting for the first time, you are indeed starting from scratch, and may even be starting as a perceived adversary. They may view you as an agent of change who threatens the comfortable work flow they have followed as long as they've been with the company.

In this case, begin by explaining your role on the project. Summarize how the goal is to improve things for them (for example, making more information available, cutting back on voluminous reports, or simplifying screens). But don't be so extreme in your description that it backfires. If you describe a potential system as "incredibly effective and streamlined," your interviewees may fear their jobs won't be needed anymore once it's installed. Instead, let them know that you are there because you want their ideas on how the current problems can be solved. And you anticipate in the end that their jobs will be easier.

Take Notes

Oh, what boring advice; it sounds like school. But it's true. You must document your interviews! You may understand exactly what is being said at the time. But the reality is that you will not remember it two weeks from now. And you'll either have to go back and get the information again, or make assumptions that may not be true.

If you feel that taking notes will hinder the flow of the interview or you know that you absolutely cannot listen, write, and talk at the same time, then bring along another person to document the interview.

Some may say, "I'll just jot down some notes as soon as I return to my desk." That sounds like a responsible thought; but if your job is like ours, you probably don't have the luxury of scheduled solitude where you can count on returning to a predictably uninterrupted work space and then adequately document your interview. Do it there in the interview, while the conversation is transpiring.

Reviewing and *updating* your notes after the interview is an excellent idea. Make sure you do this within 48 hours or you will not understand what you had written.

Listen Carefully

Yes, you have prepared your interview questions and have clear expectations of what you want to gain from the meeting. But don't let this structure hinder your ability to listen. When your interviewee gets off the track, as inevitably will happen, listen to the digression. Is this tangent uncovering (or leading to) information that will help in your objectives? Perhaps this person is revealing a problem you never considered or maybe is describing work-flow implications that you would not have thought to ask about. So listen carefully, with natural interest and empathy. Control unproductive diversions but, at the same time, listen for digressions with substance.

Restate What You've Heard

A good interviewer does more than ask questions and listen to the answers. Miscommunication can occur when either you or the interviewee misunderstands a question or an answer. One of the best ways to guard against these sources of error is to confirm your understanding of what's been said by restating it to the interviewee. An experienced interviewer will confirm his understanding with phrases like: "So what you're saying is . . ."; "Let me see if I understand you . . ."; and "In other words . . . ." When you restate in this fashion, you give the interviewee the opportunity to confirm that you've grasped his point ("Yes, that's right"), or if not, to clarify what you've missed ("No, what I really meant to say was . . ."). Restating also strengthens your retention of the material. There's an old saying among educators: A person hasn't really learned something unless he can say it, write it, or do it.

Make One More Phone Call

It's a good idea to make at least a brief follow-up. A phone call will suffice. After reviewing the notes you made in the interview, you will undoubtedly have a question or two that need clarification (for example, "Who actually uses the information on this report?"). Furthermore, this communication gives you a chance to thank them for the time they spent in the interview and it gives them a chance to share any afterthoughts they may have as well.

With your management interviews complete, you are prepared to produce the Management Definition Guide and schedule the session.

THE MANAGEMENT DEFINITION GUIDE

Management Definition Guide: Could a more mundane title for a document ever be found? Doesn't it sound like something to read when you can't sleep and have already tried counting sheep?

Despite the dryness of its title, the Management Definition Guide contains important substance. It defines what management wants from the project. It is written from management's perspective and includes the purpose, scope, and objectives of the project. It communicates management's direction and commitment.

Contents of the Document

The contents of this 10- to 20-page document come from the interviews you have completed in the business areas. (Sometimes a complete JAD session is held for the sole purpose of preparing the management perspective of the project.) The following describes what you gather in these interviews and how it comes together to build the Management Definition Guide.

This example is based on the project described in Chapter 1, where your company wants to design a robot to cater meals for company functions. This example shows what each section of the document accomplishes and clarifies such concepts as purpose, objectives, and functions. Once these concepts are clear, you then need to know how to complete each section of the Management Definition Guide for the actual projects you are faced with.

Title Page

The title page begins with the document's prosaic identifier, "Management Definition Guide," followed by:

- The project name
- The publication date
- The names of contributors
- The company name

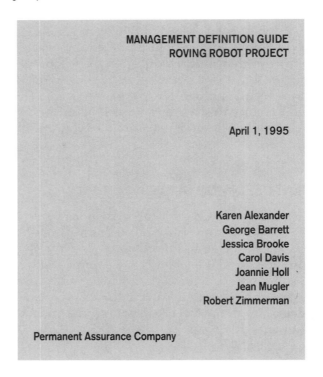

MANAGEMENT DEFINITION GUIDE
ROVING ROBOT PROJECT

April 1, 1995

Karen Alexander
George Barrett
Jessica Brooke
Carol Davis
Joannie Holl
Jean Mugler
Robert Zimmerman

Permanent Assurance Company

Preface

This summarizes how the Management Definition Guide fits into the JAD process. For example:

PREFACE
This document results from the first phase (JAD Project Definition) of the JAD process. Information gathered in interviews with the executive sponsor, key users, and IS managers has been compiled into this document, the Management Definition Guide.

Table of Contents

A table of contents is optional, but nice. It lists the document sections and their page numbers. You can divide more extensive sections into subsections, as shown with the items listed under the heading *Business Processes* in the following sample.

TABLE OF CONTENTS

Purpose 1

Scope 2

Management objectives 3

Business processes 5

    Plan meals 5

    Prepare meals 7

    Serve meals 8

    Clean up afterwards 9

Constraints 10

Resource requirements 11

Assumptions 12

Open issues 15

Session participants 18

Purpose

This tells *why* the project is being done.

PURPOSE

The company faces increased demands for catering services at company functions. Senior management has determined that a Roving Robot system can fulfill these culinary needs in a cost-effective manner. The robot will prepare and serve meals for breakfast and luncheon meetings as well as cater larger social functions, usually held in the evenings.

Scope

This tells *who* will use the new business processes and how often—which departments, divisions, and off-site locations. It lists the areas indirectly affected, such as those that will either provide information or receive it. Scope describes what existing computer systems are affected and identifies products that will be impacted. Scope can also identify business processes that are *not* included in the JAD.

SCOPE

The Roving Robot will be administered by the Corporate Services department to provide food services throughout the company. Ninety percent of the robot's services will be used by the following departments:

- Communications
- Sales and Marketing
- Human Resources

The expected volume of requests for catering can be estimated based on last year's volume, which totaled:

- 55 breakfast meetings averaging 15 people per meeting
- 80 luncheon meetings averaging 20 people per meeting
- 30 evening functions averaging 40 people per function (20 events were for drinks and appetizers; 10 included full-course dinners)

We expect these requests to increase 10 percent this year, 10 percent next year, and (due to a planned subsidiary acquisition) 20 percent the year after that.

The robot system will receive orders from the Information Desk (for catering requests) and will send requisitions to the Purchasing department (to handle major food purchases). It will automatically interface with the chargeback system to charge cost centers for its services.

Management Objectives

This tells *what* management expects to gain from the project. Try to quantify the objectives. Include such information as expected increases in sales volumes, decreases in costs, changes in inventory levels, and measurable improvements in customer satisfaction. Quantified objectives allow you to better determine if the resulting system meets those objectives. In the following example, notice that two of the four objectives are quantified.

MANAGEMENT OBJECTIVES

The Roving Robot system will:

- Reduce by 20 percent the cost of having meetings catered by outside food services.
- Increase reliability. The company has had a long history of bad luck with local caterers. With our own robot, we will have more control over the kind of service provided.
- Decrease by 50 percent the Corporate Services work load of having to process meal requests, contact caterers, and call out for pizza when food does not arrive.
- Increase the quality of food served at company functions. Satisfied, well-fed clients translate into more business for the company.

Business Processes

Business processes define a structured set of activities with a beginning and an end. They describe inputs, outputs, and the work done in between. There is a subtle distinction between business processes and objectives. Business processes tell what the system will do (prepare meals) while objectives tell what management will gain from these processes (catering costs are reduced).

BUSINESS PROCESSES

The Roving Robot will do the following:

Plan meals. The robot prepares meal plans based on:

- Time of day (breakfast, lunch, dinner, or snack)
- Type of attendees (staff, management, or clients)
- Season (summer, fall, winter, or spring)
- Desired ambiance (formal, informal, or festive)

After processing this information, the robot prints the following reports:

- Menu
- Shopping list, including what to buy and where to purchase it

Prepare meals. After the meal plan has been verified and supplies purchased, the robot assembles the ingredients into the appropriate cuisine. The robot will:

- Identify equipment such as pots, pans, woks, and food processors.
- Calibrate volume ranges from one pinch to six gallons. (It also handles metric conversions.)
- Distinguish between food entities such as lettuce heads and artichoke hearts.

Serve meals. The robot transports hot and cold meals to the meeting location.

Clean up afterwards. After dessert, the robot clears the table, washes the dishes, puts everything away, and prepares doggie bags on request.

Constraints

This describes limitations to consider. The most common constraint is time (the application must be installed by April 1). Others include cost (we cannot exceed a $500,000 budget), space (we have only 1,200 square feet to hold the equipment), system limitations (the software must run under UNIX), and government regulations. Sometimes time zone considerations are handled in this section (we need to handle West Coast agencies).

CONSTRAINTS

Constraints are:

- The robot must be ready for use by December 10 of next year to serve the annual Christmas party.
- The robot must perform all food preparation in the 800 square foot space now occupied by the copy center.
- The cost for the complete robot system cannot exceed $500,000.

Resource Requirements

This identifies additional resource requirements such as people, physical space, and hardware.

RESOURCE REQUIREMENTS

To implement the Roving Robot system, the following additional resources are needed:

- One part-time taster to sample new recipes and shop for the food specified on the Shopping List report
- One full-time worker to maintain quality control and service the robot
- A closet with a lock to store the robot
- A full complement of cooking equipment and supplies. (This list, which should include everything from a food processor to a stainless steel garlic press, will be finalized in the JAD session.)

Assumptions

Any general business decisions that emerge from the management interviews are included here. The list of assumptions will grow before and during the JAD session.

ASSUMPTIONS

Assumptions about the Roving Robot system are:

- Robot services will be charged back to the departments using them.
- Meals planned by the robot must meet corporate health standards (no junk food allowed).
- Equipment will be repaired only by certified robotic specialists.

Open Issues

This includes questions that have come up before the session that need to be resolved.

OPEN ISSUES

Open issues are:

- How will we handle the conflicting food and beverage preferences among departments? For example, there are several opposing views on what should be included on the wine list.
- How will we accommodate special requests, such as for vegetarian and kosher foods?
- What will we do for backup when the robot is out of service? Should we resort to food courts and pizza parlors as we do today or try to prepare meals ourselves (with real live cooks) in the newly constructed robot kitchen?

Session Participants

This lists all the participants (including the executive sponsor) who will either be attending the session or be on call during the session (see Figure 5.2). It also includes the departments they represent, their mail codes or addresses (for distribution), and their roles in the session. This preliminary roster will probably change somewhat before the actual session.

Send the completed Management Definition Guide to the contributors for their review. Give them a specific amount of time to return their comments. Two or three days should suffice. Then, send the revised document to all participants so they can read it before the session. It is the foundation of the JAD.

SCHEDULING THE SESSION

The session schedule is influenced by the scope of the project and, of course, the time constraints. Some projects can take several months to complete.

Name	Department	Mail Code	Role
Karen Alexander	Sales & Marketing	4	Team
George Barrett	Corporate Services	7	Executive Sponsor
Enya Brennan	Facilitities Management	2	Observer
Jessica Brooke	Communications	3	Team
Carol Davis	Corporate Services	7	Team
Joannie Holl	Research & Development	10	Team
Stella Kowalski	Communications	3	Team
Martin Major	Corporate Services	7	Team
Jean Mugler	IS	9	Team
Renee Rudolph	Business Systems Engineering	9	Facilitator
Terry Silver	IS	9	Scribe
Cindy Zonies	Sales & Marketing	4	Team

Figure 5.2 Session participants.

Others must be done in less time. One project in our company involved adding major enhancements to five separate application systems. Using JAD, we defined the business requirements in four months. This involved user and IS interviews, 25 back-to-back full-day sessions, and six final documents.

The Length of the Session

The time required for the session depends on the project. One-day sessions are not uncommon and certainly can produce good results. For example, we have held several one-day sessions to select among software packages. But three- to five-day sessions are more typical. They tend to enjoy more success because of some basic principles of group dynamics: The participants need about three days to work most effectively as a team. On the first day, the group gets acquainted. On the second day, they begin sharing perspectives. And by the third day, they are in a consensus-building mode. Consequently, the fourth and fifth days can be extremely productive.

It's hard to sustain the group for sessions longer than five days. And anytime a weekend interrupts your session, momentum decreases. It's difficult to decompose a business process when people are thinking about basking in the sun.

How Much Time Does Each Phase Take?

Figure 5.3 shows how much time typical JAD phases might take. Of course, depending on the project, the contents of these phases will vary. For example, Phase 2 (Research) will vary dramatically between a complex system design project and a simple package evaluation.

As you can see from Figure 5.3 most of our JAD projects last between three and nine weeks. But plenty of projects have fallen outside these typical ranges.

Sue Leonard (of Amoco Oil Company) suggests that lead time (that is, the three JAD phases that precede the session) can safely be minimized:

> Two years ago, we reduced our lead time requirement to a maximum of three weeks, with a goal of two weeks. With experience, you should get to the point where you can facilitate a meeting with only a few days notice. You may have to bypass interviewing every participant, but experience and organizational knowledge will teach you when you can do that without jeopardizing the quality of the JAD. (Leonard 1993)

Some JAD users and consultants often give much lower time estimates because they may not include the up-front work to the extent that others do. They may omit certain things, such as preparing the Working Document. In this case, a JAD project involves much less time but may not cover the same level of detail.

No.	Phase	Step	Work Days
1	JAD Project Definition	Interview management Produce the Management Definition Guide Schedule the session	1 to 3 1 to 3 1
2	Research	Get familiar with the existing system Document data requirements Document business processes Gather preliminary information Prepare the session agenda	1 to 4 1 to 5 1 to 5 2 to 4 1
3	Preparation	Preparing the Working Document Prepare overheads, flip charts and magnetics Hold the preseason meeting	2 to 5 1 1
4	The Session	Hold the session	1 to 5
5	The Final Document	Produce the final document Participants review the document Hold the review session Update and distribute the final document	1 to 5 2 1 2

Figure 5.3 Time required for each JAD phase.

Half-Day or Full-Day Sessions?

In the first edition of this book, we recommended half-day sessions over full days. If you have the luxury to choose either approach, we still recommend half days. Recently, however, we have found ourselves holding full-day sessions more often than before. Perhaps this is in response to downsizing, budget cuts, and tighter time constraints. Since we must complete projects in shorter times, we cannot always afford the half-day sessions.

We have talked with some people who feel that full-day sessions are the only way to go. They feel that groups lose momentum in the half-day format. Some say that what takes three full-day sessions can require as much as seven to ten half days to accomplish. It takes time each morning to bring the session up to speed.

We feel there is credence to this, *sometimes*. For example, a session with stamina and strong group identity can easily keep the momentum of the full-day pace. However, the time saved in less lost momentum during full days is offset by the challenge of keeping that motivation going for three to five days straight. No matter what the setting, full days are strenuous for everyone. By mid-afternoon, unless you can add scintillating humor and spellbinding enchantment to the subjects of data models and screen design, you will probably lose at least some of the participants to cognitive burnout. Productivity diminishes and afternoon caffeinated cola can recharge only the most resilient.

With half-day sessions, participants are more attentive and less preoccupied with what might be happening (or not happening) back at the office. They still have the non-JAD part of the day for other responsibilities. Also, when people need to get information about a particular item discussed in the session, they have time to make contacts and do research in their own environment rather than making hurried phone calls during a break or staying after normal work hours.

Facilitators benefit from half-day sessions as well. They have time to review the scribe's documentation and research questions. They can prepare flip charts, magnetics, or overhead transparencies showing, for example, the new data models that may have emerged via the CASE tool in that day's session.

Another advantage of half-day sessions is scheduling. Bringing together a group of key company people for up to five days straight is challenging enough, let alone trying to arrange all *full* days. With half days, the participants still have some time for their other work.

Sessions are more productive in the morning than in the afternoon. Early in the day, people are more awake and ready to get started. For example, sessions can be held from 8:30 to 12:30 with a 15-minute mid-morning break.

In summary, full-day sessions can offer higher momentum for certain groups and an earlier JAD completion date. Also, if you use a consultant, this is the best approach. On the other hand, half days are easier to schedule, not as subject to burnout, and allow other work to continue in the non-JAD part of the day.

Being Off-Site and Inaccessible

Sessions can be held anywhere you have sufficient space, magnetic boards, and a place to project overhead images. However, holding them off-site in a separate building has several advantages. Of course, you pay the charges for the room, coffee, and audio visuals. And participants must take time to travel to the off-site location. But these inconveniences are worth the benefits gained.

The main advantage of being off-site is simply stated: *out of sight, out of mind*. Being away from work prevents distractions such as co-workers who just want to "check on something" or pass along phone messages that you might want to follow up on.

Another advantage is partly psychological. Most people enjoy getting away. The change in environment frees the mind to focus more completely on the project at hand. This makes for a more productive session. Anthony Crawford (leading JAD expert) describes a JAD project involving an insurance company:

> [The session was held at] a management training center some ten miles out of the city. The location was idyllic—with spectacular views. It was a perfect setting for creating a sense of remoteness from work pressures and for people to become creative thinkers and deal with situations otherwise thought of as beyond their scope. (Crawford 1994)

Finding a Room for the Session

When evaluating meeting rooms, whether on-site or off, look for:

- *Large tables.* Participants like to have many items in front of them, such as JAD documents, data dictionary listings, notes, mugs of coffee, donuts, and name cards.
- *Audio-visual accommodations.* If you want to rent equipment, check the models and prices. Evaluate the room for projection conditions. Is there enough space to project a sufficiently large screen image? Do they have an overhead projector available?
- *Board space.* The more board space the better. To use the magnetic techniques described in the "Visual Aids" section of Chapter 7, you will need a white magnetic board. This allows you to write with colored pens as well as to move magnetic shapes around the board when designing screens and creating lists of items to prioritize.
- *Storage space.* Having a locked area allows you to store your supplies and equipment overnight.

- *Food services.* What refreshments are available? For example, it is nice to have coffee and pastry for morning sessions and soda for afternoon sessions.
- *Flexible scheduling.* Can sessions be scheduled on consecutive days (to keep the momentum going) and in the same room (to save setup time)?
- *Comfort.* Good ventilation and climate control are also important.
- *Convenient location.* Being close to the office is nice, but not as important as the other considerations.

Although hotels are relatively expensive and generally do not have good board space (flocked wallpaper just doesn't work for flip charts), some companies use hotels. Sometimes, these companies arrange for the participants to stay overnight (sequester them!) for the duration of the session. In this way, the session timetable becomes more flexible. If good progress is being made, the group can continue the session and keep the momentum going. If the session drops behind schedule, they can squeeze in some extra time in the early morning or evening. And many an open issue has been resolved over a good spaghetti dinner.

If the cost of hotels is prohibitive for your company, try buildings that lease office space to small businesses. They often have available meeting rooms. Colleges and universities are sometimes suitable, but the challenge is finding a room that has tables (most have only desks) and that is available for several consecutive days. Also, some colleges rent only to nonprofit organizations. If you do find a room on a campus, you will probably have excellent board and wall space (not to mention the inspiring environment of a college campus).

When all else fails, open your wallet and rent a hotel room. For rooms with little or no board space, you can rent or buy portable magnetic boards from audio-visual or office supply companies.

When to Hold the Session

Determining when to hold the session depends on whether the target date for completing the project has been set. Target dates are either flexible (people have not set a firm date) or mandated (upper management or "Uncle Sam" says implement the new procedures by July 1).

For *flexible* target dates, management can wait until after the session to determine a realistic implementation date. This is by far the best way to set target dates. Once the session is complete, the complexity of the requirements is known, which enables management to set more realistic target dates. Also, with flexible dates, you have time before the session for more detailed analysis of the requirements.

For *mandated* target dates, plan the project working backward from the final date. For example, you might have a mandated target date of January 1. Working backward from that date, you can calculate when the JAD session must be held.

Once you set the session dates and select the meeting room, send a memo (from you, the facilitator) to the session participants with copies to:

- The executive sponsor
- Your manager
- Any others who should be advised

Figure 5.4 shows a sample of this memo.

Having completed the JAD Project Definition phase, you are ready for Phase 2: Research.

August 20, 1995

To:	JAD Participants
From:	Renee Rudolph
Subject:	The JAD Session

The Roving Robot system JAD session will be held in the Liberty Building at 3600 Market Street. To determine the complete business requirements, it is vital that all participants attend.

Location:	Liberty Building (Room 101) 3600 Market Street
Dates:	September 26 to 30 (8:30–12:30)
Phone:	Messages can be left at 555–2200.
Public Transportation:	Market–Frankford Elevated A-train to 34th Street
Parking:	Across the street.
Snacks:	Coffee, tea, and Danish.
Copies:	(executive sponsor) (your manager) (others who should be advised)

Figure 5.4 JAD session memo.

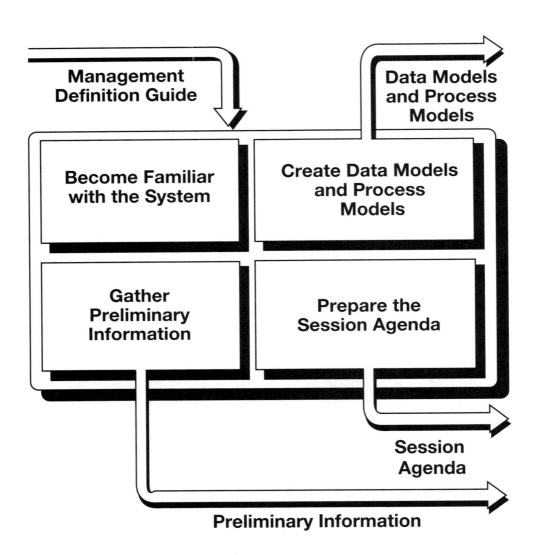

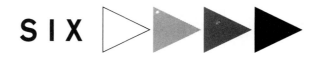

SIX

PHASE 2: RESEARCH

Having selected the JAD team, prepared the Management Definition Guide, and scheduled the session, you are ready to:

- Become familiar with the business area or system
- Document data requirements
- Document business processes
- Gather preliminary information (for example, screens and reports)
- Prepare the session agenda

The information gathered in this phase goes into the Working Document prepared in Phase 3.

GETTING FAMILIAR WITH THE BUSINESS

The best way to familiarize yourself with the functions of the business is to set up meetings with the people in the business area and IS (if a computer system is involved). You need to learn enough about the business to be comfortable with the terminology and buzzwords. And you need to know enough about how the current work flow and computer systems work so that you can effectively facilitate the session.

Meeting with the Business People

Hold the meeting in the business area. Meet with those who actually do the work. The ideal person is a working supervisor who has performed all of the business functions.

1. *Observe the working environment.* Take a user-guided tour through the workplace. Some facilitators take photographs of the key business areas. Then during the session they project the slides to allow participants to see a visual image of the area being discussed.

2. *Observe the overall work flow.* How do they do their jobs? What roles do people play? Observe the activities they perform. *Why* do they do these particular activities? Sometimes the "why" of an activity is more illuminating than the "what."

    If there is an existing computer system, have the users log on to it. Spend some time with the main menu and submenus, as these often summarize the business functions. Have them enter some real data. Ask them to perform their functions as they normally would, including handling phone calls, sorting through mail, and reading reports. Where do they get the information they need to accomplish their tasks? What is the volume of activity? Discuss the processing; in other words, what happens to that data?

3. *Review the output.* This includes anything they create in their work: manual forms, tally sheets, and hardcopy computer reports. Tell the people well before the meeting that you are interested in seeing these reports. Find out the frequency of distribution.

4. *Discuss the business changes.* Do they like the way things are now? What are the problems? What causes time delays? What solutions do they envision?

Meeting with IS

Your goal for this meeting is to get a more technical overview of how the system works. You want to fill in the gaps from a data-processing perspective. Therefore, arrange the IS meeting not only with the project manager, but with the programmer analyst who works directly with the programs.

1. What is the project history? What are the current weaknesses in the system and how can they be addressed?

2. What problems do they envision in implementing the requirements we have identified so far?

3. Will existing hardware be able to support the new system?

4. Which IS representatives should participate in the JAD session to provide technical information about the system?

Does the Facilitator Have to Know Everything?

As you gather information you (the facilitator) will come face to face with the question, *how much do you really need to know?*

The more of a perfectionist you are, the more you are burdened with the quest to know everything. There may be a compulsive part of you that wants to learn every detail about every function in the business and in the system. You want to know it as a user or programmer would.

The best thing you can do is to divest yourself of this self-imposed burden right now. The facilitator does *not* have to know everything. By realizing this, you will save yourself a lot of time and energy plodding through piles of forms, reams of source code, pages of calculations, and other details that can only bog you down.

Keep your perspective on a higher level. Yes, you need to know the business functions. You need to know generally how the system is used. But you do not need to know every value that a field can have. You are not preparing to fill in for fallen programmers. You are preparing to lead a session in a room full of participants who already have their heads filled with such details as how the program performs commission calculations and which amounts are valid for the cash-value field. These system experts will handle the details. One application system could have a project team of 10 people whose sole purpose in life (so to speak) is to know the definition for every data element, complex calculation, and other nuances. You, the facilitator, could be dealing with six major systems in one year. How could you possibly learn all the details? Your job is to keep sight of the big picture, run the JAD using the resident experts, and move on to the next project.

DOCUMENTING DATA REQUIREMENTS

There are many ways to document what data the business area needs and how this data interrelates. Most companies build these data models using entity-relationship diagrams (ERDs). The goal of data modeling is to:

- Identify the groupings of data used in the business area.
- Define the data element (or attribute) names and descriptions.
- Define the relationship between the data groups.
- Correctly structure (that is, normalize) the data.

You can build prototype data models in small meetings prior to the session or you can have an entire JAD session whose sole purpose is to create these models. In either case, you can use the same technique as described in the next section (Documenting Business Processes). The Post-it™ notes can

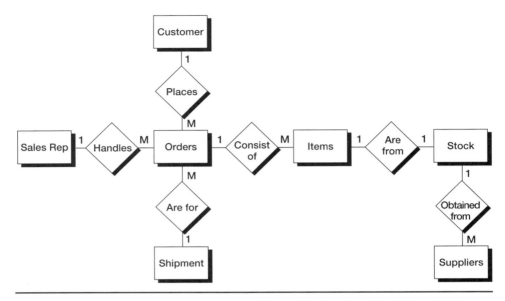

Figure 6.1 Sample entity-relationship diagram.

represent the data entities. These data models are best designed with the aid of automated tools. Figure 6.1 shows a portion of an ERD for an order entry project.

DOCUMENTING BUSINESS PROCESSES

While the data model tells us what information we need, the business process models define the rules for using the data. To document the inner workings of a business process, many types of diagramming techniques are available. Some companies use decomposition diagrams, some use process dependency diagrams, and others build matrices. No single graphic technique is the best. To capture business processes, we use data flow diagrams. People can understand these pictures and easily modify them.

Data Flow Diagrams

This method, which comes from the world of structured analysis and design, documents the flow of information between business processes. The most common methods for creating data flow diagrams are those of Yourdon and Gane & Sarson.

To create these diagrams, we use a CASE (Computer Aided Software Engineering) tool. Although such tools make the job easier, they are not absolutely essential. But they do help when it comes to revising and analyzing the diagrams. As the CASE salesperson will tell you, people are reluctant to change system designs because it means having to redraw all those diagrams. CASE tools make this easier and can save a lot of pencil lead and eraser crumbs. Also, most of these tools have a data dictionary—a central repository for storing information about the diagrams for later use.

Parts of a Data Flow Diagram

To set the stage for describing how to identify business processes and create data flow diagrams, it will help to talk about the kind of information you are dealing with. Data flow diagrams contain four kinds of information:

- Data flows
- Processes
- Data stores
- External entities

The following describes each of these parts. Figure 6.2 shows a data flow diagram that uses "Pay Bills" as an example. Refer to this diagram as each part is described.

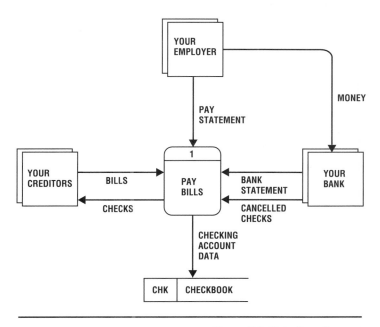

Figure 6.2 Data flow diagram.

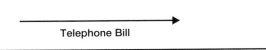

Telephone Bill

Figure 6.3 Data flow.

- *Data flow.* This is the information that moves through the system. For example, your telephone bill is a data flow. It contains pieces of data moving from the telephone company to you. Data flows can be drawn at any level of detail. Just as your telephone bill is a data flow, so is each piece of information on it, such as your account number, name, address, and the amount due. In the diagrams, data flows are shown as arrows (see Figure 6.3).

- *Process.* This is what causes data to change. Data moves into a process, is somehow changed, and then moves out of the process. For example, the telephone bill moves into a process called *Pay bills,* where the data is reorganized into the form of a personal check and sent back to the telephone company. The best way to make sure something is a process is to see if the data has, in fact, changed. If someone receives data, does nothing with it, and passes it along in the same form, then a process has not occurred. Processes are shown in a rounded rectangle (see Figure 6.4) with an accompanying number that uniquely identifies the process (more about these numbers later).

- *Data store.* This is a repository for data. Data stores usually take the form of files or data bases, but they can just as well be filing cabinets, bins, or anything else that holds information. In the "Pay Bills" example, your checkbook is a data store because that is where you store information about what has been paid (see Figure 6.5).

- *External entity.* This is anything the system interacts with that is not actually part of that system. In a typical business example, external entities might include customers, sales agents, or other computer systems. In our example, the external entities are your creditors, employer, and the bank. They are shown in Figure 6.6.

Figure 6.4 Process.

CHK	CHECKBOOK

Figure 6.5 Data store.

Figure 6.2 (the data flow diagram for paying the bills) includes a process, several data flows, a data store, and three external entities.

In data flow diagramming, processes can be *decomposed* into more detailed levels. For example, in Figure 6.2, the process "Pay Bills" can be decomposed into several subprocesses such as sort the bills, write checks, and balance the checkbook.

To identify the level of decomposition, the processes are identified with numbers. If the "Pay Bills" process is process number 1, it could decompose into the following processes:

1.1 Sort Bills

1.2 Write Checks

1.3 Balance the Checkbook

For some other project, process number 2 might decompose into a diagram containing these processes:

2.1

2.2

2.3

Then process 2.1 could, in turn, decompose into these processes:

2.1.1

2.1.2

2.1.3

2.1.4, and so on.

Figure 6.7 shows how these decomposed processes are numbered.

Figure 6.6 External entity.

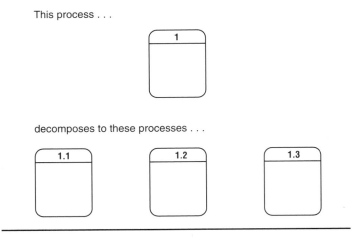

Figure 6.7 Numbering processes in data flow diagrams.

What we have shown is one way to diagram business processes. You may already be using this technique or some other approach that works for you. This brief description of data flow diagrams is just the tip of the iceberg. Complete books have been written on this and other structured analysis techniques.

Capturing the Business Processes

Now, how do you get the business flow out of the peoples' heads and onto paper? You can do this in the session. Or, if you want to come into the session with proposed business processes, then you can lead a series of small design meetings beforehand.

What about tools? Using a CASE tool is the obvious approach. But there are plenty of ways to do it without CASE. We'll describe an effective way of using overhead transparencies, a whiteboard, flip charts, and Post-it™ notes. Enthusiasts refer to this approach as PASE (Post-it Assisted Software Engineering).

The following description shows you how to *capture business processes,* whether you use data flow diagrams, decomposition diagrams, or whatever. This four-step method uses an example involving the design of an Order Processing system.

1. Identify the First Level of the Business Process

   Arrange a meeting with the two or three people who really know the work flow. They are usually a manager or supervisor and perhaps someone from IS. Also, have a scribe attend to assist in documenting decisions. You will see the importance of this in a moment.

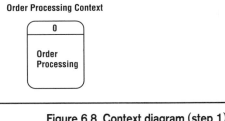

Figure 6.8 Context diagram (step 1).

Open the meeting by explaining how the business processes will be diagrammed. If you are using data flow diagrams, for example, describe the technique as we did beginning on page 85.

Start with the first level of business. This is the *context* diagram; that is, the highest-level diagram that shows the scope of the system and the net flow of data in and out of it. In our example, the scope of the system is "Order Processing." Therefore, the context diagram is named *Order Processing Context*. Write that name at the top of the board. Draw a rounded rectangle in the middle of the board with the system name and a zero for its number, as shown in Figure 6.8.

Order Processing is shown in a rectangle because it is a process in the broadest sense; that is, something is happening to the data.

Next, identify the data flows. Ask the group, "What comes into order processing and what goes out? We are not concerned with details here. If we have one line of data flow coming into the process and one going out, that is sufficient." Keep the diagram as simple as possible.

The group will probably ignore your plea for summary information and try to give you the whole enchilada: "Well, we get requests for new orders, order changes, order cancellations, address changes, and . . . ." After you ask them to summarize all that into just a few data flows, they suggest that *order information* comes into the system and the following goes out:

Invoices

Billing information

Packing slips

Shipping labels

Reports

Add these flows to your diagram (see Figure 6.9).

Ask the group where this information is coming from and going to. They may tell you that "order information" comes from customers and

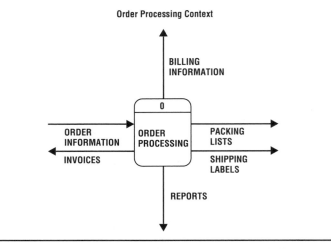

Figure 6.9 Context diagram (step 2).

"billing information" goes to Accounts Receivable. The other informa-tion goes to the Sales Manager and Shipping Department. These are the external entities because, although they interface with the process, they are not part of it. By adding these four external entities, you have a complete first-level data flow diagram (see Figure 6.10).

2. Identify the Second Level of the Business Process

Keeping the first-level diagram on the board, move to the flip chart. Tell the group the next step is to define the second level of the busi-ness process. In other words, you are going to decompose process *0—Order Processing* into a second level.

Label the diagram at the top of the flip chart as *0—Order Processing*. (The zero at the beginning of the title identifies the process from which it was decomposed.)

Now, ask the group, "What is involved in Order Processing? What functions do you want to do?" After much discussion on the many detailed tasks, they come up with three general ones:

Enter orders

Maintain customer file

Print reports

These are the processes for your new diagram. This time, however, you will not use the board to build the diagram, for the following reasons:

• You usually do not have sufficient board space to draw another level *and* keep the previous level in place for reference.

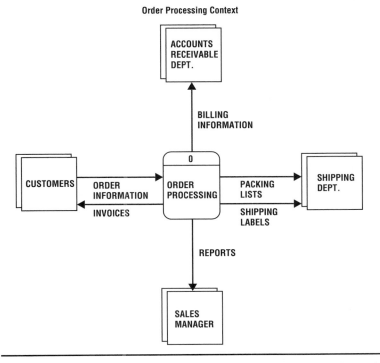

Figure 6.10 Completed context diagram (step 3).

- As discussions progress, diagrams can change to such a degree that if you were using the board, you would be driven mad by having to constantly erase and relocate the shifting parts of the diagram.

So you need an easy way to move the parts of the diagram around. To do this, use a flip chart and the Post-it notepads. For simplicity, we will call them "notes." As this second-level data flow diagram develops, the scribe writes the data flows, processes, data stores, and external entities on the notes while you place them on the flip chart. When a new process arises, the scribe makes a new note. When a location changes, you move the note to its new place.

Now that the group has identified the three processes for the second-level data flow diagram, you put these processes on notes and place them in the middle of the chart. (At this point, you have no idea what other processes might be added or where they will end up.) The contents of the flip chart are shown in Figure 6.11.

Ask the same questions as you did for the first level. "What data comes into these three processes and what data goes out? And where does the data go from here?" Several data flows and the data store *Cus-*

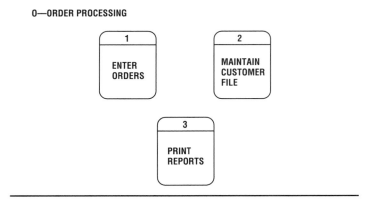

Figure 6.11 Three processes.

tomer File are identified. The complete second-level diagram is shown in Figure 6.12.

Two levels may be all you can accomplish in the first meeting. Do not keep the group more than two hours. You want to leave them at a point where they feel they really accomplished something rather than in the unresolved depths of a third-level data flow diagram.

After the meeting, you translate everything from the board and flip chart into two data flow diagrams. Either use a CASE tool or draw them by hand. Put them each on separate pages and title them:

Order Processing Context

O—Order Processing

Then copy these diagrams onto overhead transparencies.

The next day, hold a second meeting with the same group. Begin by reviewing what was done in the previous meeting. Using an overhead projector, show the two levels. Note any additional changes on the transparencies.

3. Identify the Third Level of the Business Process

The next step is to decompose from the second-level diagram into several third-level diagrams. A separate diagram is created for each process. So the third level includes three diagrams named after the processes they decomposed from:

1—Enter Orders

2—Maintain Customer File

3—Print Reports

0—ORDER PROCESSING

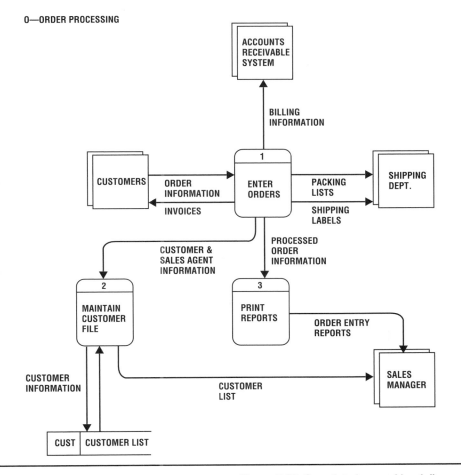

Figure 6.12 Completed second-level diagram.

Tack the original flip-chart diagram to the wall for reference. On a blank flip chart page, write the title for today's first diagram (see Figure 6.13).

Discuss the process called *1—Enter Orders*. In the same way as before, ask the group to break down this larger process. Perhaps they identify six subprocesses:

1.1—Add Orders

1.2—Change Orders

1.3—Print Orders

1.4—Print Packing List

1–ENTER ORDERS

Figure 6.13 First diagram title.

1.5—Print Labels

1.6—Print Invoices

Put these processes in rectangles on notes and stick them to the flip chart. Identify the data flows, data stores, and external entities. In the previous level, notice the data flows coming in and out of the process. These must all be included in this diagram as well. In structured analysis and design, this is referred to as "balancing."

When this diagram is complete, continue with the second process, *Maintain Customer File*. Write the title on a blank flip-chart page as shown in Figure 6.14.

Break down this process into its subprocesses. They might be:

2.1—Add Customer Data

2.2—Change Customer Data

2.3—Delete Customer Data

2–MAINTAIN CUSTOMER FILE

Figure 6.14 Second diagram title.

Put these processes on the flip chart and identify the data flows, data stores, and external entities. Is this beginning to sound repetitive? You bet! Once you get past the second level, a pattern develops where you identify, review, identify, review, and so on.

4. Continue the Levels

The number of levels you diagram depends on the size of the business and amount of detail you need. As before, guide the attendees through defining these levels. At the end, you have a series of data flow diagrams showing the business processes. You can take these diagrams into the JAD session as a starting point for discussion with the full group. The diagrams will probably change some more, but you will not be starting with a blank board. You can imagine how difficult managing this process would be in a full session with 18 participants. Situations do arise, however, where you must define segments of processes in the session. For example, sometimes new processes are hinged on the outcome of open issues that are not resolved until the session.

Decomposition Diagrams

A decomposition diagram can show the hierarchy of the processes involved in a system or business area. A decomposition diagram breaks down the work flow into manageable pieces. This helps you get a broad overview of a complex system. You can use the same technique described in preparing data flow diagrams with the Post-it notes. Figure 6.15 shows a simple decomposition diagram you might create for an order-entry project.

GATHERING PRELIMINARY INFORMATION

This part of the Research phase involves gathering information about the business requirements. This can include any preliminary information that will be further defined in the session. For example, for a systems development project, you may want to gather information on screens, reports, or processing requirements.

The kind of information to gather depends on what you want to accomplish in the session. Do you need to gather mission and goals information for a strategic plan, vendor information for a package evaluation, or calculations for a new insurance product? Or will you only be defining a few new screens for an enhancement? For example, the following summarizes what you might want to gather during this research phase for designing text-based screens for mainframe applications:

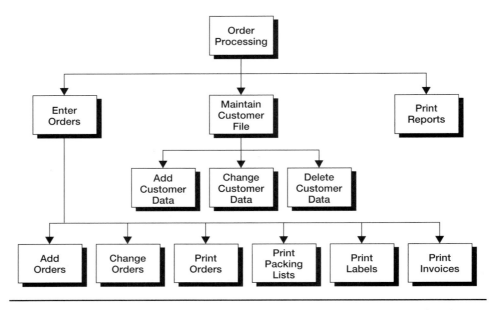

Figure 6.15 Decomposition diagram.

- *Screen flow.* This diagram shows how the screens branch.
- *Screen descriptions.* These describe the function of each screen.
- *Samples of existing screens.* These can be used in the session for reference or as a basis for creating new screens.
- *Prototypes of new screens.* These are preliminary designs of how the new screens might look.
- *Screen messages.* These messages display on the screen and identify error conditions or confirm that an action has taken place (for example, a new order has been accepted).

The following summarizes what you might want to gather for designing reports:

- *Report descriptions.* These describe the function of each report, including report name, general description, frequency of distribution, number of copies needed, distribution list, and sort specifications.
- *Sample of existing reports.* These can be used in the session for reference or as a basis for creating new reports.
- *Prototypes of new reports.* These are preliminary designs of how the new reports might look.

THE SESSION AGENDA

Although the session agenda has been evolving and probably will continue to change somewhat, now is the time to put it into as close to final form as you can. The agenda is based on what you have learned from:

- Preparing the Management Definition Guide
- Doing familiarization interviews
- Documenting the data requirements
- Documenting the business processes
- Gathering preliminary information

By now, you should have a good idea of what needs to be accomplished in the session. List everything that must be covered, then organize these items into a logical order. Figure 6.16 shows a typical agenda for a system design session.

Notice that the agenda items in these samples begin with verbs such as *define, design,* and *review.* These words further explain how each agenda item will be handled. If prototypes are available, you will probably be *reviewing* them. If not, then you will be *designing* from scratch.

No Two JAD Agendas Are Alike

An agenda can include anything. It depends on what you want to accomplish in the session. Each of the following types of JAD sessions would have a unique agenda:

- Prepare a strategic plan
- Brainstorm a reengineering project

AGENDA
COMMISSIONS JAD SESSION

1. Overview of existing Commissions system
2. Define new data elements
3. Design new screens
4. Review and modify existing reports
5. Define calculation routines
6. Resolve open issues

Figure 6.16 Agenda for the Commissions JAD session.

AGENDA
CORPORATE STRATEGIC PLANNING SESSION

1. Overview of session scope and objectives
2. Define financial goals and objectives
3. Discuss how to reduce costs
4. Define marketing goals and objectives
5. Discuss problems with the company's image
6. Define enterprise model
7. Define time frames for achieving each goal
8. Discuss how to measure the plan's success
9. Prepare action plan

Figure 6.17 Agenda for a strategic planning JAD session.

- Define corporate policy
- Build a project plan
- Define data requirements
- Define business processes
- Identify regulations
- Resolve security issues
- Create a manual form

AGENDA
DATA REQUIREMENTS SESSION

1. Discuss problems with the existing system
2. Define and describe each entity type
3. Describe the relationships among entities
4. Define the volumes for each entity type
5. Prepare data element descriptions
6. Review the entity-relationship diagram

Figure 6.18 Agenda for a data requirements JAD session.

For example, an agenda for defining a strategic plan might include the items in Figure 6.17.

But an agenda for defining the data that the users need to perform their job might look like Figure 6.18.

Having completed the Research phase, you are ready for Phase 3: Preparation.

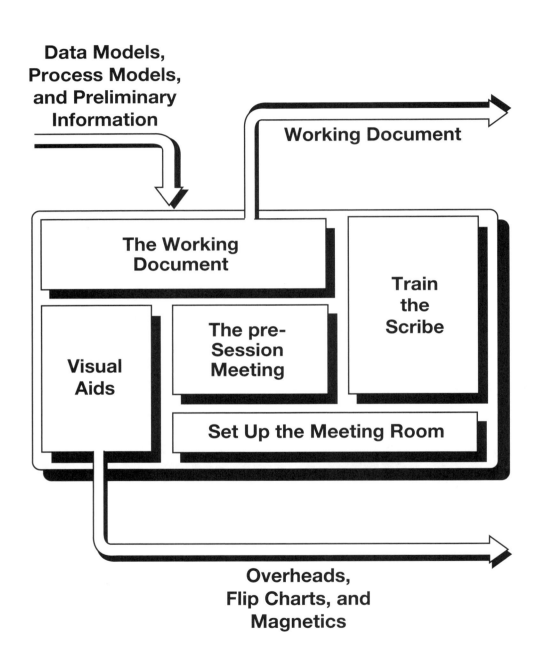

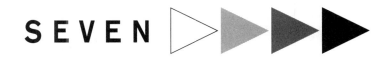
PHASE 3: PREPARATION

You have now interviewed the business area people and, in many cases, IS managers and programmer/analysts. You have documented data requirements and business processes, gathered preliminary information, and prepared the agenda for the session. Having spoken with the people who know the business best, you should have a level of understanding ("cocktail party knowledge") sufficient to talk intelligently about the project. Now, moving into Phase 3, you have pages and pages of *proposed* requirements which might include definitions of business processes, data models, screens, and reports. Also, assumptions and open issues have been accumulating throughout the first two phases.

All this information needs to be compiled into a document that can be used in the session. Also, you train the scribe, create visual aids, hold a pre-session meeting, and set up the meeting room the day before the session begins.

THE WORKING DOCUMENT

The Working Document is just that, something to work from in the session. It is a point of departure for making decisions. Although this document may have the look of a final copy (especially if you've used the most advanced formatting features of your word processor), everything in the document is *proposed*. It contains the lists, diagrams, and text that people suggested during small meetings or phone conversations before the session. You should emphasize this point in the pre-session meeting (discussed later in this chapter) so that people do not go into the session thinking that final decisions have already been made. Don't make the Working Document *too* pretty—so as to retain its tentative character. You might, for example, forgo fancy fonts and right justification.

The Working Document should be in the same format as the final JAD document and can include:

- Title page
- Preface
- JAD overview
- Agenda
- Session participants
- Distribution for the final document
- Assumptions
- Requirements (such as data requirements, business processes, and screens)
- Open issues

The following sections describe each of these parts.

Title Page

This includes the document title, project name, and date.

Preface

This describes how the document fits into the overall JAD process.

> **PREFACE**
>
> **This is a working document for the Order Processing project. It includes proposed requirements to use as a starting point in the JAD session.**

JAD Overview

Some companies include a summary (about two pages) just after the preface. It summarizes the JAD process for people who have not yet participated in a session. It gives them the background they need to understand how JAD fits into the overall project.

Session Agenda

This describes what will be covered in the session.

SESSION AGENDA

The following items will be covered in the four-day JAD session to be held July 7 to 10, 1995.

1. Overview
2. Discuss assumptions
3. Define data requirements
4. Define business processes
5. Design screens
6. Design reports
7. Resolve open issues

Session Participants

This tells who is attending the session, their departments, mail codes, and roles (see Figure 7.1). The same list was included in the Management Definition Guide. You can copy that one and update it with any changes in participants. Also include the executive sponsor even though she may not be attending the session.

Distribution for the Final Document

This lists all those who will receive the final document. This includes the participants and any others who should receive it.

Assumptions

The Assumptions section includes the sum total of business decisions agreed upon so far. These should be considered during the session. For example:

ASSUMPTIONS

1. All checks from the Cash Disbursement System will be printed at the home office.

Name	Department	Mail Code	Role
Ryan Barrett	Ordering	3	Executive Sponsor
Allison Brooke	Ordering	3	Team
Martha Clancy	Business Systems Engineering	7	Facilitator
Sally Doehnert	Law	3	On-call
Barbara Haber	Accounts Receivable	2	Observer
Michael Kowalski	Customer Service	4	Team
Sarah Major	IS	9	Team
Linda Morgan	Shipping & Receiving	1	Team
Charles Mugler	IS	9	Scribe
Patricia Noar	Marketing	2	On-call
Robin Rosen	Ordering	3	Team
Anna Schwartz	Sales	4	Team

Figure 7.1 Session participants.

Requirements

These sections of the Working Document tie directly to each particular agenda item covered in the session. For example, they might include data models, business processes, or screen designs. The details of how to handle these agenda items and what the Working Document should contain are described in Chapter 8, which includes complete descriptions and actual Working Document samples.

Open Issues

The Open Issues section includes the complete list to date of all unresolved questions that need to be answered either during the session or afterwards. For example:

OPEN ISSUES

1. How will we handle the different customer numbers that vary in size among divisions? For example, Milwaukee uses seven digits while Hoboken uses two letters followed by three digits.

Sending Out the Document

Send the document to all participants at least one week before the session begins. This gives them time to review the document and do any research or preparation necessary. If the timing works out, you can distribute it at the pre-session meeting. Include a cover memo as shown in Figure 7.2.

With the Working Document complete, you have accomplished a task that is as important as the session itself. The more clearly you can present these proposed requirements, the smoother the decision-making process will go when all the participants are together.

Now you are ready to continue with the other pre-session preparations.

TRAINING THE SCRIBE

Training the scribe may be exaggerating the task. It is not exactly an Olympic event. But unless the scribe is part of your staff and has done this role before, you do need to prepare the scribe for his role. This involves one meeting, at least a week before the session, where you:

1. Summarize the role of the scribe

The first question the scribe asks will probably be, "Why me?" and then, "Do I have to know how to take good notes?" Explain that the role does not involve note-taking in the traditional sense. Stress the importance of the role. You may be dealing with someone who is not pleased with being asked to record the session decisions. Also, the person may not be aware of the critical impact he will have on the final product. This person was probably

---

June 30, 1995

To: Order Processing JAD Participants

From: Martha Clancy

Subject: Working Document

Attached is the Working Document for the Order Processing JAD session. This document, along with the Management Definition Guide distributed on June 16, will be the basis for our discussions in the session.

See you Monday at 8:30.

Figure 7.2 Cover memo.

selected to scribe because of familiarity with the business and good communications skills. Explaining this may make the scribe feel more positive about the task. The scribe's functions in the session are detailed in Chapter 4.

2. Describe the JAD process

If the scribe has not been in a JAD, walk him through the five phases, emphasizing how the scribe's role fits into the process.

3. Discuss the project

Because of being familiar with the business, the scribe will also know about the project to some extent. This is a good opportunity to get the scribe's comments. Make sure the scribe reviews the Management Definition Guide.

4. Describe the session

Show the scribe the printed agenda and discuss how each item will be handled. This is where you get into detail. Show what visual aids will be used. Point out when to make revisions directly in the Working Document and when to use specific forms or tools. Explain the task of making magnetics as new data elements or screen names arise.

In closing, ask the scribe to arrive at the session early to help set up the visual aids. Make plans to meet shortly after the session to review what was documented that day. And, of course, show appreciation for his help. You will be relying on the scribe a great deal throughout the session.

Daily Session Meetings with the Scribe

After each day of the session, meet with the scribe. Review all completed notes. Are they understandable? (If they do not make sense now, they will have absolutely no meaning in three days.) Has all the information from the board been documented accurately? (Never count on the board information remaining overnight. It might get erased.)

Promoting the Role of the Scribe

Sometimes companies have trouble finding people willing to scribe sessions because the role is often perceived as a menial, note-taking function that nobody wants to do. It's unfortunate that this perception exists because, on the contrary, the role is important. Scribing is the link between the session decisions and the final documentation.

If you feel the scribe's role has a negative image, here are some ways to help promote it:

- *Give the role another name.* If you feel that the name "scribe" demeans the image, call it something else. Other names used are "documenter," "documentation specialist," and "recorder." Some use "design analyst," although this title should be reserved for people with analysis skills and perhaps CASE tool expertise. Changing the name, however, is only a surface cure. You need to do more.

- *Enhance the scribe's role.* Sometimes the scribe does nothing more than push the pen when prompted. This could be the problem. In this case, beef up the role. Give scribes more responsibility. Have them participate in some of the "boardtalk" endeavors (the scribe can fill in information on the board while the facilitator guides the discussion). Ask them to read back decisions to confirm accuracy, or have them write the open issues on the flip charts.

- *Involve them in the tools.* Perhaps you can have the scribe operate any of the various tools you use in the session. This includes anything from overhead projectors to computer screen projection units. Depending on their skill level, some scribes can become CASE tool experts. This way they can perform such tasks as creating data flow diagrams and actually building the prototype.

As in any situation, respect is earned. If your scribes take an active, significant role in the session, others will acknowledge it, and people will be more willing to take on the role.

VISUAL AIDS

This is the part of the process where you can roll up your sleeves and be creative. You can draw pictures on flip charts, write words in colored ink on magnetic shapes, and prepare overhead images that fill half the wall. The latent artist emerges here.

Visual aids help keep the participants focused and can clarify the decisions being made. You can build a picture of the business, step by step, as it evolves.

Flip Charts

Use flip charts for information that you want displayed throughout the session. Good candidates for flip charts are:

- Session agenda
- Management objectives
- Graphics for the business overview
- Open issues

The following sections describe each of these flip charts.

Session Agenda

On a full flip-chart page, list the agenda items. Throughout the session, you can refer to this list so people will always know where you are in the agenda. Since you must accomplish a lot of work in a short time, it is important to display the agenda to help keep the discussion on track.

When new subjects arise that you had not planned for, you can note them on the agenda flip chart to assure they will not be overlooked. For example, someone may want to discuss the test plan. You can add this to the agenda flip chart, just before open issues.

Management Objectives

These are the objectives included in the Management Definition Guide. Since they describe what management expects to gain from the project, these objectives tie into the entire agenda. Having them on a flip chart keeps them visible so that participants maintain their perspective on the project.

Graphics for the Business Overview

Near the beginning of the session, you or someone in the group will present an overview of the system, the work flow, or the business area. It's often said a picture is worth a thousand words. Whatever concepts you want to communicate in this overview, you will probably want to come back to them throughout the session. Take the time to show these concepts graphically.

People's familiarity with the project will range from those who are very involved in the details to those who have virtually no experience with it. It takes time to assimilate new concepts. These flip charts will help. For an example of a business overview chart, see Figure 8.1 in Chapter 8.

Open Issues

As described in the "Open Issues and Assumptions" section of Chapter 5, open issues arise throughout the session. You need a way to note them and refer to them as the session progresses, and to review them on the last day. As issues come up, note them on the flip chart and number them sequentially. By the end of the session, you may have several pages of issues.

A note about writing on flip charts. Make sure you put an extra page behind each one so the ink does not go through. Here is how one company learned the hard way:

. . . the design team had a suite of brand new rooms in an office building. There were flip charts everywhere covering the walls. Unfortunately, they didn't realize that flip charts should be double thick, otherwise the marker goes through to the next page (or in this case, the wall). Repainting the walls was not a budgeted cost, but the positive results of the team sessions made it easier to explain to the steering committee. (Corbin 1991)

Magnetics

Now is the time we finally talk about these things called *magnetics*. They are thin sheets of vinyl cut in various shapes, sizes, and colors. Magnetic material, which comes in a long coiled flat roll (like masking tape) about .5 inches wide, is cut and attached to the back of the vinyl shapes. This is what makes the magnetics stick to the board. You can then move the shapes around and place them anywhere you want. With special pens, you can write on the magnetics and remove the ink later with water (unless you mistakenly use pens that are not water soluble, in which case your magnetics are dedicated forever to whatever profound words were written). Suppliers for these magnetic materials are difficult to find. One such supplier is:

Ryan Screen Printing, Inc.

5412 West Burnham Street

Milwaukee, WI 53219

Figure 7.3 shows some typical magnetic shapes we have used.

One use of magnetics is for data elements. You can put data element names on magnetics that are 1 to 1.5 inches by 8 inches. Different colored shapes can be used to distinguish existing, changed, and new data elements. Then you can use them in your screen designs. Another common use of magnetics is for defining the entities in an entity relationship diagram.

One comment on preparing magnetics: Make sure you print large enough for everyone to see clearly. This may involve abbreviating somewhat. For example, instead of trying to fit "Increasing Death Benefit Rider" on one magnetic, you could print "Inc Death Ben Rider."

Overhead Projection

Most of you have probably used overhead projection in one way or another, or have been to a meeting where it is used. It involves copying images of presentation material onto clear sheets called transparencies, foils, or overheads. Then, these transparencies are projected onto a screen or wall using an overhead projector. With special pens, you can write on the transparencies in various colors. You can erase these ink lines with moistened paper

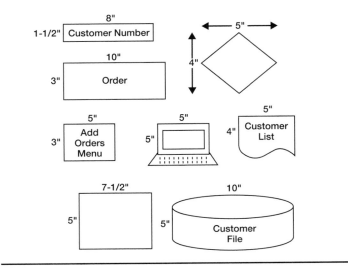

Figure 7.3 Sample magnetic shapes.

towels. This is not a particularly graceful process if you are trying to delete a tight area of small lettering. But it does work for simple edits.

In JAD sessions, transparencies work well for any situation where you are presenting something for *review*. In other words, you expect that most of what you display on the transparencies will remain, with only a few parts needing change. For example, you can use transparencies to show proposed work flow developed before the session or you can use them for reviewing screens and reports that will, at the most, have minor changes. As these changes are decided in the session, mark them on the transparencies with the pens. The group can easily see the results displayed.

When making transparencies, copy the image as large as possible while still staying within the frame of the transparency. In other words, don't try to squeeze a short six-line report on a portrait-oriented transparency. Instead, turn the image sideways (landscape), enlarge it (if your copier permits), and print it across the full length of the paper. In the same way, enlarge screen images to fill the whole transparency. The group can see more easily and you have more space to note the changes. Figure 7.4 illustrates two ways to put the same image on a transparency. The first one shows the image squeezed into the transparency (not a good use of space), while the second one shows the same image turned sideways and enlarged (much easier to see).

If you are showing many overhead transparencies, tape a yellow transparency on the flat bed of the overhead projector where the light comes through. Then, place your transparencies for viewing on top of that yellow transparency. This softens the harsh white light of the projector and is much easier on the eyes of your viewers.

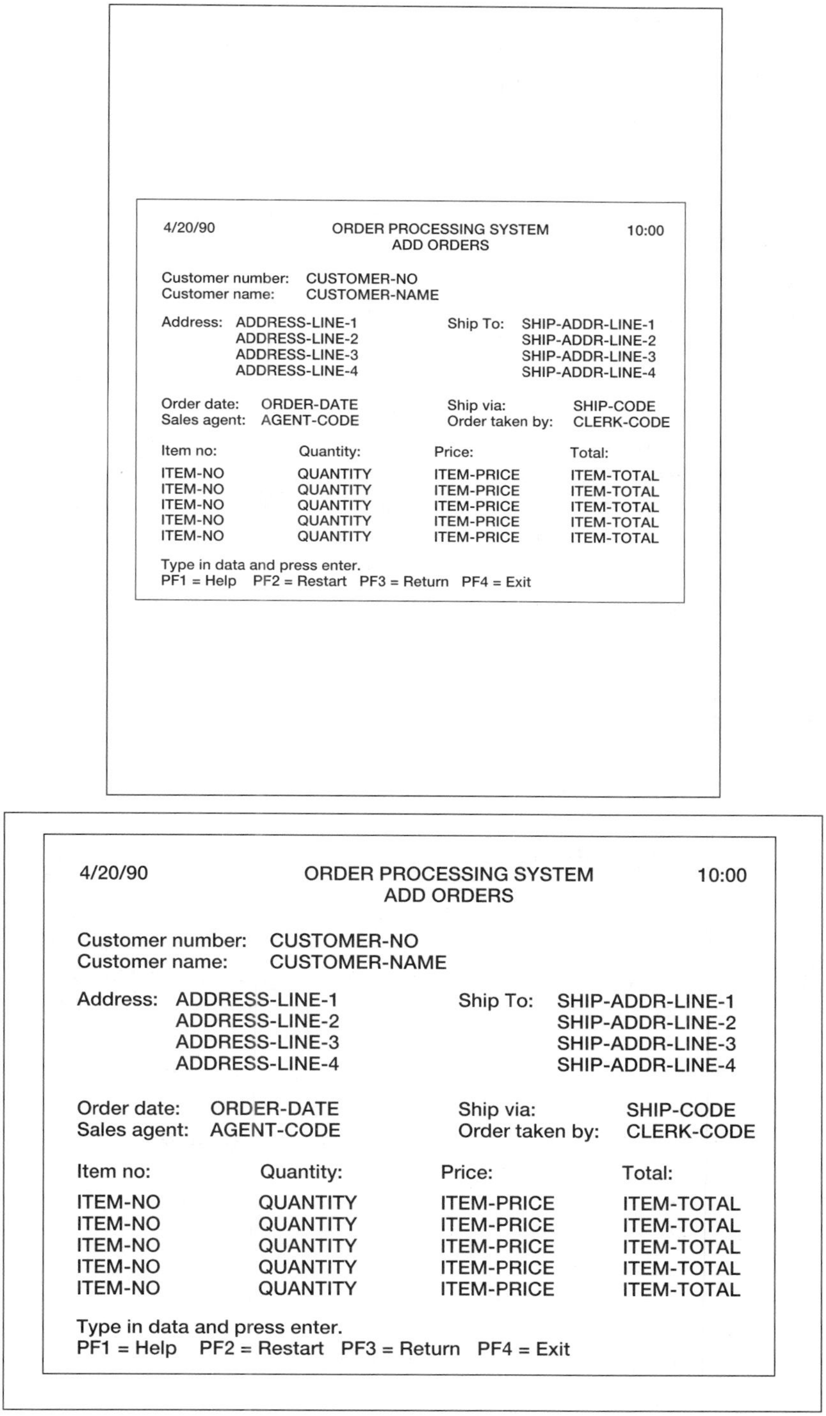

Figure 7.4 Putting images on transparencies.

And finally, do not begin your overhead presentation with the statement, "I know this is too small to see . . . ." Either make it large enough to see in the first place, or if that is not possible, don't use it at all.

Electronic White Boards

Some people use electronic boards not only as a visual aid, but also as a way to document decisions in the session. These boards are free-standing and can easily be moved around. They have white surfaces, like traditional white boards, except the surface is scrollable. In other words, a fresh, clean panel can be scrolled into place, without having to erase the previous panel. Some boards, for example, have enough scrollable length for six complete panels.

The other feature of these boards is that you can print the contents of any or all panels. By pressing a button, a copy of exactly what you've written on the board prints out on a sheet of paper. You can also tape flip charts to the electronic board and print them as well.

Betty Johannessen (of Connecticut Mutual in Hartford, Connecticut) describes an example of how she uses electronic boards in her sessions.

> We recently used the electronic white board in a series of sessions to define several key business processes. The participants were able to leave the sessions with the results in hand, instead of waiting for the documentation package.

Computer Screen Projection Units

Computer screen projection units display images from a PC onto a surface large enough to be viewed by the entire group of participants. These portable units (small enough to fit into a briefcase) have replaced the larger, more expensive projection units (that typically were suspended from ceilings).

The projection unit sits on the flat part of the overhead projector and interfaces with the PC. Through liquid crystal display technology, it displays the PC images onto a large screen or wall. This image can come from a PC application, or from a mainframe application that has been routed through the PC.

This tool is useful if you want to display screen images for a particular computer application. You can also use it to display any diagrams created from a CASE tool, such as entity-relationship diagrams, data flow diagrams, or screen and report designs.

However be warned: If you plan to use any kind of PC tool to display and update images in the session, make sure you can make those changes smoothly and quickly. You do not want to hold up the session while you plod through nested menus, stumble through move and copy commands, and apologize for slow response time. If this is the case, you are better off *not* using the PC and using traditional overhead transparencies instead.

Tape Recorders

Sometimes JAD participants ask why you are not tape recording the session. After all, the scribe wouldn't have to write down all those decisions and you would be assured of capturing every word.

We recommend *not* tape recording the sessions. Tape recorders inhibit discussion. Would you want to voice your opinion on a sensitive, political matter if you knew that at a later time your comments could be replayed? Even those aggressive dominator types might reserve expressing their viewpoints when the tape is running. People will simply tout the company line rather than probe into why a particular policy is not working.

Another reason to keep tape recorders out of your session is that they really don't help the scribe. The scribe is not taking dictation, but is being prompted by the facilitator and using other aids such as CASE tools, scribe forms, and flip charts. A tape recorder may even bog you down. As Judy August, JAD consultant, says:

> If the [scribes] were to rely on the taped material, they would add considerable time to the documentation effort. During wrap-up, they would have to run through all of the taped discussions in order to extract the appropriate output. (August 1991)

THE PRE-SESSION MEETING

This kickoff meeting is held at least a week before the session. The purpose is to establish management commitment, summarize the JAD process, and distribute and discuss the Working Document. Also, this is the first time all the participants will be together and have a chance to establish group rapport. For that alone, the meeting is worthwhile.

What Happens in the Meeting?

The following describes what to cover in the meeting.

1. Establish Management Commitment

Introduce the executive sponsor who should summarize the objectives and benefits of the project in a five- to ten-minute presentation. Perhaps this person can talk about how the project came to be and how it will solve certain problems. The sponsor can describe the time and resources that have been committed to the effort and how each person was selected for individual skills and experience. "People are relying on the session participants to define the new business processes." The executive sponsor can emphasize how the JAD process, particularly the session, is a key part of the whole development effort.

2. Summarize the JAD Process

Now the agenda turns back to you. Discuss how JAD is being used to support this project. Review the five JAD phases, highlighting the participants' responsibilities in each one. For an experienced group who has been through JADs before, this discussion might not be required. For example, we do many JADs for new insurance product introductions that involve the people from the same business areas. Participants who have recently endured a five-day session do not need to hear that "the session" is Phase 4 of the JAD process.

3. Distribute the Working Document

Explain with emphasis that everything in the document is *proposed*. You might say:

> "Although this Working Document appears to be in final form, it is only a starting point for the session. Everything in this document is *proposed.* It includes requirements that have come from you.
>
> "For each section, we may be simply modifying the requirements or we may be starting from scratch. When we cover screens, for example, you may find that the proposed screen designs are close to what you need. In that case, we can just review them and change some fields. Or, you may find that the screens have nothing to do with what you require. In that case, we can start at the beginning, with a blank board and new ideas. It's up to you."

Have the participants turn to the table of contents as you summarize what is contained in the document. Do not rush through it. Even though you are intimately familiar with the document, no one else has ever seen it. So avoid breezing through in a whirl of details.

Highlight the sections you want the participants to spend the most time reviewing. Only the most conscientious (or those who also enjoy reading procedure manuals) will read every word of the document. So show them what areas to concentrate on. Make their review as productive as possible. For example, you might say:

> "Spend time reviewing the data and process models. In the session, be prepared to confirm or change them. Are these existing processes consistent with how you do things? Also be prepared to model the new accounts receivable process from scratch."

SETTING UP THE MEETING ROOM

It is now the day before the session. The Working Document has been prepared and distributed. The visual aids are ready. You have several rolled-up flip-chart pages and a JAD supplies box filled with magnetics, overhead transparencies, board pens, and so on. Now, all you have to do is set up the room to accommodate all these items as well as the session participants. This is where you can set aside your mental efforts for some physical activities: moving chairs, adjusting tables, setting up the overhead projector, dragging flip chart stands across the room, and lugging a few boxes around.

Arrange to have access to the room on the day before the session. If possible, avoid setting up the day of the session. These activities are a burden you do not need at a time when you have the agenda for a five-day workshop rolling around in your head. Running back to the office 10 minutes before the session to get the overhead transparencies you left next to the copy machine does not add to your composure as you open the session.

To set up the room:

1. Arrange the tables in a hollow square

In other words, the tables should create a complete square with an open space in the middle. Break the square toward the front of the room (by leaving one table out) so that you can go inside to project the overhead transparencies. You, the facilitator, along with the scribe, are the only people on the front part of the square. Any participants sitting there would not be able to see the board. We usually use two tables for the facilitator and the scribe and a small table or a couple of chairs off to the side for the box of supplies. Figure 7.5 shows how tables are arranged for a typical session.

Facilities management will usually set up the tables for you. But more often than not, you will need to make some minor adjustments.

2. Hang the flip charts

Place the "Agenda" flip chart in a visible place toward the front of the room. You will refer to it often. "Open Issues" should be on a regular flip-chart tablet placed on a stand in a front corner, in an easily accessible spot. Other flip charts are taped on the walls or boards along the sides.

3. Check the things that can go wrong

This refers to the typical, but often overlooked, *mechanical* things that can go awry in any kind of session. This includes checking items such as overhead projector bulbs and board pens that may have run dry since the last session.

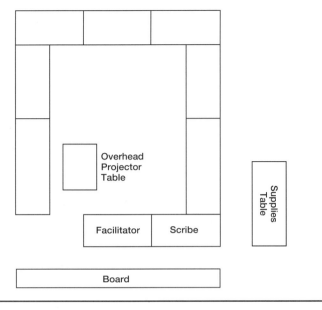

Figure 7.5 Table arrangement for a JAD session.

All this may sound trivial and perhaps overly obvious, but these are just the kinds of glitches that can throw off your rhythm. It's worth a test run.

Set up the overhead projector. Check both the in-place bulb and the spare. Project the image and focus it. Walk around the room. Will everyone be able to see? If you are projecting from the middle of the room, will any seat be in the path of the light? You will need to ask that participant to relocate while you project transparencies or that person will be jolted by a beam of blinding light. Make sure that the surface you project upon does not produce a glare that has that high-beams-in-your-eyes effect. Most white boards do not work well for this reason. Instead, use a projection screen, light-colored wall, or boards with a photo-gray projection surface.

Know where the light switches are. Test which lights can be dimmed, if any. The lights should be low enough for your participants to see the projection image clearly, but not so low as to create the kind of "mood lighting" that has them nodding out by the second transparency. Finally, determine where to place the "props" you need for overhead projection. These include the transparencies, pens, water, and paper towels to erase the water-soluble pen lines. Keep lightweight items away from the rear of the projector where the fan blows. Otherwise, you will begin your presentation with a dramatic storm of windblown transparencies flying across the room.

Check all pens. Do the flip-chart pens work? Will the board pens carry on for more than a couple of words? Do you have plenty of them along the board rail? (You may be one of those with the strange habit of carrying the

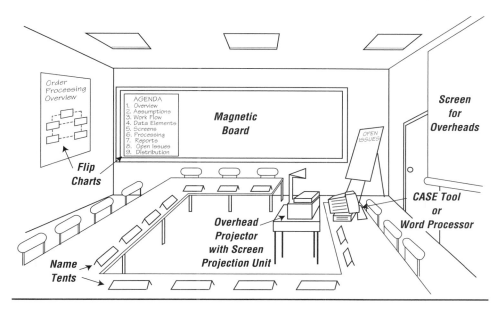

Figure 7.6 JAD sessions meeting room.

pens away and depositing them in other parts of the room. This results in your dashing about searching for pens.) And, if the boards require a liquid solution to erase, do you have sufficient "erasure juice"? This is a small detail, but essential.

A note on pens: You have flip-chart pens, board pens, and pens for overhead transparencies and magnetics. Be sure to keep them straight. For example, using anything but the correct water-soluble pens on the magnetics will create permanent images. And if you use a flip-chart pen on the board, make sure you write something worthwhile, because it will be there for good.

4. Distribute name tents and pens

Place the blank name tents and some marker pens around the tables so the participants can fill them in when they arrive. No preplanned seating arrangement is required. One interesting thing you will notice: More often than not, people will take the same seat every day of the session. The habits learned in grade school are with us all our lives.

Figure 7.6 shows how the meeting room can be set up.

HOW TO PREVENT PSS (PRE-SESSION STRESS)

Some JAD projects can get intense. The most stressful times are those days before the session when you are earnestly involved in getting ready for that room full of participants. The session dates have been set, so you can't tell them you're not quite ready to begin. What you *can* do is take steps to prevent unnecessary stress during your earlier preparation time. Here are some tips.

Set Realistic Schedules

Do not let the person requesting the project coerce you into unrealistic JAD dates. Certainly there are times when target dates drive your schedule, in which case there's not much discussion on dates. But in most cases, you have at least some flexibility.

When you are asked to estimate the time to accomplish a JAD project, gather certain information about the project before giving an estimate. Do not feel pressured into giving dates before you really know the project scope and objectives. Explain that you will look at the project requirements, time constraints, and perhaps consult with some others as well.

When people demand certain JAD dates, explain the impact of these dates in terms of what can be accomplished. For example, you might say, "If we hold the JAD in September, we can handle *this*. If we hold it two weeks later, we can also handle *that*." Or it may be a matter of adjusting resources. For example, "We can hold the JAD two weeks earlier, as long as we have one more person to work with us."

Avoid Overkill

Carefully evaluate every aspect of your preparation. Do you truly require this particular analysis or that particular chart, or is it just "nice to have"? Tie every preparation effort to the objectives of the project. Don't let yourself fall into carrying out tasks just because you did them on the last project. Evaluate the need for all preparation tasks.

Ask for Help

Compiling information before the session is not the sole function of the facilitator and staff. Rely on the subject-matter experts to help compile information. For example, you do not need to spend time plowing through reams of documentation. The session participants are more familiar with these items and can help in your analysis.

Scale Back the Working Document

Based on how much time you have, determine how you will handle the Working Document. Figure 7.7 describes four possible approaches to documenting preliminary information. When you have sufficient time, use the first one. Use the others as your available time and resources become progressively less.

When you have . . .	*Handle the Working Document like this . . .*
Plenty of time	Distribute the Working Document *before* the session. (This is the approach we have used for most of our projects.)
Less time	Distribute the Working Document *at* the session.
Much less time	Instead of creating a Working Document, have IS and business area people prepare handouts to distribute at the session.
No time	Do everything from scratch in the session using flip charts and board space. This is extreme, but it can be done.

Figure 7.7 Adjusting the Working Document based on time.

All these tips for preventing pre-JAD stress need to be balanced against your goal of providing quality service to your customers. Of course, you want to give your customers everything they want, need, and ask for. At the same time, you want to minimize your stress and craziness prior to the session.

CHECKLISTS

Another way to simplify and organize the tasks before the session (and help prevent PSS) is to use checklists. Over the course of our JAD projects, we have developed a couple of checklists that have helped. These include checklists for JAD tasks and for JAD supplies. Following are descriptions of each one.

JAD Tasks Checklist

This checklist shows all the tasks that could be required for doing a JAD. It is the basis for creating work plans as described in the "Work Plans That Work" section of this chapter. You can use this checklist as a starting point. The last column, called *Required?*, allows you to note whether you need to do that particular task for this project. By checking the required tasks, you will know what to include in the work plans. Figure 7.8 shows a sample of this checklist.

JAD Supplies Checklist

You do not want to run out of certain supplies during a JAD session. If you run out of rubber bands, staples, or No. 2 pencils, you can almost certainly scrounge some up around the office. But let's say that on the day before the session you need to make overhead transparencies for five pages of data models, eight proposed screen designs, and ten existing reports. You go to

JAD Tasks Checklist

Task	Required?
Phase I: JAD Project Definition	
Interview executive sponsor Interview user managers Interview IS managers Create the participation list Prepare the Management Definition Guide Schedule the session Reserve meeting room Send JAD session cover memo to all participants Take inventory of JAD supplies	
Phase 2: Research	
Interview users Interview IS Define and document data requirements Define and document business processes Gather preliminary information Prepare session agenda	
Phase 3: Preparation	
Schedule the pre-session meeting Send memo on pre-session meeting Prepare the Working Document Meet with the scribe Prepare flip charts, magnetics, and overheads Hold pre-session meeting Set up the session meeting room	
Phase 4: The Session	
Follow the agenda	
Phase 5: The Final Document	
Schedule the review meeting Prepare draft of the final document Distribute the final document and memo Hold the review meeting Update and distribute the document, if necessary Get signatures on approval form	

Figure 7.8 JAD tasks checklist.

the copy machine and, lo and behold, there are no blank transparencies. You ask the administrative assistant for some more. She tells you she gave the last ones away yesterday, but they are on order and will be in next week.

To avoid this unnecessary stress, take an inventory of supplies as soon as the project begins. At that time, determine what you need, check what you have, and order what you don't have. Figure 7.9 shows the JAD supplies checklist that we use to check our inventory. This checklist helps you track items on order as well as remember what to bring to the session.

JAD Supplies Checklist

Need to Order	Date Ordered	Date Expected	Item
Overheads			
			Bulb and spare
			Blank transparencies
			Yellow transparency
			Transparency frames
			Pens
Magnetics			
			1.5" by 8" shapes
			5" by 7" shapes
			3" by 10" shapes
			CRT shapes
			Disk file shapes
Flip Charts			
			Flip chart paper
			Pens
Final Document Assembly			
			Binders
			Tabs
			Cover, back, & spine
Other Supplies			
			Board pens
			Erasers
			Eraser juice
			Pencils
			Tablets
			Tents
			Masking tape
			Scotch tape
			Stapler and staples
			Scissors
			Rubber bands
			Paper clips
			Company telephone book

Figure 7.9 JAD supplies checklist.

Having compiled the Working Document, trained the scribe, created the visual aids, held the pre-session meeting, and set up the meeting room, you are ready for Phase 4: The Session.

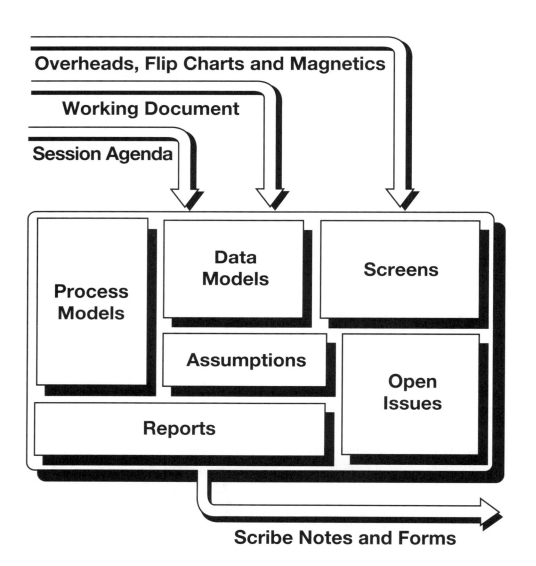

EIGHT ▷ ▶ ▶ ▶

PHASE 4: THE SESSION

In the JAD process, the session is the main event. Up to this point, all efforts have been in preparing for the session. Now, all the information gathered in interviews, compiled in the Working Document, and illustrated in visual aids, comes together to support this one- to five-day structured workshop.

No two JADs are alike. Describing a "typical" JAD is like trying to describe a typical football game. In football, you know both teams are trying to win (objectives). All the players know their positions (roles) and the rules of the game. But no one has any idea how the game will play out (the session). So for our JAD description, we will use one agenda and carry through with that. We'll use an example from a systems development project—the Order Processing example we started with earlier. And we'll carry that through the session, from start to finish, beginning with the agenda:

- Discuss assumptions
- Define data requirements
- Design business processes
- Design screens
- Design reports
- Resolve open issues

In the session, you will use the Working Document as a basis for defining the final requirements. As you embark on each agenda item, different levels of detail are available from the document based on how much pre-session "homework" you have done. For example, in the Screens section, you could find yourself in any one of the following situations:

- You have already gathered proposed designs for new screens and now the group need only review them and make some minor changes.

- You have gathered proposed designs (as in the previous example), but in the session, the group agrees that these screens do not meet the needs of the new work flow revised earlier in the session. In other words, you must start over.

- You come into the session with few or no screen requirements at all. The only thing certain is that screens must be designed.

Whether you have comprehensive requirements or none at all, the descriptions in this chapter apply. For each agenda item description, you will see two parts. The part *before the session* shows all the requirements you could possibly have gathered coming into the session. The part *during the session* describes how to define requirements from scratch as if you came in with nothing at all. This way, you can tailor each agenda item to the level of preparation you have done. Also, if the participants decide to abandon the requirements proposed in the Working Document (leaving you with a large blank board and four colored pens), you are prepared to start at the beginning for any item on the agenda.

OPENING THE SESSION

The first two minutes of any session can be the most tense. Leading a session is in part a performance, like teaching a class. It's normal for the facilitator to have "opening-night" butterflies. Anyone who has had a speaking part in their fifth-grade school play knows the feeling. Vice Presidents are there. Your boss's boss is there. And users and IS people are there, sitting in close proximity.

Everyone has their eyes on you. Can you pull it off? You close the door, clear your throat, and say, "Welcome . . ."

1. Administrative Items

Begin by reviewing the "administrivia," those items that answer questions about how the meeting will run. This includes:

- *Schedule.* Tell what time sessions begin and end, and when the breaks occur.

- *Rest rooms.* Tell where they are located.
- *Phone calls.* Provide the phone number where people can leave messages (no calls directly into the room). Tell them where they can make calls during breaks.
- *Introductions.* Introduce those people with particular roles, such as the executive sponsor (if he is attending), the scribe (the one either sitting at the PC or at the desk with the 12 sharpened pencils), and the observers (the ones sworn to silence). Ask the participants to fill out the name tents that you have placed on the tables. These should suffice for other introductions. Also, refer them to the Working Document, which lists the participants and their departments.

2. Session Objectives

Describe what you expect to accomplish in the session. You might say:

> "We are here in this session to define your requirements for order processing. This new process will replace the existing order processing systems (both manual and automated) across all divisions of the company. We will use the Working Document (distributed last week) as a basis for each item on the agenda.
>
> "As decisions are made, Charles, our scribe, will record them. He will read them back to confirm the accuracy. Then, all this information goes into a final document."

3. The Session Agenda

Walk through the session agenda. Refer the group to the flip chart, elaborating on how each agenda item will be handled.

4. Ground Rules

Summarize the session rules. Although some people are already aware of these rules from having attended previous sessions or from your conversations with them before the session, you need to summarize them again. We put these rules on magnetics on the upper part of the board so they are always visible. The ground rules vary among facilitators. We use these:

- *One person speaks at a time.* This prevents multiple conversations.
- *Silence means consent.* This reminds people that when decisions are discussed and documented, unless someone speaks up, we assume everyone agrees.
- *Be on time.* This includes not only when sessions begin, but also when people reconvene after breaks and after lunch.

And to help preserve the environment:

- *Bring your own mug.* We ask people to bring their own coffee cups, so that fewer styrofoam containers are used, thrown out, and then dumped in landfills.

Feel free to include other ground rules as well. For example, if you feel the group needs to be more open to new ideas, you might add a ground rule that says, "Consider all possibilities." Or if you are concerned about group reticence, perhaps you could try, "Question anything," or "Assume nothing." Your ground rules will evolve to suit your needs and the characteristics of your participants.

5. Business Overview

You or someone in the group now presents an overview of the business area. This high-level summary answers such questions as: Which departments are affected by the business processes? What are the major functions? What problems are you dealing with? Figure 8.1 shows a diagram that could be used for the business overview in the Order Processing JAD.

Also in this overview, you can clarify the terminology that will be used throughout the session. Remember that people's familiarity with the business under review may vary tremendously. Keep this overview brief and as free of technical jargon as possible.

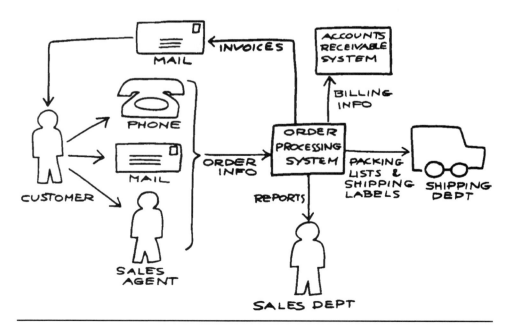

Figure 8.1 Business overview flip chart.

6. Management Definition Guide

Although the participants received this document before the session, reviewing the main points helps reinforce why the participants are here. Read aloud (verbatim or in paraphrase) the purpose, scope, and objectives sections. You may have prepared a flip chart of these objectives, which you can refer to now and throughout the session.

You are now ready to delve into the Working Document and start making those decisions we have been alluding to. This begins with a look at the assumptions.

ASSUMPTIONS

The length of time spent on assumptions depends, of course, on how many assumptions you bring into the session. If an assumption turns into an open issue (or if some issues must be addressed at the beginning of the session), much more time may be required. In such a situation, the participants may become skeptical about the session's progress when the first day ends with their having covered only three pages of a 100-page document. Assure them that this is not uncommon. These important assumptions are the basis for defining the rest of the requirements.

Assumptions have been accumulating since the JAD project began. The Working Document lists them all, including the assumptions from the Management Definition Guide (which you copied directly into the Working Document) and those that may have surfaced after that.

Again, remind the participants that all these assumptions are for review—they can be changed. Read each assumption to the group, then open it up for discussion. Each assumption will either:

- Stay as it is (if everyone agrees with the wording).
- Be revised.
- Become an open issue (if group consensus cannot be reached).

The scribe documents the minor changes directly on the pages of the Working Document. He documents new assumptions, either on a scribe form or the PC, and reads them back to the group. These new assumptions will continue to arise throughout the session.

DATA REQUIREMENTS

In this part of the session, you define the data needed to support the business processes. Depending on the scope of the project, you may build a complete enterprise model or you might simply define five new data elements.

Data Models

Data models are handled similarly to process models (described after this section). In summary . . .

In small meetings before the session, the facilitator guided a few key people through defining proposed data models using entity relationship diagrams or other techniques. These diagrams were put into the Working Document as well as onto overhead transparencies to use in the session.

Now in the session, with everyone present, the facilitator walks through the data models. The participants verify the accuracy and completeness of the data groupings and relationships as well as identify any missing data.

Data Elements

Every piece of information that will be entered, processed, stored, displayed, and reported is packaged into units called *data elements* (or *attributes*). These are the building blocks the group will use throughout the session to design screens and reports and build the data dictionary.

Before the Session

Proposed data elements may have been defined and listed in the Working Document. For example:

DATA ELEMENT DESCRIPTIONS

Name:	Customer Number
Length:	7
Format:	Numeric
Description:	A unique number assigned to each customer.

Name:	Customer Last Name
Length:	20
Format:	Alphanumeric
Description:	The last name of the person ordering the item.

These definitions can include other information such as allowable values (for example, the allowable values for Customer Number could be 1000000 to 5999999).

In the Working Document, data elements are organized into three groups:

- *Existing data elements.* These are current data elements that already exist somewhere in a data base or file. Even though these data elements will not change, review them to familiarize the group with their definitions.

- *Changed data elements.* These are current data elements that can be used in the new system by changing the definition or range of values. For example, the existing data element called Customer Region might have two new codes added for the two new additional regions.

- *New data elements.* These are data elements proposed for the new system. Their definitions include data element name, length, format, and a short description (as previously shown).

The required data elements have been written on magnetics. Different colors (of the magnetics or of the ink used to write the names) indicate which group the data elements are from. For example, white magnetics could be for existing data elements, yellow for changed, and blue for new.

During the Session

Arrange all the magnetics in columns on the board. To find them easily, sort them first by color (existing, changed, or new), then alphabetically. Figure 8.2 shows what the board might look like.

Review each data element for its correct name, length, and definition. New data elements will arise and others will be removed. For example, the new system might use the logon ID code to determine who is accessing a particular application. Therefore, it is no longer necessary for the clerk to enter a separate code to identify who is entering the data. The separate data element, Clerk Code, may no longer be needed. These kinds of changes occur throughout the session.

As new data elements are defined, the scribe makes a magnetic to add to the list and documents the data element definition. As data elements are deleted, the scribe pulls them from the board to keep in a separate pile in case they are called back. (One data element could be removed and reinstated three or four times before the participants make up their minds.)

Now, the magnetics on the board display a complete list (to this point) of data elements required by the new system. These data elements will be used to build the screens and reports later on.

BUSINESS PROCESSES

In this part of the session, you define the business processes—the collection of activities relating to the business and the system.

During interviews before the session, business processes were identified.

Existing Data Elements	Changed Data Elements	New Data Elements
Customer First Name	Agent Code	Clerk Code
Customer Last Name	Agent Name	Commission Pct
Customer Address	Customer Number	Credit Limit
Customer City	Item Description	Region Code
Customer State	Item Number	Terms
Customer Zip	Item Price	
Customer Phone	Item Quantity	
Discount Rate	Item Total	
Invoice Date	Shipping Address	
Order Date	Shipping City	
Shipping Date	Shipping State	
	Shipping Zip	

Figure 8.2 Magnetics showing data elements.

In small meetings, the facilitator guided a few key people through defining existing and proposed processes. (See the "Documenting Business Processes" section in Chapter 6.) Data flow diagrams or other techniques were used to document the business processes. These diagrams were put into the Working Document as well as onto overhead transparencies to use in the session.

Now in the session, with everyone present, the facilitator walks through the data flow diagrams of the *existing* business, using an overhead projector. Participants may have comments or minor changes on these diagrams, but generally there is not much discussion about what already exists.

In contrast, *new* data flow diagrams can generate lively debate. Here you are talking about changes that will directly affect the participants' working environments and daily procedures. Will they need to hire new staff, decrease existing staff, or completely reorganize the department? There is much at stake.

Present the new work flow one step at a time (or in data flow diagrams, one level at a time). Do not imply that any of the processes have been finalized. Use phrases like, "This is how the procedure *could* work . . ." or "One approach is . . . ." After all, some participants have not yet been involved. They need to establish ownership in the concept by seeing their ideas included in the diagrams.

As participants agree on changes, note them on the transparencies so everyone can clearly see the decisions. Your diagram could end up looking something like Figure 8.3. The scribe notes these changes in the Working Document.

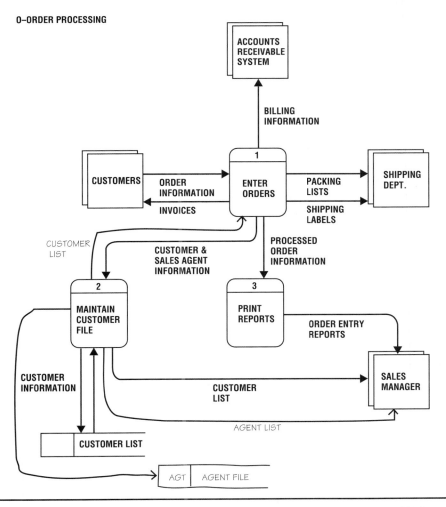

Figure 8.3 Data flow diagram with changes.

After this first walkthrough, move through the new business processes one more time, reviewing for accuracy and consistency. Changes made in one area may now affect another.

Of all the agenda items, business processes are the most important to define in small groups. You can do this either before the session or during. For example, some facilitators assign specific business processes to several groups of three or four people. Each group works together to prepare their diagrams. Then the participants reunite and review each business process for consensus.

SCREENS

This part of the session involves defining how people enter information into the system via computer screens. There are two parts to defining screens: you need to define *screen flow* (how users branch from one screen to the next) and *screen design* (what actually displays on each screen).

Screen Flow

Screen flow uses a series of menus or other branching techniques to define how people will access the various functions. Let's assume you have done no preparation and that the Working Document has nothing on screen flow. In the session, you can do this from scratch.

We are also assuming you are designing the screens in a low-tech (or no-tech) mode—that is, without PC tools. You can certainly follow this approach with hi-tech tools. But for now, let's say you have a pile of magnetics and some colored markers. You can work just fine with that. To define screen flow, follow these steps:

1. Identify the main menu selections.

Ask, "What are the *main* functions the screens will handle? In other words, what options should be on the main menu?" The work you have done to document the business processes will help here. For example, the main menu might mirror the second level of your data flow diagram.

As the participants identify these functions, make 5-by-7-inch magnetics for each one. Place them on the board and draw lines that show the screen flow. Figure 8.4 shows what the board looks like.

For larger systems, you may have several menu levels. This is when the phrase *sufficient board space* takes on meaning. For example, you may find the submenu levels stretching clear across two or three board panels.

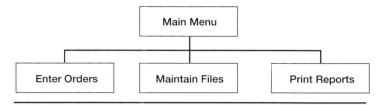

Figure 8.4 Magnetics showing menu screen flow.

2. *Identify submenu selections.*

Ask, "What is involved in the first function called *Enter Orders?* What options should that submenu contain?" (Once again, do you see how these questions echo the same ones you asked when documenting the business processes?) Write these functions on smaller magnetics and place them below the menus. When all functions are identified, the board is filled with magnetics, as shown in Figure 8.5.

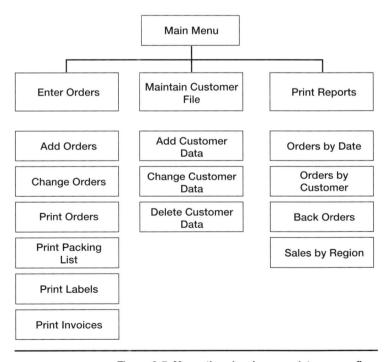

Figure 8.5 Magnetics showing complete screen flow.

Putting this information on magnetics works much better than just writing it on the board, because with magnetics you can:

- Make changes more easily by simply moving the magnetics as requested.
- View the entire screen flow. When the screen flow is complete, you can move the magnetics in their final arrangement over to a corner of the board. Then, as you design the actual screens, the overall screen flow will be available for reference.

3. Describe the screens.

For each screen, have the participants finalize the screen names and create descriptions of the functions. The scribe documents this as shown in Figure 8.6.

4. Review the complete screen flow.

When the group feels the screen flow is complete, ask, "What tasks have been overlooked in these screens? Can any of the screen functions be combined? Are the screen names simple and clear, accurately reflecting their purpose? Will the data entry clerk know exactly what these names mean?"

Now, with screen flow defined and documented by the scribe, you are ready to design the actual screens.

Screen Design

If there is a high point for the users in a JAD session, it is this portion of the agenda: *screen design*. Here, the group determines how the screens will actu-

---

SCREEN DESCRIPTION

Name: Add Orders

Description: Allows users to enter and validate new orders. The customer must already be on the file. The system automatically retrieves a price for the order and does a credit check on the customer.

Estimated
Volume: 200 orders per day.

Figure 8.6 Screen description.

ally look. This can be fast-paced and animated as the facilitator moves magnetics around the board while participants command what fields to add and relocate. Following is a description of how it works.

Interviews before the session can generate samples of existing and new screens. Any existing screens that relate to the system being designed can be included in the Working Document. In the session, these screens might be used as is or updated to reflect new enhancements.

We keep online files of screens that frequently come up in JADs. For example, we have complete screen samples for the online policy inquiry system. When we need to bring certain screens into a session, we print them out, ask the appropriate project manager to review the screens to assure they are current, and add them to the Working Document.

Again, let's assume you are coming into the session with no proposed screen designs. You are beginning with a blank board. Some say you can plan on designing about three screens per half-day session, but this can vary tremendously. You can use a prototyping tool or other PC technology to work with the group to design the screens and display the results on a large screen for all to see. But, as we have said before, you can do just fine in the no-tech mode as well. Follow these steps:

1. *Set up the board.* Draw two large empty frames (representing screens) on the central panels of the board. If you have enough board space, draw three or four frames. Arrange the magnetics of data elements (defined earlier) off to the side on a separate board panel.

2. *Define the headers and footers.* This is the information that displays at the top and bottom of every screen. It may already be determined by your company standards. Write the headers and footers directly on the board at the top and bottom of the screen frames, not on magnetics. This may include the business process name, screen name, and perhaps the date and time. Figure 8.7 shows an example of what it might look like. These headers and footers remain on the board throughout the screen definition process.

3. *Design the menus.* Begin with the main menu and continue through the submenus. For simple menus, write the design directly on the board. For complex menus, magnetics allow you to move the selections around, experimenting with different arrangements. While defining a particular screen, keep the design of the next highest level displayed on the board. For example, while designing submenus, keep the main menu in view. This puts the screen flow in context. Figure 8.8 shows what the main menu design might look like.

4. *Select the fields for the screens.* Begin by adding the screen title. Then, ask the group, "Which fields should display on the screen?" As participants call out the required fields, move the corresponding data ele-

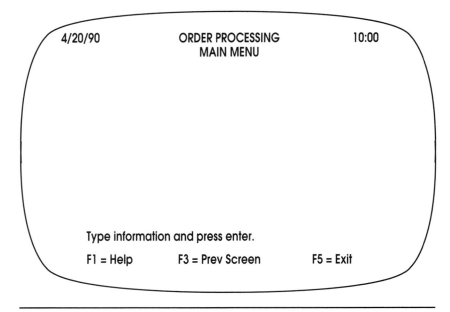

Figure 8.7 Headers and footers for screen design.

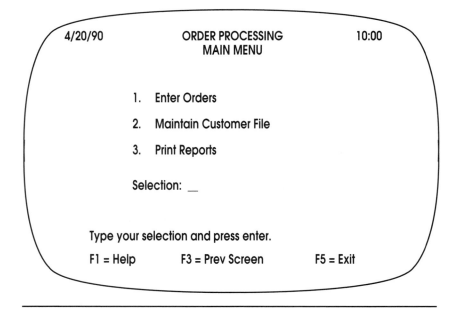

Figure 8.8 Main menu design.

Order taken by: | CLERK-CODE |

Figure 8.9 Field label.

ment magnetics into the screen frame. Arrange them in their general locations. When all the fields are there, adjust their positions.

5. *Define the field labels.* For each field, define the field labels that prompt users what to enter in that field. For example, the field CLERK-CODE might be labeled "Order taken by:" as shown in Figure 8.9. Write the field labels on magnetics of different colors to set them clearly apart from the fields. If you are confident there won't be many more changes, you can write the field labels directly on the board.

6. *Fine-tune the placement of the fields and field labels.* Consider space limitations. Most text-based screens are 80 characters wide and 24 lines long. This is the point in the session where the group splits. There are those who say, "I don't care where you put the fields, let's get on with it." Others really get into the details, offering such comments as "Move that field up a little and to the right . . ." as if they were hanging a picture on the living room wall. But these comments are worthwhile. Good design results in screens that are easier to read and more efficient to use.

Now, within the frame drawn on the board, you have a completely designed screen with:

- Headers, footers, and a screen title (written on the board)
- Fields (shown on data element magnetics in their proper location)
- Field labels (shown on magnetics of a different color or just written on the board)

The scribe documents the screen design or you can take a Polaroid® picture of the results. Figure 8.10 shows the completed screen design. You can follow the previous six steps to design the remaining screens.

7. *Determine screen messages.* Identify all the messages that could display on the screens. Then for each message, identify its type: Is it for confirmation (acknowledging that a certain action has been taken) or for errors (the data entered has not passed all the edits)? Next describe the conditions under which the message displays and how it will be worded. The scribe documents this information as well. Figure 8.11 shows a scribe form you can use to document screen messages.

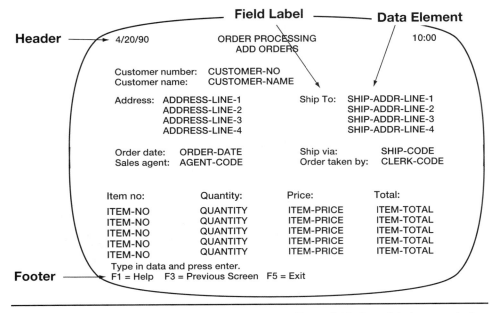

Figure 8.10 Completed screen design.

8. *Determine screen access.* If there are security requirements, now is a good time to define them. Let's say you want to define which job functions can access which screens. On the board, create a large chart. Across the top, list the screen names. (You can use the already created mag-

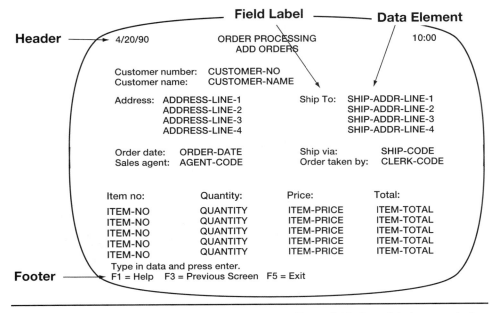

Figure 8.11 Screen message description.

netics for this.) Then, down the left side of the chart, list the job functions. For each job, ask the group, "Which screens can this job access?" Some screens are designed to be used for either inquiry (people can read the screen but not add or change data) or update (people can read *and* update information). In this case, mark the space on the chart with either "I" (for inquiry) or "U" (for inquiry and update). Figure 8.12 shows how this chart might look.

Now your screen design is complete. But before going on to reports, let's explore another area of screen design.

Human Factors in Screen Design

When designing screens, there is a whole area of screen design that is critical, but often inadequately considered—the area of *human factors*. This is the aspect of screen design that deals with how people interact with the screen. Much research has been done in this area. The resulting guidelines can be applied to your screen design techniques. Here are some human factors tips to consider when designing your next batch of screens:

Screen Access by Job Function

Job Function	No. of Locations	Add Orders	Change Orders	Print Orders	Print Packing List	Print Labels	Print Invoices	Update Customer File	Print Customer File	Orders by Date	Orders by Customer	Back Orders	Sales by Region
Order entry clerk		U	U	U	U	U	U	U	U				
Order entry supervisor		U	U	U	U	U	U	U	U	U	U	U	U
Order entry manager		U	U	U	U	U	U	U	U	U	U		U
Shipping clerk				U	U	I	I					U	
Shipping supervisor				U	U	U	U			U	U	U	
Shipping manager				U	U	U	U			U	U	U	
Sales agent										U	I	I	
Sales manager		U	U	U				U		U	U	U	U

I = Inquiry   U = Update

Figure 8.12 Screen access by job function.

- *Uppercase versus lowercase.* Lowercase letters are easier to read. If this is true, then why do we see so many mainframe system screens in uppercase letters? Years ago, computer systems could handle only uppercase. But now, even though most systems can handle both, many of us continue in the uppercase tradition because "that's the way we always did it"—or programmers find it's too much trouble having to press the shift key.

  To see the difference in clarity, compare the following two passages. They both have the same text. The only difference is that the first one is all in uppercase letters and the second has upper- and lowercase.

> TO THE LOOKING-GLASS WORLD IT WAS ALICE THAT SAID
> I'VE A SCEPTRE IN HAND I'VE A CROWN ON MY HEAD.
> LET THE LOOKING-GLASS CREATURES, WHATEVER THEY BE
> COME AND DINE WITH THE RED QUEEN, THE WHITE QUEEN AND ME.
> THEN FILL UP THE GLASSES AS QUICK AS YOU CAN,
> AND SPRINKLE THE TABLE WITH BUTTONS AND BRAN:
> PUT CATS IN THE COFFEE, AND MICE IN THE TEA—
> AND WELCOME QUEEN ALICE WITH THIRTY-TIMES-THREE!
>   —LEWIS CARROLL

> To the Looking-Glass world it was Alice that said
> I've a sceptre in hand I've a crown on my head.
> Let the Looking-Glass creatures, whatever they be
> Come and dine with the Red Queen, the White Queen and me.
> Then fill up the glasses as quick as you can,
> And sprinkle the table with buttons and bran:
> Put cats in the coffee, and mice in the tea—
> And welcome Queen Alice with thirty-times-three!
>   —Lewis Carroll

  Chances are, your system can handle lowercase letters. Even if you do nothing else to improve your screen design, using upper- and lowercase alone makes the screens much easier to read.

- *Error message location.* Traditionally, error messages appear at the bottom of the screen. But consider the users' eye movement. They fill in the screen information and press Enter. Then, expecting the next screen to appear, their eyes naturally move to the top left corner of the screen. When an error message displays, they must move their eyes down again to the bottom of the screen. Many human factor specialists suggest putting error messages at the top to save eye movement.

- *Indents.* The more unique indentations you have in your screen design, the harder it is to use. Minimize the indents by lining up fields and field labels. Combine field labels of similar lengths, where possible, without sacrificing the logical order. And place the colons directly after the field labels.

    This screen has multiple indents:

Customer Info:
     Number: 901851   Phone: (215) 555–2600
     Name: David Lieberman

Address: Street: 14 Maple Terrace
City/State: Strawberry Fields, NJ   Zip: 08099

The following screen is easier to read. It has only two indents.

Customer Information
     Number: 901851
     Name: David Lieberman
     Phone: (215) 555–2600

Address
     Street: 14 Maple Terrace
     City: Strawberry Fields
     State: NJ
     Zip: 08099

- *Field prompts.* If space allows, use complete words. When you need to abbreviate, do not punctuate. For example, for the word "application," use "app," not "app." Do not hyphenate words as in Cobol names. For example, use "Policy Date" not "Policy-Date."

- *Consistent words.* Always use the same word for the same concept. For example, do not use "Date of Birth" on one screen and "Birth Date" on another. In your instruction lines, do not tell users to *"Depress* the Enter key" in one place, *"Press* the Enter key" in another, and *"Hit* the key" in a third. (Anyway, keys don't get "depressed"; only people do.)

- *Highlighting.* Use highlighting for emphasis, but only to a point. Excessive highlighting dilutes the effect. For example, overuse of blinking, color, and reverse video can make screens "noisy." Instead of getting the people's attention, you give them sensory overload. To prevent this, use lower levels of highlighting most of the time. Save the more

Most	blinking
Intense	color
	size (e.g., large lettering)
	reverse video
	boxes
	underline
	boldface
	dim (lower intensity)
	uppercase
Least	brackets, parentheses, and asterisks
Intense	white space (indents and blank lines)

Figure 8.13 Highlighting techniques in order of intensity.

powerful highlighting for when you really need to get their attention. Figure 8.13 lists some highlighting methods in order of intensity.

- *Headings.* Many screen headings are too complicated and contain superfluous information. They are filled with information that is there just because it's always been there. Certainly some of this information is necessary, but some of it may only be taking up valuable screen space. For example, do people really need to see the date, time, and internal program number at the top of every screen? You can often simplify these headings.

When screens are well designed, users don't need three-day training sessions and one-inch manuals to learn the system. Nor are they confused by alien mnemonics, cryptic messages, and mysteries such as, "How do I get out of this screen"? A good screen is intuitive and self-explanatory.

Designing a screen with human factors in mind saves a few seconds here and a few spaces there. All these nit-picking adjustments can add up to significant improvement over the lifetime of the screen. However, introducing these changes into your organization can be difficult. You will find resistance. People like things the way they are. Users become comfortable with meaningless field labels. And programmers find it easier to work in all uppercase mode. You may get resistance from your technical staff as well. They might tell you, for example, that lowercase lettering is impossible with the existing hardware, while further research might reveal otherwise. Try to overcome this resistance. People eventually adjust to the changes and productivity will increase.

GUI Screen Design

What about GUI (graphical user interface) screen design? More and more systems are being developed to use Windows or other visual presentations.

This kind of screen development differs from text-based development in the following ways:

- Prototyping takes on a different flavor. You don't need screen builders to prototype screen look-alikes. With object-oriented development tools, you can use point-and-click technology to interactively build production-ready screens.

- For screen flow, branching is more liberal. You can use such things as action/menu bars, icons, windows, and buttons. You are not as constrained by the more rigid hierarchy of text-based systems.

- Most mainframe screens are 80 characters wide and 24 lines long. GUI environments use horizontal and vertical scroll bars to expand the window size to a much larger range.

- Screen messages use different formats. You can use microline help, online help, balloon help, cursor-over-icon descriptions, pop-up messages, and so on.

- In the GUI world you can do a lot with the text. For example, you can change the font type style, adjust the size, or make it bold, italic, or underlined.

GUI screen design is more often done in smaller groups (of two to four people), all working around the PC. For example, the group might include a GUI design expert, a person from the business area, and a systems person to document what the user expects the screen to do. But if you prefer to design your GUI screens in a JAD session using a screen projection unit, here are some things to consider.

In the text-based world you are limited by what you can do with the screens. Consequently, in the session, you focus more on titles and headings, function keys, error messages, highlighting, and navigation through the menus.

With GUI design, you can select from an overwhelming number of options. GUI screen design has its very own language: You can point and click, drag and drop, or maximize and minimize. Things pull down, pop up, and scroll. So in your JAD session you have a lot of decisions to make. Do users want action/menu bars, pop-up menus, or buttons? Do they prefer radio buttons or butted boxes? Which font is easier on the eyes: Helvetica or Times Roman? And what use can they make of that *right* mouse button? GUI design does a lot with color and depth perception. Books have devoted entire chapters to such color considerations as whether to use warm versus cool colors, what are the best hues for adjacent areas, and which colors work well for the foreground and background. You might want to include a graphic designer in the session to help with such graphical tasks as customizing icons, designing screen layouts, and making effective use of color.

All these varied and complex choices create the potential for even more screen clutter. You, as the facilitator, must be careful to guide the group in the right direction. Like with text-based screens, focus on building screens that are clear, easy to read, not distracting, predictable, forgiving, consistent, and friendly. Graphics screens do provide that "slick" appeal and enable you to develop your own unique style. However, the basic characteristics of screen design should not be forgotten.

The following books provide details on GUI screen design:

- *User-Interface Screen Design* by Wilbert O. Galitz (a complete reference book on screen design)
- *Secrets of Effective GUI Design* by Mark Minasi (a style guide for designing GUI screens)

Now that the screens are designed and documented, you are ready to design the reports.

REPORTS

This part of the agenda defines all output from the system. Besides standard reports, this includes any other printouts generated in the process, such as invoices, statements, checks, and labels. Again, let's assume you are beginning with a blank board in low-tech mode.

Ask the group, "What printed documents do you need?" Here's where you trot out the speech about killing trees to make paper to print reports that collect dust on a shelf. Ask, "Do you really need this report? Could the report be microfiched? Could you view the information online?" There are laser printers that kick out more than 750 pages per minute. That translates to more than a million pages per day! How the business world loves those printed reports! Let's get rid of as many as we can.

On a flip chart, write the report names and short descriptions. The result is the report list shown in Figure 8.14.

After the group agrees on the reporting needs, complete the detailed report descriptions. Begin by deciding which of the following to include in the detailed description:

- Report name
- Description
- Frequency
- Number of copies
- Distribution list
- Selection criteria
- Sort criteria
- Data elements

REPORT LIST:

Orders by Date:	Lists all orders (sorted by date) in the date range specified.
Orders by Customers:	Lists all orders (sorted by customer) in the date range specified.
Back Orders:	Lists all orders (sorted by product number) that have not been filled because the items are not in stock.
Sales by Region:	Lists all orders (sorted by region) for the current month and year to date.
Customer List:	Lists all customers and their profiles. These are leads that the salesman can follow up on.

Figure 8.14 Report list.

Then fill in this information for each report. The scribe notes the decisions. Figure 8.15 shows a resulting report description sample.

Having described the reports, you are prepared to design the formats. You will either update existing reports (in which case you can use overhead transparencies to review and update the reports) or define new ones.

REPORT DESCRIPTIONS

Report name:	Customer List
Description:	Lists all customers and their profiles.
Frequency:	Monthly
Copies:	3
Distribution:	Sales Manager Marketing Manager Order Entry Supervisor
Selection:	All customers that have made purchases within the last five years.
Sort:	Sort alphabetically by customer name.
Data elements:	Customer Number Customer Name (first and last) Customer Address (street, city, and zip) Customer Phone Number Region Code Discount Rate Credit Limit Terms

Figure 8.15 Detailed report description.

Defining New Reports

Defining new reports from scratch is similar to designing screens. Follow these steps:

1. *Set up the board.* Draw a large empty frame (representing the report) on the board. Arrange the magnetics of data elements (defined earlier) off to the side on a separate board panel.

2. *Define the headers.* (Reports generally do not have footers.) Write the header on the board at the top of the report frame. Add the report title.

3. *Define fields for the report.* Move the data element magnetics across the width of the report, indicating which fields print on the report. (This is the information that prints below the column headings.)

4. *Define the column headings.* You can do this in the same way that you defined field labels for the screens. For example, column headings might be Customer Name, Customer Number, Item Name, and Quantity.

5. *Fine-tune the placement of the fields and column headings.* Consider space limitations. Most reports cram 132 characters on 8.5-by-11-inch paper. With laser printers, you can save paper by printing in duplex or quadriplex (thereby increasing the need for reading glasses).

6. *Add summary text and totals.* In a report sorted by region, for example, you may want to include subtotals for each region as well as grand totals at the end. Summary text can be added to help clarify the subtotals. Again, you can use sample data or symbols (such as xxx, 999, or mm/dd/yy) to fill the body of the report. The result is a completely designed report containing:

   - The header (including the report title)
   - Column headings
   - Fields shown as either symbols (such as xxx) or data elements on magnetics indicating what is contained in each column
   - Summary text and totals

   The scribe documents the completed report design or takes a Polaroid picture. Figure 8.16 shows a completed sample.

OTHER AGENDA ITEMS

Depending on the kind of JAD you are running, there are all kinds of other items your agenda might include. For example, for systems development projects, you could define records, transactions, detailed calculations, or manual forms.

APRIL 20, 1995	ORDER PROCESSING SALES BY REGION		PAGE 1

REGION 99

ITEM NO.	DESCRIPTION	SALES MTD ($)	SALES YTD ($)
9999999	XXXXXXXXXXXXXXXX	999,999	9,999,999
9999999	XXXXXXXXXXXXXXXX	999,999	9,999,999
9999999	XXXXXXXXXXXXXXXX	999,999	9,999,999
9999999	XXXXXXXXXXXXXXXX	999,999	9,999,999
9999999	XXXXXXXXXXXXXXXX	999,999	9,999,999
9999999	XXXXXXXXXXXXXXXX	999,999	9,999,999
TOTAL SALES FOR REGION 99		99,999,999	99,999,999
GRAND TOTALS		999,999,999	999,999,999

Figure 8.16 Completed report design.

OPEN ISSUES

Open issues are added throughout the session. When you see that a discussion is going on for a while and the answer to that issue is not immediately needed, recommend making it an open issue. For example, say the participants are discussing screens, particularly the data element called Customer Number. The discussion might go like this:

Sherry:	We can put the customer number as the first field on the screen, followed by customer name and address.
Ned (from IS):	How long is the customer number field?
Sherry:	Seven digits.
Irene:	But we use eight digits at our location and the Boston division uses one letter followed by six digits.
Sherry:	Well, it seems more people use the seven-digit format, so shouldn't that be the standard?
Irene:	No way.
	This is where the facilitator steps in.
Facilitator:	Since we do not have enough people here to represent the various customer number formats, perhaps we could make it an open issue. At the end of this session, when we discuss open issues, we can identify who will meet to resolve this issue and when. Meanwhile, let's get back to the original question about what information displays at the top of the screen.

At this point, someone from the group puts the issue into words while the scribe documents it in detail. The facilitator writes a one-line summary of the question on the Open Issues flip chart:

> **OPEN ISSUES**
>
> 1. What will be the standard format for customer numbers?

Then the session moves on.

At the end of the session, you address all those open questions that you have "put off until later." For each one:

1. The scribe reads the issue and the facilitator opens it up for discussion.
2. If participants can resolve it, the scribe documents the agreement.
3. If they cannot resolve it, the question is left as an open issue. The group determines who will resolve it and when it should be resolved.
4. If more than one person is assigned to an issue, an issue coordinator is designated.

For the customer number issue, Figure 8.17 shows how the completed scribe form might look.

After the session, these smaller groups meet on their own to discuss the issues. The facilitator is not involved. When an issue is resolved, the issue

OPEN ISSUE

Issue number:	1
Issue name:	Standardizing custormer numbers
Assigned to:	Allison Brooke (coordinator)
	Arthur Dent
	Joannie Hall
	Ruth Noble
	Janice Siegel
	Fred Weber
Resolve by:	9/15/95
Description:	What will be the standard format for customer numbers? The current formats in the six divisions are:

Boston: X999999
Denver: 99-999-999
Hoboken: XX999
Miami,
Milwaukee,
and Seattle: 999-9999

Once the numbers are standardized, all customers will have to be renumbered to prevent duplicate numbers.

Figure 8.17 Documented open issue.

coordinator sends a written copy of the outcome to the executive sponsor and to all the people on the distribution list. Meanwhile, the IS project manager monitors the resolution of these issues and follows up on those not resolved by the date determined in the session.

Make sure that the IS project manager *and* the participants are clear about who is responsible for monitoring the resolution of these open issues. Years ago, we had a JAD project where several issues remained unresolved long past their due dates. Thinking that the facilitator was the one accountable for these open issues, a key user complained about this flaw in the JAD process. Meanwhile, the facilitator was off on another JAD project. To prevent this confusion, clearly delegate this role to the project manager at the end of the session.

WHEN SHOULD THE SCRIBE TAKE NOTES?

Very simply, the scribe takes notes whenever a prompt is received from the facilitator. The scribe of a session is not like the student of Sociology 101 who writes everything down because he doesn't know what will be on the test. Instead, the scribe can save pencil lead until you indicate what to write. Then, the scribe records either exactly what the participant says or the facilitator's paraphrased version of it.

This is where you may need to slow down the person doing the talking. For example, when you ask the participant most familiar with the agreement to summarize it for the scribe, the participant might begin with an elaborate exposition on the subject and then jokingly ask, "Did you get all that?" Tell the participant to go slowly, as the scribe needs to record it. Make sure the scribe is bold enough to say, when necessary, "Could you please repeat that a little more slowly?"

EVALUATING THE SESSION

The evaluation form is used to measure the success and participant satisfaction, not of the agreements made, but of the session itself. This evaluation allows the person managing the JAD process to monitor how the participants perceive the sessions, as well as how the facilitator is performing.

The evaluation form is most beneficial when you first bring JAD into the company. You especially need this feedback for the first few projects. As the use of JAD progresses and the process becomes an accepted tradition, you still need to keep this feedback mechanism in place. Although you may not ask the participants to fill out evaluation forms after every session (after all, sometimes the same people participate in several sessions), you might want periodic feedback at least twice a year.

When Should You Pass Out the Evaluation Form?

Most evaluation forms at seminars or conferences are distributed at the very end, when people are looking at their watches and thinking about lunch. If you pass out the evaluation form at this time, you will not get helpful feedback.

Instead, pass out the evaluation forms on the last day of the session, but before the last break. Ask the participants to take a few minutes to give you their comments on how JAD has worked for them. Figure 8.18 shows a sample evaluation form.

Then, after the session, read the evaluation forms carefully. Evaluate the comments and use what you can to rework and improve the next session.

CLOSING THE SESSION

At the close of the session, you need to:

- Determine who receives the final document.
- Discuss how the participants will review the document.
- Give some closing remarks.

Determine Who Receives the Final Document

With everyone together in the room, finalize the list of who receives the final document. Have them refer to the page in the Working Document that shows this list. Figure 8.19 shows a sample.

Explain that this list includes all participants and the executive sponsor. Ask if anyone else should be added to the list and who needs extra copies. After updating the names and confirming the mail codes, you have a finalized distribution list.

Discuss the Review Process

Describe how the document will be reviewed and finalized. Tell the group that they will receive a copy of the document for their review. Then you will all meet again to discuss the changes people would like to make to the document. Once the changes are agreed upon, key participants sign an approval form.

At this point in the session, discuss who should be designated to sign the approval form. These signatures will represent consensus of all participants. Suggest one or two key managers from the business area and an IS project manager. The executive sponsor should always sign the approval form. These signatures will be obtained only after the review meeting, at which

JAD Evaluation Form

Name (optional): _____ Date: _____

JAD Project: _____

JAD Facilitator: _____

Please rate the following from 1 to 5, where 5 is the best.

Low – – – – – – – High

Rate the quality of the . . .	1	2	3	4	5
Contents of the agenda					
Working Document					
Meeting room					
Audio visuals (flip charts, overheads, and magnetics)					
CASE tool use in the session					
Meetingware use in the session					
Degree of group consensus					
Facilitator					

Answer the following questions:

Did the session meet its objectives? If not, why not?

Did the session stay on track? If not, what prevented it from doing so?

Were you able to freely contribute your thoughts and opinions? If not, what prevented you from speaking?

Did all participants contribute equally? If not, what would have made this possible?

Were areas of disagreement addressed? If not, what was overlooked?

How can we improve future sessions?

Figure 8.18 Evaluation form for the session.

Name	*No. of Copies*	*Mail Code*
Ryan Barrett	1	3
Allison Brooke	2	3
Martha Clancy	1	7
Sally Doehnert	1	3
Barbara Haber	1	2
Elvira Kipnis	1	8
Michael Kowalski	1	4
Sarah Major	1	9
Linda Morgan	3	1
Charles Mugler	1	9
Patricia Noar	1	2
Robin Rosen	1	3
Anna Schwartz	1	4

Figure 8.19 Distribution list for the final document.

time everyone has agreed with the document contents. See the "Approving the Document" section in Chapter 9.

Closing Remarks

It is 12:25. Stomachs are empty and growling. Heads are filled with business processes and screen fields. The final moments are here. The agenda is complete. The session is over, almost. All that is left is for you to say a few parting words. You want to leave them on a positive note, thanking them for their efforts. You might say:

> "Okay, that wraps it up. I think this has been a really productive session and I hope you're as satisfied with the results as I've been with your commitment and enthusiasm. The draft document will be out in a couple of days and I look forward to seeing you at the review meeting."

Having completed the session, you are ready for Phase 5: The Final Document.

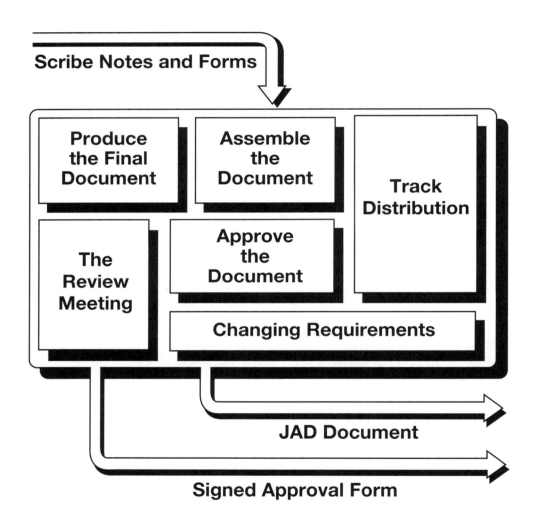

Scribe Notes and Forms

Produce the Final Document

Assemble the Document

Track Distribution

The Review Meeting

Approve the Document

Changing Requirements

JAD Document

Signed Approval Form

NINE ▷ ▶ ▶ ▶

PHASE 5: THE FINAL DOCUMENT

When the session is over, you have all the information you need. You have gotten through the hardest part of the project and the part you probably had the most uncertainty about—getting all the participants to agree on an outcome. Having done that, you naturally have a feeling of accomplishment. It is easy to say "Ah, we did it!" and simply let up on the project throttle. Don't do it. A critical part still remains. You must put all the information that came out of the session into a format that can be used by the people in the business area, the programmers, and all those involved in the next phase of the project.

In this, the final JAD phase, you transfer all the agreements made in the session into the final document. You assemble and distribute that document to the participants for review. Finally, you get signatures to approve the final document and, for systems development projects, authorize the development team to begin the next phase of the life cycle.

PRODUCING THE FINAL DOCUMENT

The session is over, the boards are wiped clean, and the participants (filled to the brim with Danish and data models) are headed back to the office. Perhaps you have a bag full of used magnetics, a collection of rolled-up flip charts, and a stack of notes from the scribe. Maybe you have a series of PC files that were prepared during the session using a word processor or CASE tool. Whatever you have, you need to turn all this material into the final JAD Document.

Consultants estimate that for each full day of the session, you can anticipate one to one-and-a-half days of documentation time. The amount of time depends on the tools you use, the quality of the scribe, and the complexity of the project.

Why the Final Document Is So Important

The JAD Document is the culmination of all that has gone into the JAD project. It is a comprehensive synthesis of agreements made in the session. It is the one resulting document, the one final product, that represents JAD's role in the process. For the people (particularly in upper management) who were not participants but have a line of responsibility for that project, the final document may be the only evidence they have to judge the status of the project after the session.

A good final document answers the business needs that were originally identified. Unless these requirements are clearly and completely documented, they are lost as soon as the session is over. No one will remember the details of what the participants decided even two days later. And after a month, you might even wonder, "What JAD session?" This highlights the importance of completing the final document as soon as possible after the session is over. Presumably your scribe has taken good notes, but they are nevertheless notes and not complete texts. Your work will be harder if you go on vacation and then return to the task. So get the document written. *Then* fly off to that tropical island.

Producing a quality final document requires certain techniques in compiling the assumptions, data models, business processes, screens, reports, open issues, and whatever else comes out of the session. The following sections describe how to do this.

Converting the Working Document

Since the Working Document was set up to mirror the final version, you already have a good starting point. You need only update that document with the additions and deletions noted by the scribe in his copy of the document. More than likely, you have the Working Document stored in files on a PC word processor. To convert these files from the Working Document to the final version, change the following:

- Title page
- Preface
- Section introductions, if necessary

The following describes changes to the title page and preface.

Title Page

Make these changes to the title page:

1. Replace "Working Document" with "JAD Document." (Leave the project name as it is.)
2. Replace the Working Document date with the final document date.
3. Add the names of the session participants in alphabetical order.

Your title page now looks like this:

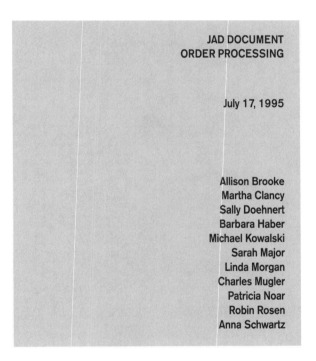

JAD DOCUMENT
ORDER PROCESSING

July 17, 1995

Allison Brooke
Martha Clancy
Sally Doehnert
Barbara Haber
Michael Kowalski
Sarah Major
Linda Morgan
Charles Mugler
Patricia Noar
Robin Rosen
Anna Schwartz

Preface

Replace the Working Document preface. The new one might say:

PREFACE

This document describes all decisions made in the Order Processing JAD session held July 7 to 10, 1995. When the participants approve this document, IS can continue the next phase of the life cycle based on its contents and the resolution of open issues.

Organizing the Source Documents

To organize the source documents, work at a large table. Sort the scribe's notes into sections and subsections. Consider such things as: Do you want the data elements in alphabetical order? Should the screens be grouped by function or do you want all the existing screens first, then the new ones? How will you present the reports?

By organizing all the information into the order you want, you will have determined the complete table of contents. (The page numbers will be filled in later.) It might look like this:

TABLE OF CONTENTS	
Session Agenda	xx
Session Participants	xx
Distribution of the Final Document	xx
Assumptions	xx
Data requirements	xx
Business Processes	xx
Screens	xx
Existing	xx
New	xx
Reports	xx
Existing	xx
New	xx
Open issues	xx

Now you are ready to expand the table of contents into the final document.

Entering the Information

With the scribe notes organized and the table of contents complete, you can enter all the information from the scribe notes into the document. Standard template files (for various parts of the document) can be set up for this step. Then you copy these templates and add the variable information from the scribe notes.

Add the text carefully, making sure it is correct, complete, and clear. The next step has some ideas for presenting your information.

INFORMATION MAPPING

When preparing the final document, you deal with all kinds of information. Innovative approaches can help present the information in clear, effective ways.

We often use various kinds of tables to present information. Several of these tables are based on techniques called Information Mapping®, which help turn ongoing, perhaps rambling text into clear, meaningful chunks. Information Mapping techniques offer an entire array of ways to format information. We'll show you the few that we use most often.

Decision Tables

You can use decision tables whenever various conditions require specific actions. For example, to tell people how to arrange a room for various kinds of meetings, you could use a decision table as shown in Figure 9.1.

Procedure Tables

When you need to explain how to do something, procedure tables can help. Procedures involve a series of sequential steps, which you can put into a table as shown in Figure 9.2.

Process Tables

Process tables also tell how to do something, but they also include who does each step (for example, several people in the Purchasing department pro-

If you want to . . .	*Then . . .*
Encourage interaction	Arrange tables in a U-shape or a square.
Teach concepts that require doing tasks	Arrange tables in straight rows that run parallel to the front of the room.
Present (but not discuss) information to many people	Don't use tables at all. Instead put the chairs in theater style (lining them up side by side in rows parallel to the front of the room).

Figure 9.1

To view a VCR tape:	
Step	*Action*
1	Turn on the TV by pressing the blue button on the TV remote.
2	Turn on the VCR by pressing POWER on the VCR remote. (The VCR is on when the channel number displays on the right side of the VCR panel.)
3	Set the TV to channel 3 by pressing 03 on the TV remote.
4	Put the tape into the VCR.
5	Press PLAY on the VCR remote.

Figure 9.2

cessing an order). Figure 9.3 is an example of a process table we prepared to explain how new chapters are produced in our online automation standards manual.

Block Labels

Block labels make it easier for readers to scan information and identify which parts to read in detail. This involves chunking information into segments according to the text's purpose, function, or content. Then you create a short label describing that chunk of text and set it off to the left of the block of text it describes.

STEP	*WHO*	*DOES WHAT*
1	Author	Prepares a detailed chapter outline
2	Standards Committee	Reviews and approves the outline
3	Author	Writes the chapter (or updates the previous version)
4	Editor	Edits the chapter
5	Standards Committee	Reviews and approves the chapter
6	Editor	Puts the chapter online

Figure 9.3

BLOCK LABELS

Definition	Your metabolic rate is the total amount of energy your body uses in a given period of time—that is, the number of calories it burns, either at rest or while active. It is usually measured by an indirect method, whereby your oxygen intake and carbon dioxide output are measured and the results plugged into a formula . . .
Effect on Weight	In general, if your resting metabolic rate is high, you may find that you can eat a lot, exercise little, and still not gain weight. Conversely, if your resting metabolic rate is low, you may eat relatively little and be fairly active but still not lose weight.

Figure 9.4

In Figure 9.4, we excerpted some text from an article on metabolism (Shelby 1994) and added block labels to identify the content.

With this approach, you sacrifice a certain amount of space because you must indent the text so the labels fit. But it's worth using the narrower margins if, as a result, your information is clearer. If you are using tables or other graphics, however, you may find this limited space a problem. Block labels are excellent when you have text that runs on with no headings or graphics to break it up. Labels break your material into meaningful chunks.

We have shown some very basic examples of a few Information Mapping concepts. You can modify these techniques to meet your needs. For example, you can combine procedure tables with decision tables as shown in Figure 9.5.

In Summary

Creating the actual boxes for these various tables is easy to do. For many word processors, making a table is a matter of selecting a function, specifying how many columns and rows you want, and filling in the information. Once you start using Information Mapping techniques, you might even catch yourself thinking in these formats!

EDITING

After adding all the information from the scribe notes, you have the first draft version of the final document. Edit this version to ensure that it is clear and consistent with the scribe notes.

This involves editing for clarity (the grammarian slaughter). With a critical eye, review the document from the perspective of the reader. Who is

To travel from the Princess Palm Hotel to the Evergreen Corporate Center:		
Step	**Action**	
1	As you exit the parking lot, turn RIGHT onto State Street and go 3 miles.	
2	Turn RIGHT onto the Sunset Freeway and go 5 miles.	
3	Exit at Highland Avenue.	
4	*If the traffic is . . .*	*Then . . .*
	Light	Turn RIGHT on Highland Avenue and go 2 blocks.
	Heavy	Go straight for 1 block, turn RIGHT on Rose Street, and go 2 blocks
5	Turn RIGHT on Main Street.	
6	Turn LEFT into the Evergreen Corporate Center and park by the brick building.	

Figure 9.5

your audience? Will the document be understood by people in the business area (who are more procedure-oriented) *and* by IS (who is more systems-oriented)? Is the text written in clear English? (Or is it loaded with unexplained technical jargon?) Are acronyms spelled out at their first mention? (Or do you say things like "The INV records of FAS must be revised to accept the MUN-SPLIV files.") Are tables titled and labeled with meaningful column headings? These are the details that are sometimes overlooked in the scribing process because everything seemed so clear at the time.

An excellent book to help in this technical writing task is *The Elements of Style* by William Strunk, Jr. and E. B. White.

ASSEMBLING THE FINAL DOCUMENT

To prepare the document for distribution, put the copies into three-ring binders. You can use 1-inch binders with clear plastic for holding preprinted covers. This allows you to insert front and back covers as well as a spine. These inserts can be set up as follows:

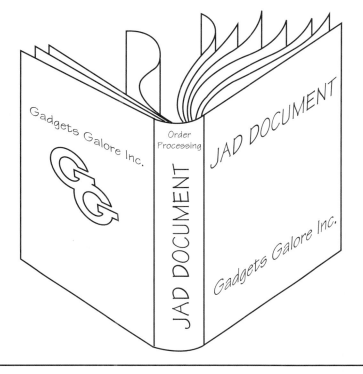

Figure 9.6 Binder for the final document.

- *Front cover*—the main title (JAD Document) and company name (for example, Gadgets Galore, Inc.).
- *Back cover*—company name and logo.
- *Spine tab*—project name (Order Processing) and title (JAD Document).

Figure 9.6 shows how the binder would look.

The front and back covers are generic and can be used for any JAD projects. The spine tab is customized by including the project name, such as Order Processing. Without this customized spine tab, some participants (who have been involved in several JADs) will have a row of binders that cannot be distinguished.

Within the document, you can separate the sections with preprinted tabs. This is one of those "not necessary, but nice to have" features. We keep generic tabs on hand so we don't have to order them for each project. Figure 9.7 shows how these tabs might look.

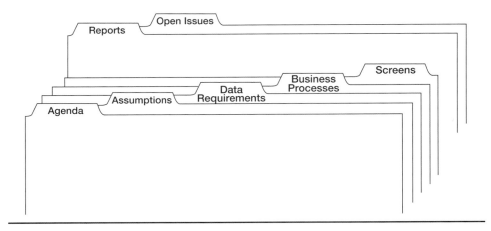

Figure 9.7 Tabs for the final document.

The full package includes the binder (with covers and spine tabs), pages, tabs, and a cover memo. A sample cover memo is shown in Figure 9.8.

THE REVIEW MEETING

This one- to two-hour review meeting is held in an on-site conference room. The facilitator presides and all participants and the executive sponsor attend. Even those who are already in complete agreement with the

---

July 17, 1995

To: JAD Session Participants

From: Martha Clancy

Subject: JAD Review Meeting

Enclosed is a draft copy of the final JAD Document for you to review. To assemble your document, please insert the tabs before each document section. (For example, insert the Assumptions tab before the Assumptions section.)

A review meeting has been scheduled to discuss changes and to approve the document. The meeting will take place Monday, July 20, at 10:00 in the main conference room.

It is important that all participants attend. If you have a conflict, please let us know. Otherwise, see you Monday.

Figure 9.8 Cover memo for document review.

document should be there, because they could be affected by other people's changes.

In the meeting, highlight the fact that although requirements will continue to change, this document represents a specific point in time—the close of the JAD session. Requirements that have changed since then (such as an open issue that has been resolved) are not reflected in this document. If people want to add a new field to a report, for example, they would discuss it with IS. Making this clear prevents new discussions that could turn a simple review meeting into a mini-JAD forming in the wake of the main session. After all, these same participants just spent days, closed in a room, in an active decision-making mode. They can easily fall back into these roles. It is your job to keep them on track.

Handling the Review Comments

Walk through the document page by page. You will hear a variety of comments that involve various kinds of edits. Following are some examples:

- *Accuracy edits.* "This is not right. It should say . . ."
- *Clarity edits.* "Assumption number 3 is confusing. Can we change the wording to . . . ?"
- *Micro edits.* "Wouldn't it be better to say '*the* data base' instead of '*a* data base?'" (There is often someone present who is interested in such details.)
- *After-the-session thoughts.* "I was thinking we should add another column to the Customer List report . . ."

For the accuracy and clarity edits, get agreement from the group and note the changes. These are the kinds of comments you want from the participants. For the micro edits, go ahead and make the changes, but do not take time discussing them. For the after-the-session thoughts, explain again that the document represents agreement at the time of the session. Suggest handling these changes in a separate forum.

As participants make their comments, restate them as you make your notes in the document. Ask the group if they agree. Then move on.

Now What?

At the end of the meeting, determine how to handle the changes. In other words, should the document be reissued? If the changes are minimal (for example, the wording has been fine-tuned on several pages), then the current version (plus their noted changes) can serve as the final copy. On the other hand, if the changes are significant (several changes have been noted

---

July 24, 1995

To: JAD Session Participants

From: Martha Clancy

Subject: The Final Document

    Enclosed is the final copy of the document. It includes updates from the review meeting. Please remove your current version and replace it with this copy.

Figure 9.9 Cover memo for the final document.

that will affect the next phase of the project), you need to update the document and send it out again, along with the cover memo shown in Figure 9.9.

APPROVING THE DOCUMENT—THE FINAL OKAY

Approval represents total agreement with the contents of the final document. This includes the changes discussed in the review meeting. The people who will sign the approval form were designated in the session. If the changes in the review meeting are minor, then the end of that meeting is a good time to get these signatures because:

- The people who will be signing are present at the meeting. This prevents having to rely on the uncertainty of interoffice mail, especially when several people are designated to approve the document.

- As requirements change, people may be less likely to sign, even though the document represents a point in time before these new requirements arose.

If the changes from the review meeting are major, however, wait until after the final version is distributed. Then, send the approval form to those designated. The signed approval form resides in the document received by the executive sponsor. Figure 9.10 shows a sample approval form.

With the review complete and the approval form signed, the JAD is done. Now you are ready to begin your next JAD project. Before that, however, perhaps you can arrange a well-deserved, one-week vacation on the Riviera.

CHANGING REQUIREMENTS AFTER THE SESSION

When the project is done, the facilitator and staff no longer maintain the document. The document represents a point in time. Nevertheless,

---

JAD APPROVAL FORM

JAD Project: **Order Processing**

Authorizing User Managers:

_____   **Date** _____

_____   **Date** _____

_____   **Date** _____

Authorizing IS Managers:

_____   **Date** _____

_____   **Date** _____

The above signatures represent joint agreement by the JAD participants as to the requirements for the Order Processing system. These include the contents of the JAD Document and the changes discussed in the review meeting. With this approval, IS can continue the next phase of the life cycle based on this document.

Figure 9.10 Approval form.

requirements continue to change. For systems development projects, the IS people can use the document as a basis for updating requirements. In this case, copy the document files over to their area. The programmers will maintain them. The original files remain with you.

Keep your files for at least a year, since you may want to use parts in future documents. And always keep a hardcopy original (or a backup diskette), because just when you delete the files from your computer, it will be your luck to have a team of newly hired consultants arrive and request five more copies.

PART
3

SESSION
PSYCHOLOGY

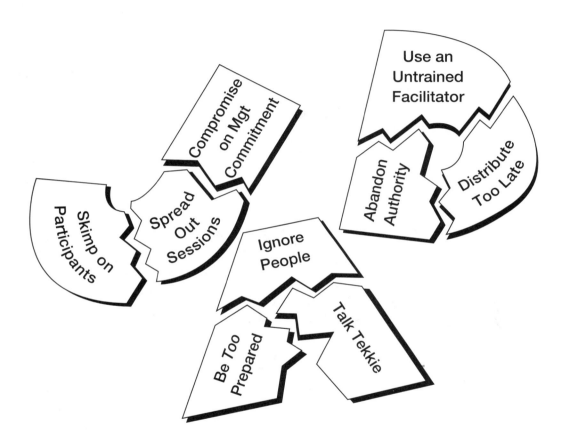

TEN ▷▶▶▶

JAD BUSTERS (OR HOW TO LEAD A GOOD JAD ASTRAY)

If you have to cross a mine field, it helps to know where the mines are buried. That is why we are devoting an entire chapter to all the ways we know of making a good JAD go bad.

The following are common pitfalls that occur even in companies that have put much effort into adhering to the JAD process. These genuine "JAD busters" can surface at any time. So don't let your resume of JAD experiences lull you into complacency.

This chapter includes advice from people using JAD in other companies. We have also drawn material from a recent study by Elizabeth J. Davidson at the Sloan School of Management, MIT. In this study, Davidson interviewed 39 people from three companies who had been involved in a total of 16 JAD projects. (Davidson 1993)

So, here is everything you need to do *if you truly want to lead a good JAD astray.*

COMPROMISE ON MANAGEMENT COMMITMENT

Of all the ways to fail at JAD, management commitment is at the top of the list. Lack of it affects almost every facet of JAD.

Compromising on management commitment begins innocently, especially if this is your first JAD. You have that initial talk with the executive sponsor who gives you a welcomed display of support. Your resulting false confidence tells you it's okay to check that step off the list. You say, "Now that we have management commitment, we don't have to concern ourselves with the sponsor's endorsement of the project anymore. Let's just go on to the next steps."

Well, the next steps are the tasks that rely directly on management commitment: selecting the participants, scheduling the session, and meeting with the executive sponsor to find out what this project is really about. Arranging time to meet with the executive sponsor is usually not a major challenge. But when it comes to committing 12 key people to five full-day sessions, then you are talking about a real quest! Often, the discussion with the executive sponsor (or a key participant's manager) is reduced to a negotiation for people's time. This is when the arena is set for the JAD-fatal compromise, where the manager says, "I can give you these people, but not those," or "Sam can come for one day, but certainly not for all three days." You may find yourself relenting and then accepting these *some*-time-is-better-than-*no*-time compromises. But with that, you also accept a higher probability of a failed session and a final product that works only for some.

When this wavering in commitment occurs, you need to point out the urgency of having all the required participants for the entire session. Explain how this can make the difference between meeting management objectives or not.

SKIMP ON THE PARTICIPANTS

No, we're not referring here to the amount of Danish and coffee you feed them. We are referring to the tendency to compromise on who attends the session. Perhaps the momentum of another hot project is preventing people from freeing up their time. A business manager describes how one company sacrificed important participation:

> We didn't use the field managers in the actual JADs. It was too much time. We met too often. We couldn't bring them out of the field that often. We knew that we (the three headquarters managers) knew 80–90% of the requirements. We felt that was good enough. (Davidson 1993)

In this case, if the meetings had been scheduled closer together to include at least a couple of field people, they might have been able to satisfy *all* the requirements.

Sometimes management will commit the participants' time, but not for the whole session. Dorine Andrews calls this syndrome "musical chairs":

> This reduces the decision quality and even results in uncontrollable workshops as people pop in and out of sessions. (Andrews 1991)

Without the right people in the session, one of two things occurs. Either you design a system that does not work for everyone, or you run around *after* the session to gather information from the people who should have been there in the first place. More than likely, these should-have-been participants suggest changes that, in turn, do not work for the others. The JAD concept is undermined and you are back to the old traditional ways of running meetings.

SPREAD OUT THE SESSIONS OVER TIME

In the midst of negotiations with management for participants' time, you might find yourself steadfast on having all the people attend, but then agree to spread out the meetings over time. A business manager explains:

> We met two to three times a week for two to three hours a session. That's not ideal, but with time constraints that's all we could do. (Davidson 1993)

Well, so much for the JAD benefit of accelerating design time. You may have succeeded in defining requirements that satisfy all the right people, but you have failed to save development time, which will surely be noticed by those you promised otherwise.

IGNORE THE PEOPLE IN THE TRENCHES

The hierarchy of an organization manifests itself in meetings (as well as everywhere else). If the vice president says to do it *this* way and the supervisor (in the trenches) says to do it *that* way, the VP usually wins.

This is where JAD sessions and meetings part their ways. But can you really tell the VP that he can't have his way? Maybe so, maybe not. But the fact is, you don't have to tell the VP anything. Your job as facilitator is not to play judge in a court of issues. You are not Solomon here. Instead, your job is to expose all views and lay them evenly on the table. In a conflict between two alternatives, you level the choices. In a struggle between two participants, you shadow the conflicting personalities, and you shine light on the facts, the issues, or whatever is in the mix.

How do you do this? Let's say the group is struggling between two alternatives. First of all, separate the alternatives from the people who are promoting them. Put them on the board where they stand on their own. Summarize them. Open the discussion to the group where others can give pros and cons for each. Also, meetingware can help level this playing field (See Chapter 16).

A good facilitator can take the organizational hierarchy out of the issues, which segues right into the next ingredient for a failed JAD session.

USE AN UNTRAINED FACILITATOR

You can see by now that the facilitator is the axis of the whole project. All tasks, in one way or another, go through the facilitator. Consequently, the quality of this person infuses the project. To put it bluntly, the facilitator can make or break a JAD session.

Here is the making of a failed session: Someone in the organization knows something about JAD. Maybe he read a few articles on the subject. So now he wants to hold a JAD for a new, highly-visible project. "No problem," he says, "We just get a room, a facilitator, and a couple of flip charts. For the facilitator, we'll just use Jennifer, the IS project leader."

A possible influence leading to use of a weak facilitator is the company's chargeback system. Let's say that your organization has a centralized JAD staff, which charges back their time by the hour. A project manager, who has experienced many successful JAD sessions, might suggest saving money by using someone in the manager's own department to lead the session.

Using a weak facilitator paves the way for a sloppy session where the guidelines of the process are not taken seriously, and where the outcome is likely to be a total flop. A bad facilitator is like a bad teacher. The session goes on, but what do you gain? With a bad teacher, the class doesn't learn. With a bad facilitator, the group doesn't decide or decides incorrectly.

If you don't already have an experienced facilitator, then invest in a good person and arrange training, if necessary. Furthermore, one good facilitator may not be enough. Take care not to rely solely on one person to make your JADs successful. This person may become burned out or may leave the job for another. Becoming dependent on one person (who has no backup and cannot be replaced) makes your JAD process vulnerable.

ABANDON YOUR OWN AUTHORITY

Because of your place in the organizational structure, you may feel that it's not your place to make certain demands. You may hesitate, for example, to request that all participants attend every session. Or in the session, you may not feel comfortable shifting the focus away from a person in a high-level position. One such facilitator describes an experience:

Everyone else in the room was high level. How do you tell a Second Vice President to shut up? If I'd had some authority, I'd be more comfortable telling him, "You're out of line." (Davidson 1993)

Remember, authority is perceived. On the organization hierarchy charts, you may be three levels below the person reeking havoc in the session. But job grade does not always determine who has authority. In the session, your perceived authority is higher because of your role as session leader. You are the one in command. Certainly, you are open to suggestions for shifting direction, but you are not open to handing over the helm to an aggressive participant just because he has a heavier title than yours.

All this sounds good in theory, but what about in practice? At the start, the theory and reality of your authority are the same. Your leadership role is assumed and respected by the group. People in a JAD session generally want to be led. They want structure that gives them the confidence that things will progress productively without their having to put energy into keeping things on track. But you must maintain this position. In a JAD session, you are in the lead until you give up the gavel. If you doubt your own authority and submissively relent unnecessarily, your authority will be sacrificed to whatever degree you abandon it. Don't give in. Remember, your authority derives from the executive sponsor's having delegated it to you.

STUMBLE THROUGH HIGH-TECH TOOLS

What's wrong with a little CASE tooling in the session? If done gracefully and appropriately, nothing. If you can make the tool dance the way you want (slowly enough to get it right, but swiftly enough to keep the participants' attention), then you can find great advantage in using these tools to help you document decisions. Most facilitators we talk with, however, do not use CASE tools or other design tools *in* the session. Some bring in tools but do not project the images for the participants to see. Instead, they use the tools off to the side to document decisions and perhaps review the diagrams later on.

CASE tools can be an excellent asset to a JAD project. The danger of using such tools in the session occurs if you let the tool drive the session. When doing a data flow diagram, for example, you can easily lose control as you frantically attempt to move a process box from one decomposition level to another. Likewise, you can accidently shift from the data model at hand (the big picture) to making sure your arrows are pointing in the right directions (the little picture). The tool becomes the center of attention and you have compromised that particular agenda item. More about tools is discussed in Chapter 15.

MUDDLE THEM WITH MODELING

Likewise, certain techniques can confuse the participants. Davidson comments in her study:

> The objectives of most of the JAD workshops discussed were to produce analytical IS models such as process models, data entity diagrams, functional decomposition diagrams, logical record designs, and so on. Business area participants typically received only written descriptions or a brief introduction to these techniques in a pre-workshop presentation. (Davidson 1993)

We are not discouraging the use of diagramming techniques for documenting design decisions. We use them frequently in our sessions. The point is how you use them. Be careful not to lose your objective in the confusing muddle of a structured technique. For example, one consultant laments on the problems of using data modeling in one particular session:

> The process . . . was not smooth. Jane and Carl both had real trouble distinguishing between . . . entities, attributes, and occurrences. . . . Stan . . . found it necessary to use frequent, time-consuming explanations and examples to keep the team on track. (Kerr and Hunter 1994)

Before you use modeling techniques, make sure the participants understand the basic principles and that a modeling expert is running the session.

TALK TEKKIE

The easiest way to confuse and alienate session participants is to allow the IS people to conduct a conversation amongst themselves laden with technical jargon, acronyms, and other gobbledygook. All you have to do is give the floor over to a hotshot tekkie rambling on: "In order for the application to perform properly, we need to operate the DBMS in an MVS/XA or ESA dataspace capability multiprocessor JES2 shared-spool environment supported by BDAM or VSAM/RRDS access methods. . . ." The other participants will retreat into silence, totally annoyed.

Make sure everyone understands the language being used. Don't take for granted that the business people automatically understand all those catchy data-processing phrases, such as *client server, network protocols,* and *navigating the data base.* If the technical people absolutely must use this jargon, have someone translate what they are saying into English so the rest of the group is not left in the dark. You, as the facilitator, may come from an IS background and understand much of the technical jargon. You should therefore make a conscious effort to listen with the ears of the business area people, and to interrupt when you sense the IS people are starting to talk over other people's heads.

IS tends to look at a system in terms of programs, disk packs, and nested "if" statements. Business area people, on the other hand, are concerned with business activities, rules and regulations, and project benefits. Since the requirements are being defined from the business perspective, you need to speak more in terms of the business (premium notices, death claims, and annual statements) and less in terms of the bits and bytes.

BE TOO PREPARED

And now, the most insidious of all JAD pitfalls. You can go through the entire planning for a JAD session and not realize that you have really set up your session to *review* requirements instead of *define* them.

Perhaps you are very conscientious and like to have things prepared in advance. Maybe you are absolutely terrified of conflict and want to make sure all the tough decisions are worked out beforehand. This may lead you to work out all the project requirements before the session even begins. Consequently, you are not really holding a JAD session to define requirements or decide alternatives. Instead, you are coordinating one big review session to peruse the pages of decisions that have already been made in a long string of traditional meetings with fragmented groups. All you have really accomplished is to arrange a highly-structured and well-populated walkthrough. In time, people will realize that all the session accomplished is a little adjustment here and a minor tweak there. Then they will wonder what all this JAD hype is about.

For a real-world example of this phenomenon, see "A Review Meeting Does Not a JAD Make" in Chapter 22.

TAKE TOO LONG TO DISTRIBUTE THE FINAL DOCUMENT

You can have the best JAD of your career, but until you complete and distribute the final document into the hands of the waiting participants, you haven't really brought the project to closure. As decisions are made and the resolutions captured one by one, the group may have clarity and consensus on the issues. But unless you get those documented decisions distributed *on time,* the results will become a vague memory.

Speed is essential. A month is as good as not at all. The way projects move along these days, you need to get the final document out within a week. Some people, especially those using word processors and CASE tools in the session, get the document out immediately after the session. Several days is all right, but no longer than a week.

IN SUMMARY . . .

Even where it has been successful, JAD can go sour. Over several years, facilitator C.J. "Mike" Cavanaugh, of Bolton, Connecticut, became familiar with a number of large companies successfully using the JAD process. In several companies, however, he watched JAD success go bad. We asked him about the events that led to the demise of facilitated sessions in these companies. He said that the changes were usually coincident with the downsizing of the organizations. During such times, he observed the following:

- Three-day sessions became more rare, replaced instead with shorter one- or two-day sessions.
- Management became reluctant to provide scribes.
- Top managers were less willing to become executive sponsors.
- The sessions contained fewer decision makers; those that did attend often could not stay for the entire session.
- Without the right decision makers in the session, items that normally could have been resolved were often left as open issues.
- Documentation review meetings were poorly attended.
- When automated tools came into the JAD room, they were not used well. Therefore, they impeded progress, rather than supported it.
- Users sold facilitator skills short. They tried to run their own sessions and consequently experienced failures.

After the companies fell into these JAD doldrums, Cavanaugh observed, the process fell into disuse. Dedicated JAD rooms soon became office space.

THE TEN JAD COMMANDMENTS

A successful JAD requires good planning before the session, carrying out that plan during the session, and following through with a quality design document after the session. It also requires staying close to JAD principles (while, at the same time, not sacrificing quality just to adhere to a particular principle).

Keeping loyal to JAD methods can be especially difficult when those methods are not in synch with the corporate culture. For example, it may not be the norm to free up several field people for three days straight to come back to the home office to design a system. But as we have seen, designing a good system absolutely requires their involvement. Sometimes you have to push the envelope.

If the keys to JAD success could be reduced to a few laws, they might read like those found in Figure 10.1.

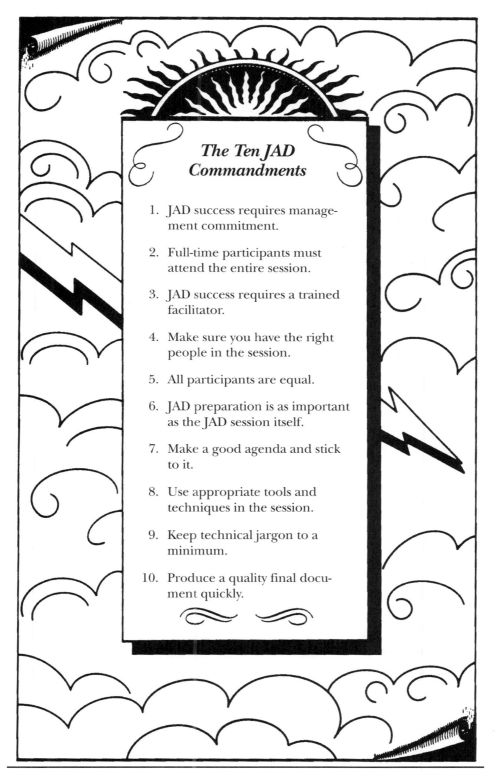

The Ten JAD Commandments

1. JAD success requires management commitment.

2. Full-time participants must attend the entire session.

3. JAD success requires a trained facilitator.

4. Make sure you have the right people in the session.

5. All participants are equal.

6. JAD preparation is as important as the JAD session itself.

7. Make a good agenda and stick to it.

8. Use appropriate tools and techniques in the session.

9. Keep technical jargon to a minimum.

10. Produce a quality final document quickly.

Figure 10.1

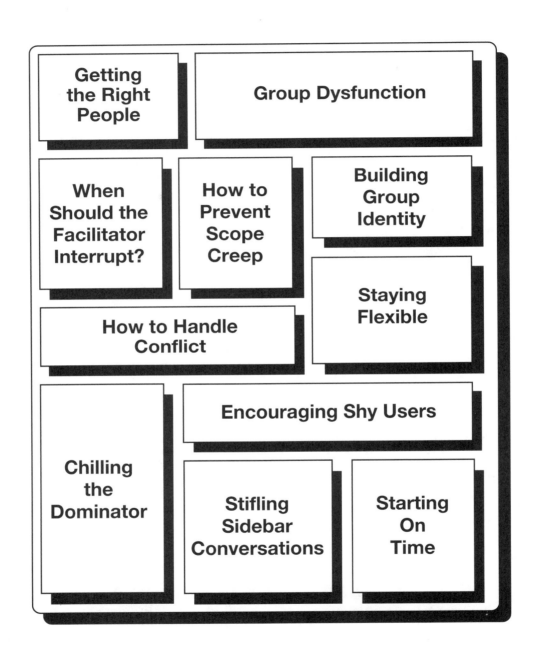

ELEVEN ▷ ▶ ▶

GROUP DYNAMICS

This chapter deals with the group dynamics involved in pulling off a successful JAD session. First, it covers how groups function and how to deal with the habits that groups naturally fall into. Then it talks about some of the individual people problems that can seriously threaten success and tells how to handle them. And it describes some ways to prevent these problems in the first place.

GROUP DYSFUNCTION

Living and working together in groups is, of course, a hallmark of civilization. Individuals working alone are limited in what they can accomplish. Even before the flowering of psychology as a science, it was well known that groups have a character or personality distinct from their individual members—and that groups can exhibit pathologies that their individual members, acting alone, might never manifest.

The violent tendencies of mobs and mass movements are well known. Charles MacKay's book *Extraordinary Popular Delusions and the Madness of Crowds* describes many examples of folly including two wildfire episodes of stock speculation that swept France and England in the early eighteenth century. He goes on to examine the "tulip mania" in Holland in the 1630s, when the price of a single bulb was bid up to what in today's terms would be thousands of dollars. MacKay's observation on the dark side of group psychology is as fresh today as ever:

> Men, it has been well said, think in herds; it will be seen that they go mad in herds, while they only recover their senses slowly, and one by one. (MacKay, 1980)

Business is certainly not immune to the consequences of bad collective decision-making. Everyone knows the saying about the camel being a horse designed by a committee. Similarly, the Ford Motor Co. in the 1950s experienced a marketing disaster with the Edsel—a car designed by a committee.

Obviously, there are tremendous advantages to working (and thinking) in groups. Tom Douglas, author of *Groups: Understanding People Gathering Together*, has summarized them as follows:

- Groups produce more and better solutions to problems.
- Groups make more efficient use of resources.
- Groups eliminate inferior ideas more effectively.
- The presence of others increases productivity.
- For tasks that can involve random errors, groups tend to make superior judgments.
- Groups achieve more than even the most superior individuals.
- Groups learn faster.
- Groups tend to make more risky decisions.
- Groups minimize the sense of responsibility of any one member.
- Groups ensure tenacity of purpose by committing members to group decisions.
- In groups, feedback of performance is from multiple sources and is therefore likely to be more accurate. (Borovits et al. 1990)

But as we've noted, groups can get us into trouble as well. Michael C. Kettelhut (of Alcon Laboratories in Fort Worth, Texas) has made a study of group dysfunction. He identifies the following five types of dysfunctional behavior (Kettelhut 1993).

Groupthink

As groups work together, they naturally develop group integrity and cohesiveness. These qualities give groups an identity and energy that benefits productivity. But, as Kettelhut describes, "Cohesive groups tend to close themselves off to unsettling information, whether from inside or outside the group." This behavior is called *Groupthink*.

This can be heightened in JAD sessions where the supposed right people with the proper authority are there to make all the right decisions. This can evolve easily into a detrimental group ego that becomes blind to new and conflicting information.

In one JAD session we held, the group (a task force of 15 people) had spent a great deal of time and research in selecting a software package. The contract negotiations were underway with the vendor of choice. Then the Vice President of IS discovered another competing package that cost significantly less. The group's first reaction was that they had absolutely no interest in looking at this new alternative. They had to be prodded into it.

To recognize and prevent this behavior, you, the facilitator, need to be alert for situations where people make decisions too quickly and ignore new information simply because it contradicts decisions that were already made. If this is happening, then Groupthink may indeed be inhibiting the potential for making good decisions. When you observe this, slow the group down. Restate the new information and ask the group how it affects their various areas of work. If they are resistant, you might point out that they seem to be rejecting good information simply because they "don't want to go down the same road again."

Risky-Shift Behavior

Groups tend to make more risky decisions than individuals. The advantage of this is that when groups get into an open, sky's-the-limit mode, decisions can be outright imaginative. Also, it's easy for groups to make risky decisions because, after all, who is really responsible? Some participants might think, "Why should I fear personal accountability or retribution if the whole group decided, especially if during the entire discussion, I kept my mouth shut!?"

In JAD sessions, this danger may cause the group to select development approaches that, when it comes time for building and implementing, simply cannot work. For example, the group may decide on an approach that does not realistically meet the time frames or technical constraints, or that may be otherwise inappropriate.

To prevent this "risky-shift behavior," make sure the group carefully evaluates each idea before deciding one way or the other. Also, as you guide the participants through their discussions, prompt them to consider the impact of their decisions. Ask questions such as, "Will this business process meet the needs of all involved?" and "Is this interface technically feasible?"

Commitment Errors

In the same way that the risky inclinations of groups can lead to bad design decisions, so can they lead to unrealistic commitments. Kettelhut describes a study where "managers who *publicly* selected certain stocks held those stocks longer than managers who made their selections *privately,* even when the stocks incurred substantial losses." Nobody wanted to admit to their peers that they had made a bad decision. Likewise, JAD participants are more likely to make (and less likely to abandon) bad forecasts under the pressure, pace, and exposure of a session.

Here is an example of a commitment error: One company held a series of JAD sessions to define requirements for a highly visible and complex application system. After these sessions, the group was asked to estimate the Specifications phase. They were so caught up in the momentum of their group accomplishments that they cockily said, "We can do the Specs phase in three months. No problem." Well, a year and a half later . . .

To prevent such commitment errors, avoid asking participants to come up with estimates in the midst of a moving session, where they may not have the time to fully consider the question. Instead, give participants adequate time to research and talk with other people when preparing their estimates.

Goal-Setting Challenges

Groups have a difficult time setting realistic goals. To make matters worse, when groups have previously not met their goals, they are likely to set *higher* goals for next time. Kettelhut offers several explanations for this odd behavior. Sometimes groups attempt to compensate for previous failures. Other times groups simply feel no shame when they do not meet a goal.

JAD sessions are particularly vulnerable to this dysfunction, especially if the group is off-site (thereby enhancing the distance between the thriving group synergy and the reality of their work environment). Furthermore, in the limelight that group projects cast upon the individual, people do not want to disappoint their fellow team members by offering mediocre promises of so-so goals. Therefore, to maintain the good graces of the group, participants sometimes extend themselves unrealistically.

As the facilitator, you need to encourage the group to compare goals with other similar projects. And always question any goals set by the group.

The Abilene Paradox

This dysfunction occurs when group members hesitate to raise objections because they do not want to create conflict or they fear disapproval from the group. The result is bad decisions followed by implied group agreement.

According to Kettelhut, this behavior takes its name (the *Abilene Paradox*) "from an incident in which a group, feuding over where to eat, accepted the idea of driving 50 miles to a restaurant in Abilene, despite everyone's better judgment." In a JAD session, similar bad decisions and assumed agreement can lead to all kinds of problems. Here is an example from one facilitator:

> The JAD team was discussing how to staff up a large, complex project. One director said, "I know this hotshot CICS guru who can do the job in three months!" The group reluctantly agreed to hire this person even though they knew that by bringing on this consultant, the business knowledge learned by him would "walk out the door" when the project was done.

To avoid the dangers of implied group agreement (let alone an unnecessary trip to Abilene), beware of alternatives being selected without serious evaluation. Do not be seduced by the group's quick consensus and easily fall into thinking, "Oh great, another decision made! Aren't we making progress!" When participants tend to quickly accept the first offered solution, query the group further. Ask questions like, "Betsy, how would this possibility affect your area?" or "What other alternatives can we consider here?"

Yes, silence means consent, but you have not really met your objectives if participants leave the session with personal reservations about the outcome. Because, chances are, these reservations are based on valid concerns that will surface as problems later on, when the solution (barely discussed in the session) is implemented.

After considering all these group dysfunctions, you might wonder, "Why would I ever bring people together for anything, let alone a JAD session? Maybe I'll just have my next Thanksgiving dinner alone as well!" Well let's put this in perspective. The fact is, the advantages of groups far outweigh the problems. Furthermore, an aware facilitator can prevent these dysfunctions, or at least recognize and counteract them as they arise.

In Figure 11.1, we have taken Michael Kettelhut's summary of the five dysfunctional group behaviors and combined them with our suggestions on how to recognize and deal with them.

BUILDING GROUP IDENTITY

In short, it's a good idea to do whatever you can to pull the group together into a cohesive unit. You can begin developing group identity even before the session convenes. When you meet with session participants, talk about how their expertise fits into the group as a whole. Before the session, send out a finalized participation list including not only the people's names, but

Behavior	Description	What to Do
Groupthink	Small groups behave and make decisions as if they were infallible.	Beware of the group making decisions too quickly or ignoring conflicting ideas. Restate new information and encourage discussion.
Risky Shift	Groups make decisions that pose higher risk than individuals do on their own.	Evaluate alternatives carefully. Consider the impact of all decisions.
Commitment Errors	Groups take on tasks that are difficult, and they fail to adjust goals or expectations as work progresses.	Give participants adequate time to prepare estimates.
Goal-Setting Errors	Groups often set unreasonable goals or set more difficult goals after a failure.	Question all goals and compare them to other projects.
The Abilene Paradox	The group as a whole adopts a course of action contrary to the desires of most or all individual members.	Encourage silent participants to share their views.

Figure 11.1 Group dysfunction and how to handle it.

also the departments they represent. (We omit titles, so as to de-emphasize where people stand in the hierarchy.)

Donna Hoffman (from Health Care Service Corporation) describes an approach for establishing group identity early on:

> I begin to cultivate the team atmosphere immediately by creating a logo for the project using a graphics package. For example, one project involved a federal employee business, so I designed a logo integrating a graphic of the capitol building along with our own corporate logo. These logos are simple, but give the group something unique to identify with.

Here is another interesting way to establish group identity. Steve Webb (of Seagram Europe and Africa in Wilrijk, Belgium) says:

> After the first day of the session, we have a group meal. As people relax with dinner and a drink, they set the stage for new ideas the next day.

Continue building group identity as the session progresses. You can do this in simple, yet subtle ways. Much of it is in the words you use. For example, you can imply group ownership in your statements. When speaking to the group, refer to "your approach," "your direction," or the "group's decision." This reinforces their ownership and responsibility in the outcome.

HAVING THE RIGHT PEOPLE IN THE ROOM

Consider the consequences of not having the right people at the session: That is, you do not have participants with the authority and knowledge to determine business requirements. This defeats the whole concept of JAD, which is to provide a concentrated workshop for making decisions with everyone present to make those decisions. If all the required people cannot attend, consider revising the JAD schedule.

To assure you have the right people, spend time in the early phases selecting the participants. Ask the business area managers who should attend. Ask the executive sponsor as well as the IS director. When you meet with various people during your interviews, review the list of participants to see if they feel anyone has been overlooked.

On the other hand, you don't want to overload the session by adding another name every time one is mentioned. It is all too easy to fall into the trap of "inviting" people for essentially political reasons, so they don't feel "left out." The JAD session is not a party. Investigate to make sure of the need for each person's attendance. Remember, some people can be designated as "on-call" to be contacted when questions arise in their area of expertise.

But What If You Missed Someone?

What do you do if you have overlooked someone who should have been included in the session? For example, several times in the session, people say, "We can't make *that* decision. Julie handles that area so it is up to her." Well then, it's time to call Julie and get her into the session. If you have selected the correct executive sponsor, he will support you in adjusting any priorities that Julie might have. If she cannot attend, make one open issue that lists all the unresolved questions where her involvement is essential. At the very least, talk with her on the phone to address the issues. Then, bring her comments to the next day's session.

How to Handle JAD Crashers

What if it's 10 minutes before the session begins and someone shows up who was not invited? You inquire as to his presence, and he tells you, "I'm substituting for Jeremy Harrison." You cannot let people take the place of other participants. No stand-ins or stunt men allowed here. These people will not have been oriented to the session's goals and objectives, may not be familiar with the JAD process, and probably won't have the power to make decisions.

Remember the Front Line

Another facet of having the right people in the room is making sure you include those who will actually use the new business processes—that is, the people who are intimately involved in the day-to-day functions.

> We have observed numerous JAD sessions in which low-level employees are overlooked as attendees. This results in a meeting room filled with middle managers and supervisors unable to specify details of day-to-day operations (for example, what 17 fields are needed to fill out form A345). (Carmel et al 1992)

So make sure you include at least some of the people who will actually read the reports, enter the data, and view the screens. You need to hear from the front-line staff.

You Need the Best and the Brightest

Selecting the right people for the session means more than just making sure all areas are represented. You also want to ensure that managers provide the best people to represent their areas. A short-sighted manager, for example, may not want to send Sally (his best, most knowledgeable, *indispensable* employee). On the other hand, he'd feel downright relieved to send Sue (his roam-the-halls, disruptive, uncooperative employee). Often the best JAD participants are those who can't be spared from their jobs.

However, don't let this example lead you to think that complainers are not welcomed in sessions. People critical of the business often have good ideas on how to make it better. Likewise, if you are looking for new, innovative ideas in your session, don't be afraid to include the person who has those off-the-wall ideas and whom others may think of as a bit eccentric. Sometimes these folks can bring exactly the perspective you need to view the business in a new light.

If you could get all the qualities you want in a participant, the ideal character would be creative, knowledgeable, vocal, optimistic, and welcoming of change. Is that asking too much? Well, perhaps you could settle for four out of five.

How Many People Should a Session Include?

In Chapter 8 we talked about the best group size being between 7 and 15 participants. On the one hand, you need enough people to make decisions, but on the other, you can't have so many people as to stifle the progress of the group. Here is a comment on group size that makes finer distinctions:

> We consider a group of 2 to 6 people to be an "intimate group," with maximum individuality, like a jazz combo that alternates from one soloist to another. Seven to 15 people constitute a "small group," in which individuality is preserved, yet true group processes emerge and exert considerable influence. Eye-to-eye contact can be maintained, and it is difficult for any participant to become anonymous. When the number of participants exceeds 15, a "large group," group processes dominate, and individuality is submerged. (Phillips and Phillips 1993)

As the research shows, 7 to 15 participants is an ideal mix to maximize creativity and decision-making. A group of this size:

> . . . is small enough to be able to work to consensus on the issues, but large enough to represent all major perspectives. (Phillips and Phillips 1993)

PREVENTING SCOPE CREEP

To stay on course, you must be able to distinguish between digressions that are necessary and those that are not. Unproductive digressions inevitably result in scope creep; that is, the project's scope migrates away from its original intent.

The natural progression is this: The group is discussing an item on the agenda. While elaborating on a particular point, someone brings up a related subject. Someone else picks up on it. The conversation digresses. The original subject is lost. You have now gone from discussion to digression to being totally off the course.

The problem is, digressions are often laced with much fervor and zeal. An apparent urgency fills the air. This intensity sometimes clouds the facilitator's ability to recognize these tangents.

Throughout the session, you will sense such strayings from the agenda. Ask yourself, "Is the discussion necessary to accomplish this part of the agenda?" If you do not know, ask the group the same question. Sometimes they will say, "Yes, we need to cover this." In this case, continue the discussion. Other times, they will cease their meanderings and get back on track. Most people in the room, having tolerated the digression in silence, will be glad to get back to the questions at hand.

The agenda is like a road map. You follow it through the course of the session. In a typical road trip, sometimes you make intentional side trips (the car breaks down and you need a new carburetor). But you still have the same destination. Other times, you get off course (you are lost) and migrate toward another destination (you head for San Diego instead of San Francisco). Now you have lost the original objective. The important thing in a JAD session is to recognize these migrations and get back on track.

Hidden-Agenda Digressions

Sometimes, people come to the session with pet gripes that have nothing to do with the session objectives. For example, one participant has, for two years, been trying to convince the home office to revise the way customer service handles complaints. This issue is not in the scope of the session. But as soon as the participant sees an opportunity, he tries to shift the agenda. Watch out for this. Bring the discussion back on course.

Merry-Go-Round Digressions

Sometimes, the group unanimously adopts a digression, professing that it is necessary. But the discussion continues in a circular fashion, leading nowhere. This is the time to make an open issue. Write a one-line summary of the problem on the Open Issues flip chart. Then come back to it later. The important thing is recognizing tangents and interrupting when necessary.

STAYING FLEXIBLE

As we have described, structure (in the form of agendas, objectives, and so on) helps prevent scope creep. In the battle against digressions, structure is your ally. Nevertheless, you must also be able to stay flexible when necessary. This sounds like a contradiction, but you can do both. You can keep on course and stay flexible at the same time.

For example, you may not run this week's session exactly as you ran last month's session. According to Alex Reinders (of IBM Consulting in Chicago, Illinois):

> The most important trait for a session leader is flexibility. This is especially true for consultants. If I say to my client, "This is the methodology and these are the work products," the session will fail. On the other hand, if I ask, "What work products do you expect from this phase of the project?" and tailor my session to that, I will have a satisfied client.

Here is another example of staying flexible. Let's say your session agenda calls for defining business processes first, then reports. You are in the midst of a decomposition diagram for the Accounting area and someone says, "If we address reports for a bit, I think we will understand the business flow better." Now, as the session facilitator, you can rigidly stick to your agenda by saying, "Sorry, we can't look at the reports now because we haven't reached that part of the agenda." In this case, you are letting structure dictate your session. On the other hand, you can say, "Although reports are not planned until later in the agenda, let's look at the ones that affect this business process." In this case, you have been flexible and made an exception to your agenda without succumbing to scope creep.

Let structure be your ally, not your burden. Use your agenda, objectives, and scope as a map for your session, but know that you can leave this planned route when opportunities arise for unplanned, yet productive approaches and innovative solutions.

WHEN SHOULD THE FACILITATOR INTERRUPT?

The most obvious time for the facilitator to interrupt is when discussions go off course. Just as important as recognizing digressions, though, is recognizing *potential consensus,* that is, detecting when a decision can be reached. This is what marketing people refer to as *closing the sale.* When a customer says, "I really think this car is right for me," the salesman does not ask, "Would you like to see the trunk?" Instead, he turns his focus to writing up the sale. You should use this same tactic in the session. Suppose someone suggests, "Well, maybe we could convert all the various customer numbers to the format used by the Milwaukee division." And someone else says, "That could work." This is when you step in and say, "The suggestion is to convert the customer numbers to the Milwaukee format. Will this work for everyone?" If so, have the scribe document the decision and read it back to the group for consensus.

Another reason for interrupting is to call breaks. Sometimes the session stays right on course, decisions get made, and you have everyone's undivided attention. Nevertheless, the participants still need a recess. Try breaking on a positive note, such as after a decision has been made and documented. But do not drag the group through 20 extra minutes of restless, fidgety discussion just to get a decision. As they say, "The mind can only absorb what the seat can endure." And the seat can usually endure no more than two hours at a time. Football games have their halftimes. Baseball games have the seventh-inning stretch. And JAD sessions have their intermissions. Maybe *you* could go on for hours. After all, you are up for the session. You are doing your song and dance, writing things on the board, and generally operating at on-stage intensity. The participants, on the other hand, have been sitting in the same position all morning, drinking lots of coffee and brainstorming. So, do not lose track of the time. Interrupt to call the breaks.

STARTING ON TIME

Let's say your session is scheduled to begin at 8:30 A.M. The first day is a test. Most everyone will arrive on time, some will be a little late, and everyone will check to see if you really start at 8:30—or if, as in many meetings, you lollygag around for 20 minutes waiting for the late ones to arrive. How late or early you start on that very first day is their gauge for when to come the next day. The point is, *always* start on time! That way, you give the punctual ones the respect they deserve. And you give the ones who come late the message they deserve—that you will not hold up the session for their fashionably late arrivals. On time today means on time tomorrow.

Judy August, JAD consultant, encourages participants to arrive at the session on time by "awarding" the latest arriver. For example, if someone shows up at 8:32, that person gets a plastic chicken (or a pineapple) placed in front of her. When the next offender arrives at 8:35, the plastic chicken is passed along to that person. (August 1991)

By starting on time, participants will show up on time. Likewise, give them the same courtesy at the end of each meeting by adjourning on time. Do not hold them for even 10 more minutes. Close on time or a few minutes early. They will be ready.

HOW TO HANDLE CONFLICT

Conflict comes in many forms. There is *gainful* conflict where a few people in the group explore and defend different ways to define the requirements. This is productive and need not be curbed. There is *stalemate* conflict where the discussion comes to an impasse. You can go no further, maybe not even to the next agenda item. This must be dealt with. Finally, there is *dogmatic* conflict which spawns the willful, headstrong kinds of discussions where egos run rampant, blood pressures rise, and people take the attitude, "It's my way or the highway." This kind of conflict is unproductive and unnecessary. When it arises, you have to squelch it immediately or it will wreck your session.

One of the jobs of the executive sponsor is to resolve conflicts when the session comes to a standstill. But you can and should try other approaches before things get to this point. The more the executive sponsor has to arbitrate, the more the results of the session begin to take on the character of a top-down decision-making process imposed from above. The following describes several conflict-resolving techniques available to you. We suggest applying them in the following sequence. If one technique does not work, move on to the next.

1. Open Up the Question to the Group

Sometimes the conflict stems from outright disagreement. For example, one person feels that the Financial Officer should approve all purchases of $50,000 or more, while another feels that the approval limit should be $100,000. When you see no resolution in sight, change the perspective. Open up the question to the others in the group. Ask, "How do the rest of you feel about this? How about you, George, what would work best in your area?"

2. Make an Open Issue

The most common way to handle conflict is to make the question an open issue. This sets the conflict aside so you can get on with the agenda. By documenting the issue and putting it on the flip chart, the group feels confident that it will not be abandoned. Sometimes, in the process of documenting the issue, the very act of trying to put the question into words somehow brings an objectivity that leads to a resolution. More than likely, though, the issue stays as an open one.

When a dispute appears to be going nowhere, some people use the "five-minute rule." Facilitators at British Telecom, for example, frequently use this technique. When the rule is invoked, participants have no more than five minutes to resolve the conflict. If they don't, the item goes on the open issues flip chart. Anyone in the group can invoke this five-minute rule (except observers, of course). After all, sometimes the facilitator does not know that a digression is in the making, while at the same time, five people in the session are silently groaning.

Beware of overusing this open issues technique. The purpose of the session is to make decisions. You don't want to be one hour into the session with 88 open issues on the board. Furthermore, when you need the resolution right then and there, talking about it tomorrow will not do, especially when everything else you need to cover today hinges upon or flows from the resolution of that particular issue. In that case, go on to the next technique.

3. Take a Break

When you are locked in a stalemate and the discussion appears unproductive, take a coffee break. During the interlude, people may get together in smaller group discussions. This more informal mode brings new perspectives. We have seen many heated conflicts resolved in the cooler environment that a break provides, as in this anecdote from Steve Webb (of Seagram Europe and Africa):

> A session involving multiple European representatives was going okay. Then the participants started to talk around and around a very small point. One representative became quite upset. I suggested a ten-minute coffee break.
>
> "Mr. Webb," she said, "I know these psychological tricks and they don't work for me! I will still feel the same after the break."
>
> When the session reconvened, the conflict was resolved in five minutes.

4. Analyze the Conflict in a Structured Way

Sometimes, applying objective analysis can clarify the issues involved in a disagreement, and thus bring participants to consensus. To handle deadlocks, we use a technique that quantifies the impact of each side of the conflict. This six-step approach is described in Chapter 14. Meanwhile, if that does not work, proceed to the next step.

5. Call the Executive Sponsor

When you cannot resolve the conflict within the confines of the session, it's time to call the executive sponsor. Usually, all the business area departments represented in the room ultimately report to that person, so he has the authority to make decisions for their areas.

The best approach is to have the executive sponsor come to the session. But if he can't come, explain the situation over the phone. Have someone from each side of the issue elaborate. Then, communicate his decision back to the group. The executive sponsor will probably resolve the issue very decisively: "The Financial Officer will approve all purchases of $75,000 or more."

Conflicts between Users and IS

Conflicts between users and IS should be handled differently, because in this case the focus is on *who* is in the conflict rather than *what* the conflict is about. Sometimes you are dealing with relationships between users and IS that are not exactly warm and cozy. For example, a programmer might carry on stubbornly about how a user's request absolutely cannot be done. Or a user might start badgering IS about a particular point and bring up other frustrations like, "What do you mean you can't do it? And what about all those other outstanding requests that never get done?"

This is where you become both facilitator and psychologist. You need to make the programmer realize that the IS department supports the users; therefore, if the users really need a certain function, then IS needs to take a close look at how to do it. In the same way, you need to make the users understand the limitations of computer systems and what may be realistically involved in implementing the requests they are asking for. In other words, try to bring both user and IS perspectives to light and break down the barrier between them, even though at times this barrier may seem like the Berlin Wall. (Remember, the Berlin Wall came down.)

CHILLING THE DOMINATOR

If you hold many sessions, at some point you are going to run into the *Dominator*. You know, the one with the loud tie, green pants, gritty voice, and muscular brain. The Dominator's the one who has to speak first and get in the last word as well. He or she (they come in both genders) tries to take over the session. The Dominator says things like, "You can't do that, it won't work!" or "I have a better idea," and speaks in paragraphs that have no end. Meanwhile, the rest of the group starts to daydream, doodle, and roll their eyes in annoyance.

The only way to deal with the Dominator is straight on. Explain to him that other points of view must be heard. When the Dominator has carried on long enough, say, "Now, how do the rest of you feel about this subject?" If the person persists in dragging down the session, speak with him at the break, explaining that this dominance is hindering the group effort. You might say, "Ken, we are fortunate to have your expertise. Your view is important to the session. But we also need to hear from others as well. Would you please give the other people more of a chance to participate? If we don't balance the session with all points of view, the results will not work."

If the Dominator persists, the choice comes down to this: Would you rather accept the consequences of running a session that meets the needs of only one aggressive participant or take the consequences of asking that person to leave the session? Depending on the political situation, you are usually better off having the person leave, unless you find yourself in the following situation . . .

What If the Dominator Is Your Boss?

Now here is a problem for you: What if your boss is the one slowing down the session because of his dominant behavior and continuous digressions? Do you tell your boss to get back on track or "exit stage right"? Euphemistically speaking, this action could have a negative effect on your career.

If your boss is a dominating digressor, you probably know that already.

Take the preventive approach. Do whatever you can to keep this person off the participation list. You can explain to your boss that his contribution would be most valuable before the session, in reviewing the preliminary requirements and contributing ideas at that time.

ENCOURAGING SHY USERS

The opposite of the Dominator is the *Shy User.* This is the person who probably comes to the session fully prepared, with several sharpened pencils and a tablet of paper. This user knows the subject matter, has good ideas, but is too shy to say anything in front of all those people.

This is a problem you need to anticipate and plan for by learning ahead of time who has the expertise for each part of the agenda being discussed. For example, Marvin has a complete understanding of how orders are processed and entered into the system and Claire knows the technical side of how the system interfaces with other business processes in the company. You may come to a point in the discussion where you realize that Marvin has an in-depth knowledge of the question at hand, but he is not speaking. More than likely, his silence is not from being without opinions, but from being too shy to speak in this forum. Nevertheless, you need his view.

Draw him out. Ask him a direct question. Stay away from open, general questions like, "Marvin, what do you think about this?" Instead, begin with a specific inquiry like, "Marvin, what process is used to sort orders before entering them?" Furthermore, ask about the department's view rather than his own personal view. Do not ask, "What do *you* do?" Instead, ask, "What does the Order Entry department do?" Try to elicit information through effective questioning without pressuring or embarrassing the participant.

STIFLING SIDEBAR CONVERSATIONS

In the session, the group must remain united. The integrity of the group dissolves when subgroups emerge. A typical scenario is this: You are covering a controversial subject that affects many people in the room. One person has the floor, talking about a particular approach. Two others start a little conversation on one side of the room. Three others start talking on the other side. You have lost group cohesion.

Maintaining this cohesion means that only one person speaks at a time and he speaks to the whole group, not just to the people sitting nearby. This way, no one misses anything. Keeping a room full of people focused on one conversation at a time for up to five days is a challenge. You need to watch for sidebar conversations and handle them as they arise. When they do, take the following two-step approach:

1. Walk toward the people who are talking. As your voice approaches them, they will probably turn their attention back to the session. This physical approach works more often than not.

2. If the conversation continues, deal with it directly, but diplomatically. There is no need to admonish them for "talking in class." This would only make them resentful. Instead, you might say something like, "Beth. Scott. We need your input on this." Or, for something stronger, you could say, "Hey folks, can we get back on track here, please?" Then, immediately turn your focus back to the session. You need only their attention, not their chagrin.

Address these sidebar conversations as they come up. You want everyone to hear what everyone else has to say. And above all, you want to keep the group together.

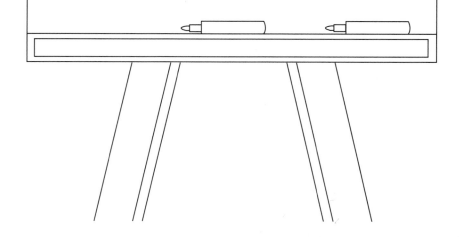

A Good Facilitator:

- Communicates well
- Separates ideas from people
- Shows a natural interest
- Listens well
- Maintains control
- Empowers the group
- Handles uncertainty
- Is quick to connect
- Focuses on the business

TWELVE ▷ ▶ ▶ ▶

THE FACILITATOR'S REPERTOIRE

If there were a college course called "Facilitating 101" designed solely for those who lead sessions, what would it cover? In other words, what skills should a facilitator possess? Following are the skills we recommend for a good facilitator's repertoire. You can use this list when you search for the ideal person to come aboard and do facilitation, or you can use it to enhance your own skills or to improve others in your group. Remember, no one can perfect all the skills on this list. Just try to hone as many as possible. Even seasoned facilitators continue to evolve. Good facilitators do the following.

COMMUNICATE WELL

Facilitators need to be able to get a point across clearly and succinctly. They need to listen to what others say, then interpret, dissect, and integrate it with the whole picture, as well as restate it so the rest of the group understands the point.

Facilitators are responsible for preparing documents—the Management

Definition Guide, the Working Document, and the final JAD Document—so they need to be good business writers. To conduct the session effectively, though, what they need most is the ability to think and speak on their feet. Like classroom teachers, courtroom lawyers, politicians, and stand-up comedians, they need to be able to "work a crowd." Without this they are weak in their role.

Many of the following facilitator abilities relate to communication skills.

SEPARATE THE IDEA FROM THE PERSON

During discussion, the facilitator should recognize spoken ideas for what they are, rather than for who is presenting them. In other words, the facilitator should try *not* to "consider the source." This is easier said than done. For example, when one idea comes from the $20,000-a-year office clerk and the next comes from the $95,000-a-year-plus-bonus vice president, it takes skill to consider all ideas equally.

Not only should the facilitator disregard *who* presents the ideas, but also *how* they are presented. One person may mumble his offerings in a monotone drone, while the next may pitch his point of view like a politician running for office. The group naturally gives more credence (or at least more attention) to the idea presented with flair. A good facilitator removes the weight from the words. He replaces the drone and the sales pitch with objectivity. How is this done? By reacting impartially to new ideas, by restating them, or at times, by writing them on the board to give them visual equality.

Remember, the richest ideas can come from the most mundane sources.

SHOW A NATURAL INTEREST

Staying objective does not mean responding mechanically and keeping your distance from the group. On the contrary! A good facilitator is naturally interested in what people have to say. For example, when a participant is laboring to describe a particular situation, doing his best to make a point, the facilitator empathizes with the participant, cares about what is being said, and wants the participant to be recognized.

LISTEN WELL

A thread weaving throughout the facilitator's repertoire is listening. The facilitator listens to distinguish unproductive diversions from those with substance. He listens for when to probe new ideas, and when to change the subject. He listens for hidden agendas and for that crucial moment when the participants have reached consensus so the decisions can be restated, agreed to, and documented. And he listens for other needs as well (for example, when the participants crave bagels in the morning instead of sweet Danish).

> Hearing is not listening. We often hear what we want to, which is sometimes referred to as "wishful hearing." Remember that you share responsibility with the speaker. (Saunders 1991)

LISTEN WITH THE EYES TOO

Listening has a visual counterpart—seeing. The facilitator looks for gestures bearing messages. Much can be gleaned from the group simply by reading their eyes. A good facilitator can tell when someone wants to speak, then prompts the person to do so. The facilitator visually senses when the group considers a discussion has digressed (rolling eyeballs, for example), confirms this possibility with the group, then gets the session back on track.

Much has been learned about the art of interpreting gestures, especially hand and eye movements. For example, research has found that much is revealed in what people do with their hands while speaking. Clenched hands indicate that the person is suppressing thoughts or holding back ideas. Open hands, particularly when the palms face up, show that the person is being candid and revealing. Watching for these gestures can help you evaluate a person's feelings.

MAINTAIN CONTROL

A good facilitator maintains authority and control in the session. He does this *not* with an iron hand, but by keeping aware of all aspects of the conversation and by following up with decisive direction. As long as the facilitator observes the forces at work in the session and understands what the session requires to meet its objectives, he can maintain good control. He can be firm when necessary without being domineering or condescending. People want and welcome the direction.

The level of control maintained by facilitators varies. Some suggest a very high level of control. For example, a JAD workshop guide prepared by British Telecom says:

> Although the concept of team working is integral to the success of a Workshop, . . . the ultimate responsibility for the Workshop lies with the Workshop Leader. As such the Workshop Leader must remain in control of events throughout, albeit as unobtrusively as possible. Loss of this control could lead to disastrous consequences. (British Telecom 1993)

Can a facilitator lead a session and contribute content at the same time? Here is an opinion:

> It is difficult to think deeply about content *and* process at the same time, just as it is difficult to write and talk at the same time. When contributing to content, the facilitator loses some ability to reflect on process, may become drawn into the group's deliberations, and may soon be treated as another participant. (Phillips and Phillips 1993)

EMPOWER THE GROUP

This may sound like a contradiction to the previous item, which counsels maintaining control over the group. But good facilitators can do both. They maintain control *and* they empower the group to consider new options, then evaluate, revise, decide, and revise again. The more this process is in the hands of the participants, the more the final product will mirror their needs. Furthermore, as Andrea Tannenbaum (from ITT Hartford in Hartford, Connecticut) says:

> When a group believes that they have had control over the effort and the content, they believe in the results as well. This sense of ownership is critical for the next step, whether it's selling the results to others or implementing them.

HANDLE UNCERTAINTY

Facilitators tend to be organized creatures. However, they should not be so organized and structured that they sacrifice spontaneity. They need to be comfortable with uncertainty. For example, they mustn't mind (too much, anyway) listening to the makings of a possible brand new agenda item or the details of work flow that they have never heard of before.

An *insecure* facilitator might steer the group away from these scary abysses of unfamiliarity and new directions that perhaps are exactly what are needed to reach the session objectives. In other words, he might miss opportunities. On the other hand, a *good* facilitator remains cautiously flexible and is comfortable with some uncertainty.

BE QUICK TO CONNECT

Good facilitators do not have tunnel vision. They see the whole picture. In the midst of discussion, the facilitator connects the subject at hand to decisions already made, to discussions held before the session, or to agenda items yet to come. The facilitator's "session memory" is like a spider web connecting all the various aspects of the project. And being quick on the feet (or is it quick in the head?), the facilitator accesses this memory with agility, quickly extracting pertinent information from a document or recalling an open issue noted on a flip chart two days ago.

FOCUS ON BUSINESS, NOT SYSTEMS

Good facilitators focus on the business, not the systems. They are genuinely interested in how the business runs, where the problems are, and how they can be resolved. Although facilitators have system savvy and often come from a systems background, the system is not their primary focus. You want a business-oriented person to lead your sessions, not a "tekkie" facilitator.

KEEP THE ROLE CLEARLY DEFINED

Be careful about the distinctions between the roles of facilitator and the project manager. The facilitator should not assimilate the project manager's responsibilities of tracking project progress. For example, systems development projects involve program design, coding, testing, and implementation tasks. These responsibilities belong with the Applications Development team. At the same time, facilitators should not be involved in *overseeing* such business area functions as preparing marketing brochures, auditing applications, and so on. It may seem obvious that these are not the facilitator's responsibilities, but it is surprising how certain obligations can improperly fall to the facilitator, simply because of the apparent leadership role and documentation skills the position assumes.

NURTURE THE INNATE QUALITIES

Are good facilitators born that way or do they learn? Although many say that it's all in the training, we feel you need to begin with a certain set of characteristics. For example, there are those intelligent beings with absolutely no inclination for planning, documenting, and communicating. These people have little hope of succeeding in facilitating sessions, and they probably have no desire to try. (Yes it's true, not everyone wants to be a facilitator when they grow up.) On the other end of the spectrum, there are extremely structured people who plan every aspect of their lives in agonizing detail, do not deviate one inch from their plan, but who are not crazy about working with other people. In the same vein, these folks would not succeed either and would be totally uncomfortable in the consensus-building world of JAD.

There is, however, a wide range of personalities in between these extremes. Many different kinds of personalities make good facilitators. We have seen high-energy, vivacious ones as well as laid back, mellow ones. We have seen those who wallow in details and others who are more comfortable with concepts. We have seen some with spotless offices and others who cannot find their stapler to save their souls. We have seen former Spanish teachers, yoga instructors, and technical writers. It's all a matter of nurturing the innate qualities and learning the skills that did not come with "the original package." Cultivating a good facilitator means mixing the natural propensities with the learned skills. It means applying the strengths and mending the weaknesses.

> In order to be a shining success, you still need your own natural style. A style is something every session leader has to acquire individually. The goal is to avoid mimicking someone else. Instead, the novice session leader should seek out a style that is comfortable for his or her personality. (August 1991)

The Psychology of Facilitators

Are facilitators truly a random mix of characters or do many of us share a common psychological make-up of inclinations, background, and yes, pathologies? Perhaps there are factors likely to foster good facilitators. No doubt many of us share similar strains in our backgrounds, in how we grew up, and in the way we were educated. For example, Dan Bartoes (an independent facilitation and Information Engineering consultant in Newington, Connecticut) observed that facilitators often come from large families and are consequently more comfortable in the domain of group dynamics and in the uncertainty that sessions produce.

The obvious generalization about facilitators is that they are an extroverted lot. But we have seen some excellent facilitators who test out as introverts. The commonality is found in how they deal with groups. For example, as Dan Bartoes says, "After a three-day session, introverted facilitators need more recovery time (a quiet weekend at home, perhaps), while extroverts, having been energized by the challenges of group dynamics, simply yearn for more."

PART
4

TOOLS AND
TECHNIQUES

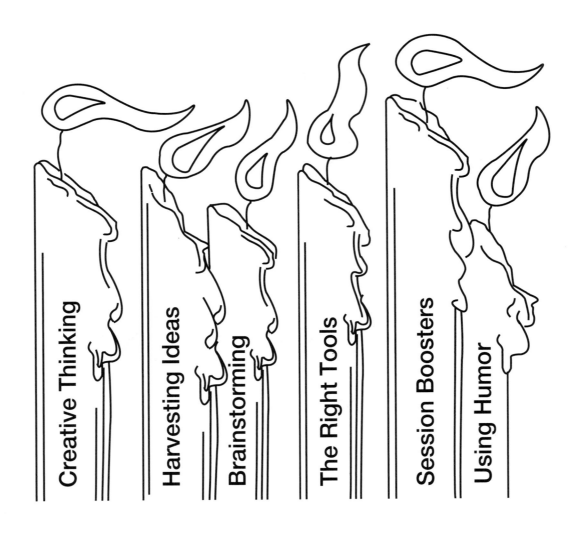

THIRTEEN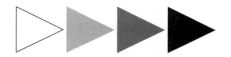

PROMOTING CREATIVITY

As children, we were *raised* in structure ("don't be late for dinner!"). As students, we were *educated* in structure ("every sentence must have a subject and a predicate," "don't chew gum in class," and above all "don't end that sentence with a preposition!"). Now as employees, we work for companies who absolutely thrive on structure ("respect the corporate culture" and "hail to the hierarchy!"). So it's no wonder that when the facilitator asks the group to be open and think creatively, the participants may not have the slightest idea how to address this foreign concept.

Yes, to some degree, we are creatures of habit, mechanical beings who have a hard time breaking the chain of structure. Naturally this affects the way we address business needs. We know how our business processes work today, and how they've been working for years. Consequently, our designs for new processes mirror the old ones. This is fine when the old way is just what we need. But in these changing times, how often can that be true? It's one thing when we are constrained by technology to use the same old computer system. But what about when we are permitted to start from scratch with no limitations? In this case, we have opportunities to create a brand new way of doing business. Furthermore, the systems we design can be based less on the old systems and more on the new work environment.

This requires creative thinking. Unfortunately, people don't think creatively on command. You can, however, jump-start creative thinking. We would like to pass along some ideas we gleaned from our survey of several facilitator user groups, conversations with other facilitators, and our own experiences.

We hope they will help promote creative thinking, get you out of session ruts, and otherwise invigorate your sessions.

CREATIVE THINKING EXERCISES

"Mental muscles" can be toned and strengthened with exercise. An excellent and entertaining collection of puzzles designed to stimulate creative thinking is found in Martin Gardner's book, *aha! Insight* (Gardner 1978). You may be able to use some of these exercises to promote creative thinking in your sessions. Meanwhile, here are some approaches that facilitators have found useful.

Truth and Lie

For sessions where the group has not worked together before, here is a little icebreaker that helps people get to know each other better. Ask the participants to introduce themselves and briefly describe their work. Then have them tell two truths and one lie about themselves. For example, "I was born in Scotland, I have five dogs, and my daughter is a neurosurgeon." Then have the rest of the group decide which is the lie. This helps establish rapport within the group.

Starting From Scratch

It's easy to get so bogged down in the details that you overlook the essence of the business. As they say, you can't see the forest for the trees. Here is a technique used by Susan Burk (of American Management Systems in Manchester, Connecticut):

> To promote creative thinking, I ask the group to imagine that there has been a corporate disaster and that all systems have been destroyed. Then I ask, "What do you really need to do business?"

To get his sessions on the right track, Kasey Reese (of Ameritech in Hoffman Estates, Illinois) asks his group, "If the CEO were the only customer of this business process, what would you do differently?" After exploring this, he asks, "Why can't we treat all the process customers as if they were CEOs?"

You can see the trend here. Facilitators use various techniques to get groups thinking about starting over, from scratch.

Invent Something New

To get people in the mood for generating creative ideas, ask them to invent something for the future that would make their lives easier. Give them some examples such as a voice-activated vacuum cleaner or virtual reality shopping where via a terminal (or perhaps a hologram) you can walk through grocery stores and pick things off the shelves without ever leaving home. The group energy created in coming up with these inventions then transfers to accomplishing your business objectives.

How Can the System Fail?

When whatever you are designing has progressed enough to view in its totality, it's time to step out of the familiar confines of the colossal structure you have created. Give the session a boost of creative thinking by asking the participants, "How can we make this system *fail?* Consider all possibilities. What can be done to crack the system that this group has designed over the last several days?" Forget functionality. Have the group go straight to the core. How can you really break the system?

This jolting question shakes the group loose and shifts its perspective. And the benefits of the *answers* to the question are obvious. You just might come up with a severe vulnerability, which you can then divert your creative thinking to correct.

Consider These Questions

Here is a way to encourage the group to think about their business before modeling it. This exercise was developed by ATLIS Performance Resources, Inc. Lucy Hancock (of John Hancock Mutual Life Insurance Company in Boston, Massachusetts) explains how they use it in their sessions:

> We call it "QDP" (Questions, Decisions and Products). Before we do data modeling, we ask the group to consider these questions: If you have improved information:
>
> * What *questions* can you answer better?
> * What *decisions* can you improve?
> * What *products* can you improve?
>
> Since this exercise works best in small groups, you can split larger groups into two or three teams.
>
> Participants use work sheets to document their ideas, including comments about priority and rationale for each item. Each team appoints a spokesperson to present the QDPs to the entire group. Comments are added, and duplicates are noted.

This decision support activity is an effective lead-in to data modeling and can be used later to validate the model.

Pass the Cube

Here's a little exercise that encourages new ideas. It works like this: Pass around an object, any object. For example, in a workshop given by Gary Rush (JAD consultant), Rush passed around a block in the shape of a cube. As the shape lands in the hands of each participant, have that person describe what new idea this shape represents and explain its advantage. Receiving the cube shape in hand, one person might say, "This is a square tomato, and its advantage is more efficient shipping." Another might say, "It's the shape for a new communications satellite, offering six different transmitting surfaces."

People have used other objects as well, such as paper clips or water glasses. You can see that, although the exercise is simple, it encourages the exact kind of thinking you need to incite creativity.

How Bad is It?

Kasey Reese (of Ameritech) gets his group rolling by asking the participants to break into small groups and draw a picture (or create a skit) showing how bad the current process really is. For example, to describe the existing system, one group drew a picture of blindfolded customers wandering around a maze with high stone walls. Within the maze they drew skeletons of customers who never made it out. Those few who did manage to escape were shown confronting several unfriendly dinosaurs, which represented the existing monolithic systems.

Next, Kasey repeats the exercise, asking them to show how good the new process can be in the future.

"It Can't Be Done"

Larry Konopka (of Advanced Computing Techniques in Glastonbury, Connecticut) explained how he sometimes comes up with ideas "on the fly." For example:

> During one session, people kept restating what they had already said, and insisted that the solution couldn't be done any other way. During the next break, I drew a picture of a rocket, the earth, and the moon. When the group returned, I explained how years ago, a lot of people thought landing on the moon was impossible, and how it took a different kind of thinking to challenge the established rules and boundaries. It worked. The group came up with a new approach and a successful solution.

Changing Hats

To help get sessions back on track, Donna Hoffman (from Health Care Service Corporation) relies on the aid of baseball caps:

> In a discussion of two complex topics, the teams tend to wander from one topic to the next. When this happens, I print the names of each topic on paper and attach each one to the front of a separate baseball cap. If anyone wanders into the other topic, the rest of the group is quick to pass the cap with the proper name on it. This keeps the team focused and prevents them from "constantly changing hats."

For example, in one project Donna labeled the baseball caps "Host" and "Home" to differentiate which company was providing and receiving services (as in Figure 13.1).

Fill in the Blank

We've all taken those tests that ask you to fill in the next character in a series. For example, in the number series 113355_, the blank calls out for a "7" since the series appears in ascending odd numbers. Well, let's say instead, you give them a character series like this: JJTTVOO_. Ask the group to identify the next letter in the series. The point is, there is no correct answer. But when Gary Rush presented this idea at a training session, it became clear how this exercise challenges the participants' minds as they attempt to solve a puzzle that has no answer.

Draw a Floor Plan

Here's a little exercise that turns up from time to time in various seminars. Its purpose: to expose the challenge we face in communicating with each other.

Have the group team up in pairs. For each pair, one person is the

Figure 13.1

speaker, the other is the listener. The speaker describes the layout of the first floor of his own home, while the listener draws the floor plan, based on the speaker's description. The speaker cannot look at the drawing or use any hand gestures. This prevents him from saying things like, "No, make the living room a little bigger," or "Move that wall to the right." The listener cannot ask any questions. When the drawing and attempted communication is done, the listener shows her drawing to the speaker. Of course, the drawn floor plan is always a far cry from reality.

This exercise shows how difficult verbal communication can be. We might think we have clearly explained something, when in fact the listener hears it quite differently. In the candlelight of a romantic restaurant, a handsome suitor dined with the woman he hoped to make his wife. "I simply adore you," he said softly, at which point the lovely lady commenced to crawl around upon the oriental carpet. She thought he had said, "There's something on the floor for you."

Pavlovian Rewards

If you want to encourage new ideas, try this: Have a big bowl of candies (M&Ms®, Hershey's® Kisses, or candy corn will do) on the table. Whenever someone contributes a new or creative idea, hand out a sweet. Or for that matter, pass along the candy to the whole group, showing that even one person's good idea benefits everyone.

Out of the Box

Here is an exercise to help the group get free of the same old way of thinking. Have the participants draw nine dots, as shown in Figure 13.2. Tell them to connect these nine dots by drawing four straight lines. Also, tell them not to pick up the pencil once they start. (Adams 1974)

Since we have been programmed since childhood to "stay within the lines," participants have a hard time getting free of this constraint to come

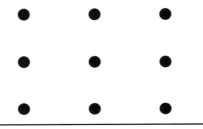

Figure 13.2

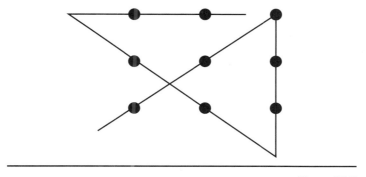

Figure 13.3

up with a solution of drawing lines that go "out of the box" as shown in Figure 13.3.

This exercise encourages transcending the old assumptions, lifting the rules, and coming up with creative ways of doing things. In fact, this solution isn't the only way to connect the nine dots. Kasey Reese (of Ameritech) describes other solutions that various people have tried:

- One person cut out the nine dots and stuck a pencil through them all.
- Another person wrapped the paper with the dots around a cylinder and just kept moving the pencil around and around until all nine dots were connected.
- Others have folded the paper in various ways.
- And there's rumor that a child wrote in a solution saying to use a very large pencil that in one stroke would cover all nine dots.

You can see how this exercise shows us that the box exists only in our minds. The trick is getting out of the box by thinking outside of the perceived assumed constraints.

BRAINSTORMING

Brainstorming is problem-solving without criticism. It is simply a way for groups to identify new ideas, while holding off judging them until later. In brainstorming, the facilitator solicits new ideas. There are no constraints for the moment. Solutions of any sort are accepted. As participants offer ideas, the scribe records them on a flip chart or on the board. When other participants fall into judging these ideas in any way (which is easy to do), the facilitator stops the judgment and moves on.

This approach offers an atmosphere much more conducive to creativity than the normal climate so laden with judgment. To give you an idea of how brainstorming works, here is a sample script:

To begin the session: "Okay, the question is, 'What skills and knowledge will leaders need in the year 2000?' Remember, no evaluation. Let's begin. Who's got an idea?"

When someone tries to judge someone else's idea: "Hold it, George! Don't evaluate Maria's idea. Do you have another idea? . . . Good. Who's got another?"

When the production of ideas begins to slow down, you can stir up the action: "Try to think of the question in a different way. For example, imagine what the world will be like in the year 2000. Will there be as many countries as there are today? Or one worldwide country? What kind of communication systems? What implications will things have for leaders?"

And to make a clean ending: "Okay, one more . . . Wonderful! We have seventy-five ideas. Well done. Let's close the brainstorming session. If you think of any other ideas, we can always add them to the list later." (Doyle and Straus 1993)

To help prevent people from judging ideas too soon, you can use various techniques. Alex Reinders (of IBM Consulting in Chicago, Illinois) explains how his group controlled negative comments during a brainstorming session:

We handed out nerf balls to participants. Any negative comment or judgment of ideas was punishable by a shot from anyone's nerf ball.

The Pace Can Vary

Sometimes brainstorming sessions move very fast, requiring more than one scribe to keep up with the pace. For example, your goal might be for the group to come up with 50 ideas in five minutes. The pace is up to you. The facilitator controls how fast the session moves by prompting when to go on to the next idea.

If ideas slow down and you feel you need more, have them consider variations of ideas already given. Also, do not be concerned about silent periods. Sometimes the best ideas follow silence.

Make the Objectives Clear

As the facilitator, you need to make sure the group understands exactly what they are supposed to brainstorm. For example, what problem are they trying to solve? And how detailed should these ideas be? Do you want them to come up with high-level concepts expressed in a few words or do you want more details? One approach is to first come up with brief ideas, capture the highlights, then go back and beef up these ideas by filling in substance.

As in any part of a facilitated session, there is no ownership to these brainstormed ideas. It doesn't matter whether the idea originated from the vice president or the clerk.

Also, make sure you are clear about when the brainstorming portion of your session begins and ends. You are demanding that every participant think in an entirely new way. That requires an adjustment. After describing the process of brainstorming, tell them when to begin. Likewise, tell them when it's done. Always give definite closure. Summarize what the group has come up with and explain what happens next.

Do Not Fear Conflict

In brainstorming sessions, sometimes disagreements develop within the group. Perhaps the ideas generated fall into either side of a more controversial decision. For example, half the ideas may involve moving the company to New Jersey, while the other half assume the company stays where it is. Consequently, tension brews.

First of all, you can assure the group that they will objectively evaluate all the ideas—later—and that for now, the group is free to contribute any ideas into the mix. Furthermore, you can assure the group (as well as yourself) that a bit of conflict can be a good thing:

> The most insightful and creative ideas are sometimes born of the conflict and tension created by the process. (Larsen 1993)

Evaluate the Ideas

Now that you have your list of fifteen fantastic ideas for reengineering the Purchasing department, you need to select the best one. Your inspiring, productive brainstorming session will have little value if you pick the wrong solution.

Sometimes the best alternative is obvious. For example, everyone in the group agrees that the purchasing process should be automated using a LAN-based solution. Your job, as the facilitator, is to determine if this consensus is genuine.

Other times, the brainstormed alternatives need further analysis to select the best approach. People may need to research various aspects of the alternatives and discuss each one further. Even then, when you have all the information you need, the selection may still be difficult, or even overwhelming. In this case, you need a structured approach to decide between alternatives as described in detail in Chapter 14.

When in the Session Does Brainstorming Come?

Use brainstorming when the need arises. Maybe that's an unfulfilling answer, but it's true, for the most part. Sometimes opportunities for brainstorming arise spontaneously. More often, however, brainstorming sessions are planned in advance. They are most often scheduled near the beginning of the workshop. For example, Dan Bartoes (an independent facilitation and Information Engineering consultant in Newington, Connecticut) describes a typical session:

> After a short introduction, I set up separate brainstorming steps for events, processes, data, and information needs. In this way, the group's focus is not confined to the current system. From the brainstorming results, we build a business model. After activities and data groups have been identified, I divide the group into subgroups. Each subgroup defines (on paper) a portion of the brainstormed results. Then we project the results on overhead transparencies for review by the entire group.

Should Users Really Ask for Anything They Want?

Brainstorming encourages users to ask for anything they want. You may be wondering, is this appropriate, feasible, or even sane? The idea of user requests having no limits might sound beyond comprehension. Would we not end up with a tome of requirements that are economically impossible to implement? Let's put this in context.

Yes, in brainstorming sessions, users do ask for anything they want. That's the purpose—to bring out new, unexplored ideas. But unless you evaluate the resulting wish list, you have only created a blue sky with no ground. The point is, remember to follow up your brainstorming with evaluation. This is easy to remember in *planned* sessions where everyone knows they are brainstorming. You can run into problems, though, when you slip spontaneously into brainstorming and mistake the resulting wish list for agreed-upon requirements. When new ideas are put on the table, but not adequately evaluated, guide the participants in considering how these ideas will actually be implemented and what resources will be required. Consider other alternatives as well.

As a prophet once said, "Take care what you ask for, for one day it may be yours." And as a project manager once said, "How the heck are we going to pay for this?!"

HARVESTING IDEAS

Much of our facilitation effort involves harvesting and capturing ideas from the group. Here are some techniques to help.

Affinity Analysis

You may have seen this idea described in books about creative thinking. Lucy Hancock (of John Hancock Mutual Life Insurance Company) describes how she uses this technique in her facilitated sessions:

> We use Affinity Analysis when we need to capture groupings of ideas. It's especially good for brainstorming sessions. Let's say you are defining *objectives* for a department, based on predefined *goals*. The participants write their objectives (for a particular goal) on index cards. I gather up the index cards, read each one, and let the participants determine if it is unique or similar to other suggestions. I label the flip chart paper, coat it with sticky adhesive spray, and then stick the index cards on the flip chart for that topic.
>
> Each piece of flip chart paper eventually contains one or more note cards pertaining to a particular topic. Participants combine and eliminate cards as necessary, and agree on the wording for the objective. We repeat this process for all the goals. The result: a list of all possible objectives for each department goal.
>
> Since the contributions are made anonymously via the index cards, the group remains nonjudgmental.

Storyboarding

Storyboarding is simply a way for groups to capture information by using pictures, usually displayed on a board for the whole group to see. Walt Disney invented the technique for designing his cartoon sequences. Alfred Hitchcock used it to detail all his scenes before shooting a film. Today video and film producers use it for everything from movies to commercials. After preparing the script, they create a document with pictures of the visuals on the left side of the paper, with the script running parallel along the right side.

In a similar way, storyboarding can be used in facilitated sessions to capture ideas in pictures, cards, charts, or sketches. Some people even do storyboards in slides or animation.

> Storyboarding consists of writing ideas or sketches on index cards, Post-its, or sheets of paper, and arranging them on a vertical board. If the board is porous, the ideas are fastened with pins; if the board is smooth and hard (such as a whiteboard or FoamCore), Post-its are an ideal choice. (Zahniser 1993)

In this process, the participants come up with ideas, write them down on the cards, and give them to the facilitator, who in turn reads them aloud and posts them on the board. In this way, the facilitator can guide the group through capturing, categorizing, ranking, sequencing, and analyzing ideas.

Another way to use storyboarding is to build ideas graphically. For example, either the scribe or participants draw pictures on the cards. These pictures could include trucks, people, registration desks, computer terminals, and warehouses. The resulting storyboard might be the precursor to the data model. Here is an example:

> In one hospital, storyboarding allowed a team to display a redesigned physical layout of the outpatient registration area and to visualize how patients would proceed through the new area. The redesigned registration area introduced the concept of "one-stop shopping" to outpatient testing, where patients could have basic laboratory tests and X-ray studies performed in the central registration area. (Larsen 1993)

Figure 13.4 shows a sample storyboard for designing the layout of the production, shipping, and receiving departments for a cosmetic company.

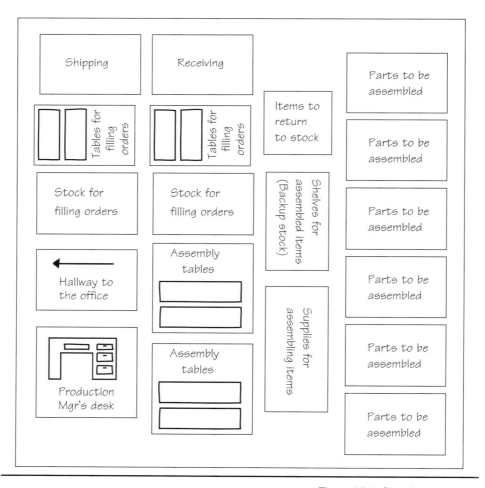

Figure 13.4 Sample storyboard.

The Stick Figure Approach

Even though we all speak English, there are times when we are not really speaking the same language. As a facilitator, for example, you might be quite comfortable with data modeling. A user manager, on the other hand, may not be as fluent using this language to describe her business. She may not see her business activities in the form of boxes, arrows, and one-to-many relationships. Certainly you can show people how to model data, but this may not be the most appropriate language for communicating.

Observe your group. In a particular exercise, how do the key people communicate? Do they convey ideas using pictures or words? If pictures, then are these graphics more conceptual (like boxes, circles, and lines) or more realistic (like people, buildings, and vehicles)? For groups constrained at first in the language of data modeling, you might try using pictures instead. You can always convert the results to another format later. For example, Gary Rush describes:

> We got the CEO and lead management of a Fortune 10 company off-site and developed their strategic plans on a big sheet of white paper with colored markers. Their "model" is a picture with trucks and roads and sunrises and pallets and stick figures. This picture captures the mission, the guiding principles, strategies, and their critical success factors. Then you turn the paper into words. (Edwards et al. 1993)

Force Field Analysis

Here is a good approach to see if a group is for or against an idea. Lucy Hancock attributes the technique to the book *In Search of Solutions* by Quinlivan-Hall and Renner. Lucy explains how she uses it:

> Let's say the group faces a question such as "Should we move the office to a new location?" I draw a vertical line on the board, then title the left side "Driving Forces," and the right side "Restraining Forces." As the group contributes their opinions, I add their comments on each side of the line. On the left side, I note the things that drive them *toward* the idea, on the right side, the things that drive them *away*.
>
> For the question about moving the office, the driving forces might include things like convenience, parking, and air quality. The restraining forces might include cost and timing.
>
> All in all, it's a good way to objectively look at a for-or-against kind of question.

Open Issues Parking Lot

Here is a way to track and sort out open issues during the session. First, draw on the board a large fish-bone shape similar to the way some parking

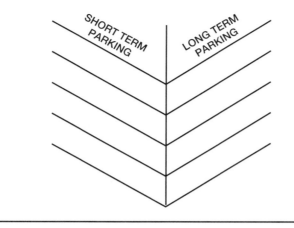

Figure 13.5

lots are designed. Mark one side "short term parking" and the other side "long term parking." This is your open issues parking lot, which looks like Figure 13.5. Paul Taylor (of British Telecom) describes what happens next:

> When an issue develops, we write its name on a Post-it note. Then, we park the issues in the lot. Issues that need to be resolved in the session get parked in short term parking, and the ones that can be resolved later on go in long term parking. Each issue takes up one parking space.

When all the issues are parked, you can use the same parking lot to prioritize issues within the short-term and long-term areas. The more important ones are placed toward the top of the lot (preferred parking). Then, once the priority of all the issues is visually displayed, the group can easily assign resolution dates.

NOMINAL GROUP TECHNIQUE WITH POST-IT NOTES

We first saw this technique at a Facilitators Network meeting in Hartford, Connecticut. Tommy Davis (of the Drake Group in South Windsor, Connecticut) captivated the group with his demo. He used an example where the objective was to identify and prioritize the issues facing the Connecticut public school system. Here is how it works (using Davis' example):

1. *Ask the group to write down their ideas.* In other words, run a mini-brainstorming session. For example, "Write down the three biggest issues that plague the Connecticut public school system today."
   Remember, after you ask your question, allow a moment or two for

Funding
Equal opportunity
Gifted children
Qualified teachers
Integration
Discipline
Overcrowding
Special needs students
Value of testing
Safety
Magnet schools
Violence

Figure 13.6

those brain wheels to start turning. That pregnant moment of silence is essential. If no one begins writing soon, however, perhaps you did not phrase your question well. Rephrase it.

2. *Ask the group to tell you their ideas.* Ask people individually; for example, "Jesse, what are your issues?" Begin with the people who you noticed (in the last step) were writing their issues more enthusiastically than others. Continue querying the group around the room—not necessarily in an ordered sequence. You can go from one side of the room to the other to add an element of unpredictability—anything to keep the momentum going. When people call out their issues, write them on a flip chart. Figure 13.6 shows a flip chart of the issues our group identified.

3. *Resolve the duplicates.* Ask, "Are there any duplicate issues?" As you identify the duplicates, combine them into one issue. In our case, we combined "Safety" and "Violence."

4. *Number each issue.* Now that all issues are identified, assign numbers to them. Now the flip chart looked like Figure 13.7.

So far nothing new, right? Now comes the good part:

5. *Give each person a set of three Post-it notes* (cut from 3" by 3" Post-its) in the following sizes:

   - A full size Post-it
   - Two-thirds of a Post-it
   - One-third of a Post-it

1. Funding
2. Equal opportunity
3. Gifted children
4. Qualified teachers
5. Integration
6. Discipline
7. Overcrowding
8. Special needs students
9. Value of testing
10. Safety and violence
11. Magnet schools
~~Violence~~

Figure 13.7

The big, medium, and small Post-it notes will be used to indicate first, second, and third choices (in the next step). Before passing out the Post-its, attach them to a sheet of paper so they don't all stick together. In our group, everyone received an 8-1/2-by-11-inch sheet of paper with the cut Post-its as shown in Figure 13.8.

6. *Have the group write their choices on the Post-its.* Tell the group, "Review the issues. Pick what you feel are the three most important problems facing the Connecticut public school system today. Write the number of your first choice on the large Post-it, your second choice on the middle-size note, and your third choice on the small note." (See Figure 13.9)

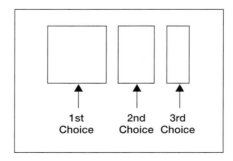

Figure 13.8

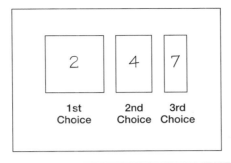

Figure 13.9

7. *Create a bar chart.* Now ask everyone to bring their pieces of paper to the front of the room (at the same time) and place them next to the appropriate issues on the flip charts, beginning just to the right of the number, and continuing on to the right across the flip chart. For each number, the Post-its form a long bar representing the group's priority of that issue. For example, our flip chart looked like Figure 13.10.

For now, don't be concerned that the growing bar charts are covering up the names of the issues.

8. *Add up the numbers.* Assign relative values to the Post-it notes. In other words, count:

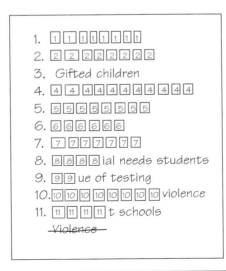

Figure 13.10

3 for the big ones

2 for the middle-size ones

1 for the small ones

For each issue, add the numbers and write the totals next to the issue. Circle the totals so they stand out from the sequential numbers already written.

9. Now, *remove the Post-its* so the group can see all the issues and their totals, as in Figure 13.11.

Groups react very positively to this technique. As people cast (or should we say "post") their choices, and the lines of contiguous Post-its dramatically grow across the flip charts, they see the unbiased, collective results of the group mind. Consensus comes easily.

This technique works well for any activity where you gather and prioritize ideas. For example, you could use it for strategic planning or ranking the criteria in a software-selection activity.

Here are some tips:

- Use colored Post-its to give contrast against the white flip-chart paper. Blue works well.

- Use 3M's brand of Post-it notes. Most others don't stick as well and you may find half of them falling to the floor instead of sticking to the flip chart.

Figure 13.11

- When you pull the notes from the chart, let them fall somewhere you won't be walking. Otherwise you'll have Post-it notes sticking all over the soles of your shoes.

- Be sure to have the group write the numbers on the Post-it notes *before* they attach them to the flip chart. Otherwise people will change their choices based on how they see other people "voting." For example, someone observing the boss put the big Post-it on issue number 6, might be inclined to do the same. Also, if the notes fall off, the numbers tell you where they came from.

- Consider the size of the group and the number of items. For example, if you have a small group with a large number of items, the results will not be as meaningful. In this case, either increase your number of "votes," or decrease your number of items to vote for.

SESSION BOOSTERS

No matter how experienced the facilitator, sessions can succumb to the inevitable lull. Some of the following ideas can help rekindle enthusiasm.

Change Seats

Session participants tend to treat their seating location as bona fide real estate. Far be it for a participant to come in on the second day and sit in someone else's seat! Along these lines, have you ever been to a meeting where, for example, 10 people are in a room with 25 chairs? Naturally, the ten people all sit in the back of the room. Then the person leading the meeting suggests, "Why don't you all come forward to the front so you can see the overheads better?" Not a move. Everyone stays right where they are. That's because they've claimed their territory and it's going to take more than a friendly suggestion to get them to move.

One way to shake up the old way of *thinking* is to change the old way of *seating*. After a full-day session, people have become quite used to their seats, their view, and the people around them. When they come in the next day, shake up the old familiarity by telling them to sit in a completely different place and next to different people as well. Or you can relieve them of that heavy decision by rearranging the name tents yourself. Or, when you feel a rut has developed in the lull of the afternoon, tell everyone to get up, change seats, and sit next to anyone they have not sat near before.

This is also useful when cliques develop that distract the session with sidebar conversations. In this case, don't wait until tomorrow. Make the change once you feel the cliques have become detrimental. But don't present it as punishment. Make it part of the natural course of things. People may moan a bit and prefer not to abandon their territory, but you will have given them a new orientation to their physical environment, which will help stimulate their mental outlook.

Acronym Alert

One rut that sessions sometimes fall into is the overuse of acronyms. No matter how many times we encourage groups to speak in English so everyone understands, participants almost always slip into babbling on in acronyms because it's their natural way of talking.

Paul Taylor (of British Telecom) has a technique for assuring that no acronym passes without being understood by everyone in the session:

> Whenever an acronym is mentioned in the session, we write it on a flip chart with its definition. When the flip chart page becomes filled, we attach it to the wall and start another page. In this way, we keep a glossary of acronyms.
>
> As the session progresses, participants take responsibility for alerting the group when new acronyms arise. They do this by calling out "Acronym Alert!" The more dramatic participants make sounds like a wailing siren to accompany the alert.

BITD (Beat It To Death)

Anyone who has held (or participated in) facilitated sessions has experienced the unproductive digression where someone rambles on endlessly and the rest of the group suppresses yawns. Here is how some people have dealt with this inevitability. At the beginning of the session, have each person write the following four letters on the back of their name tents: "BITD." Then, in the course of the session when people feel that the group has gotten off the track, they simply hold up their name tents making visible the letters BITD, which stand for "Beat It To Death."

Introducing this little gesture encourages shared responsibility for keeping the session on track. As the facilitator, you don't always know when the session has gone astray. Sometimes it takes a bored participant or two to reveal when someone is beating a topic to death.

Bag the Observer

Session observers are mandated to keep silent. Some more liberal facilitators allow them to supply information, but not to participate in decisions. In either case, sometimes these observers cannot keep quiet no matter how hard they try.

To fend off this tendency, some facilitators have been known to keep a paper bag handy, explaining to the group that you will place it over the heads of any observers who do not keep their vow of silence. Usually the bag and the comment are all that are needed in this particular approach, but some facilitators have been known to actually bag their observers. Doing this in most organizations, however, might result in the facilitator being shipped off to a three-week course in sensitivity training.

Stress Test

We all know how groups can get emotionally carried away, especially when discussing decisions that directly affect their own workplace. Sometimes the energy level rises beyond a productive point and you know you must do something. Perhaps you have recently had a recess, so the "take a break" trick won't work.

Now's the time to bring out the trusty stress test dots. Sometimes called bio-dots, these little round, dark circles are placed on the skin, usually at the wrist. The resulting change in color (of the dot, not the participant) indicates the person's stress level. After a few moments, the dot shifts colors, then settles on one hue. Colors range from black (indicating high stress), through various shades of gold, green, and blue, to violet (indicating a most mellow state).

Even if little credence is given to the results, you will find the session's intensity dissolves in the act of comparing stress dot colors.

Take a Stretch Break

Don't forget physical fitness! Phyllis Calianese (from a large service company in Mahwah, New Jersey) describes a kinetic session booster she uses in her sessions:

> We introduced stretch breaks for our facilitated sessions. At various points during the session, we take five minutes to guide the participants through some deep breathing exercises to refresh the mind. We also perform neck stretches and shoulder shrugs. And for the scribe, we have finger stretching and wrist circles to loosen up the hands. It's amazing how these quick stretch breaks energize and refresh the participants.

TIPS ON USING THESE TECHNIQUES

Here are a few things to consider when using the techniques described in this chapter.

The Right Tool for the Right Purpose

All the techniques that we have talked about in this chapter are only as good as how you apply them. An activity for breaking the ice won't do much good with a group of people who have known each other for years. First, identify your goal. What do you want to accomplish? Is there a technique that can help? For example, if your goal is to get people to come up with new solutions, try either the "Starting From Scratch" or "Invent Something New" techniques. If you are dealing with a group of people who have never worked together before, try breaking the ice with the "Truth and Lie" exercise.

Evaluate the use of any technique carefully. Donna Hoffman (from Health Care Service Corporation) says, "When time is limited and an activity does not *directly* result in a quantifiable piece of the plan or design, the participants generally feel there is no time for it." On the other hand, Andrea Tannenbaum (of ITT Hartford in Hartford, Connecticut) says, "A facilitator might need to 'waste' a little time with these exercises. Once the group is warmed up, focused, and on track, there's no stopping them." You need to find your comfort level with these exercises.

Whichever approach you take, be selective! Don't just do an exercise because you like it or because it worked before. Consider the group need first, then decide on the technique.

Don't Call Them Games

Many techniques for creative thinking have the flavor of group games. It's best, however, not to actually refer to them as "games." To some, this term implies a time-waster. Since the participants know they are in the session to "produce," they might be turned off by a suggestion to "play games." You are using these techniques to promote creative thinking that leads to productivity. Therefore, refer to them as "tasks," "exercises," or "tools."

Let Everyone Feel Creative

Is there such a thing as a "creative person"? If so, where does such a value judgment come from? The biggest hinderance to creativity is the belief that some people are creative *and others are not.*

> A team of psychologists studied the staff of a major publishing house to determine what differentiated the creative employees from the others. After studying the staff for one year, the psychologists discovered that there was only one difference between the two groups. The "creative" people believed they were creative, and the "less creative" people believed they were not! (Abuls and Leonard 1993)

So how do you deal with this phenomenon? Here is one approach that can help:

> I always mention this study before starting a creative activity, whether it's a warm-up or the actual information-gathering portion of the meeting. It affirms my belief that everyone in the room can contribute creative ideas. (Abuls and Leonard 1993)

Remember the Point

Why bother with these various exercises? After all, we're not gathered in these sessions to connect dots, draw floor plans, and imagine situations that will never be. The intent is to change the group's way of looking at things. You want them to consider solutions based on the problem, not based on the way they always did it.

A little girl asked her mother why she always cut off the end of the roast beef before putting it in the roasting pan, even though it would have easily fit in otherwise. The mom replied, "Because that's the way my mom always did it." Unsatisfied with the answer, the little girl asked her grandmother why she always cut off the end of the roast beef before putting it in the pan. The grandmother replied, "Because the roast was always too big for my pan, so I cut the end off to make it fit."

Your mission in creative thinking is to get the group to define problems at their core. A case in point:

> An automobile traveling on a deserted road blows a tire. The occupants discover that there is no jack in the trunk. They define the problem as "finding a jack" and decide to walk to a station for a jack. Another automobile on the same road also blows a tire. The occupants also discover that there is no jack. They define the problem as "raising the automobile." They see an old barn with a pulley for lifting bales of hay to the loft, push the car to the barn, raise it on the pulley, change the tire, and drive off while the occupants of the first car are still trudging toward the service station. (Rush 1990)

Your goal is to get the group to work on "raising the automobile," not "finding the jack." You want them to focus on solving the problems in their business, rather than on designing the system.

USING HUMOR

There is nothing like a good laugh to get the creative juices flowing. And there's nothing like a little humor to spice up a long session.

Through a Child's Eyes

After going through 52 data element definitions, 3 levels of decomposition, and 15 screen formats, people are ready for anything of a jovial nature that might give them some relief. When the opportunity arises and you feel comfortable with it, try some humor. For example, one Sunday when we were setting up the room for the session, the two-year-old daughter of the facilitator happened to be with us. While we arranged magnetics on the board, she amused herself by making colorful drawings on blank flip-chart paper. She made one particular drawing that we thought looked rather like a conceptual depiction of the application system we were addressing (probably because both the drawing and the system were quite a mess). We labeled the drawing with some of the system buzzwords. We hung it in the front of the room so that it was the first thing everyone saw when they arrived. It was a good ice breaker. Throughout the session, people suggested new items to add to the picture. In the end, we had an impressionistic version of the complete system.

A Champagne Finale

In another off-site session, the group had developed such a good rapport that we felt it was appropriate to offer a round of champagne on the last day. To get everyone in a festive mood, we presented several humorous data elements, modeled after the real ones. For example, we renamed the data element *Allocation Percent* to *Alcohol Percent*. *Original Issue Age* became *Original Drinking Age* and *IDB* (for Increasing Death Benefit) became *LCB* (for the Liquor Control Board). It took about five minutes to walk through them. The participants seemed to enjoy this, especially when we came to the part where the champagne was uncorked. We are certainly not recommending the bubbly stuff for all sessions. In fact, we have done it only that one time. But sometimes, going off the beaten track in one way or another can be worthwhile.

The Price is Right

In a session to review the cost benefit analysis for a new software package, we used a little humor to lighten things up. For the first agenda item, the facilitator needed to present detailed pricing information for the package. (This information had previously been prepared in a six-page spreadsheet, but had not yet been revealed to the participants.) Cost was of particular interest to the JAD group. If the package was too pricey, the steering committee would be sure to reject the purchase.

Prior to the session, the facilitator asked the scribe to draw (on a flip chart) a gift package with a big red bow. The acronym for the software package (PPS) was also written across the front of the box. The facilitator opened the session by pointing to the drawing and dramatically asking, "What is your bid for this beautiful PPS software package?" She went on to say, "The contestant who bids closest without going over the actual retail price, wins the leftover Danish from today's meeting!"

The facilitator continued in this game show mode by going around the room gathering everyone's guestimates: "$250,000;" "$300,000;" and one person yelled, "$422,000.24!" It was a good thing we softened up the group beforehand, because when the facilitator turned over the next flip-chart page to reveal the actual package price, the group gasped in horror.

Hire an Alligator

Facilitators sometimes invite session participants not of their own species. For example, Donna Hoffman (from Health Care Service Corporation) describes:

> The first JAD I facilitated involved a three-day business trip to Florida with the JAD team. At the start of the first session after we returned, I mysteriously found a two-foot rubber alligator on the overhead projector. This "gator" has since become legendary and attends all JAD sessions. I use him as a tool by "speaking through him." Via this character, I get people to speak—or not speak. We consult him on important issues, and involve him in helping the group reach consensus.

No Jokes before Their Time

Humor works best once group identity has had a chance to set in. In other words, you don't want to start right in with "a funny thing happened on the way to the JAD session . . ." or "did you hear the one about the lawyer, the minister, and the facilitator . . . ." Let the humor come naturally and take the opportunities when they arise.

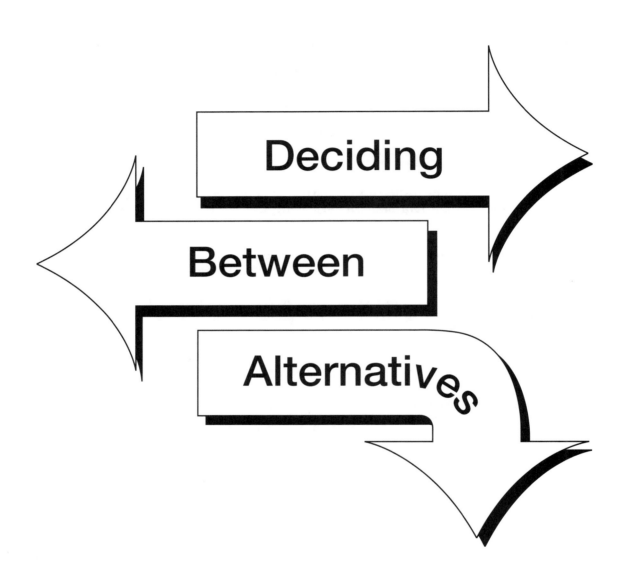

FOURTEEN

DECIDING BETWEEN ALTERNATIVES

In everyday life, we are all involved in deciding between alternatives. We use our own set of built-in criteria to make these decisions. Whenever we say, "I like that," we have compared something to our own set of preferences and found it to be a good choice.

> Most people aren't aware of their criteria, but they have them nevertheless: Jazz is better than classical music, red is nicer than blue, don't trust anything plastic, spinach is yucky, don't pick up hitchhikers.
> Most evaluations and decisions are made by testing alternatives against personal criteria and selecting the one which most conforms. (Doyle and Straus 1993)

In making mundane decisions, we don't stop to deliberate. We automatically "order peas instead of spinach and drive on past the hitchhiker." More complicated decisions require conscious thought. In group sessions, for example, paralyzing indecision can set in. You need a way to break these deadlocks. It is often useful—and sometimes necessary—to put these thought processes "out on the board" where everyone can see what is going on. We need a way to explicitly and objectively define alternatives, evaluate criteria, and make the best choice.

For years, we have been using the decision-making technique we are about to describe. It is similar to a technique that has an official name. Dr. Charles H. Kepner and Dr. Benjamin B. Tregoe, consultants in strategic and operational decision-making, invented it and appropriately called it the *Kepner-Tregoe* approach. The modified version we describe here has worked well for us in JAD sessions and in other business situations as well.

SIX STEPS TO GROUP DECISION

Let's look at a quandary that most everyone has been in—deciding which automobile to buy. Let's say you have narrowed your search down to two cars, but cannot decide between the two. You like the Volvo and the Toyota. But which should you buy? Here is how to use the modified Kepner-Tregoe method to make your decision:

1. List the criteria.

Determine what is important to you in your selection. What do you want from an automobile? Your criteria might be safety, price, gas mileage, trunk space, reliability, and color. List these criteria down the left side of the board as shown in Figure 14.1.

2. Assign weights to the criteria.

Add a new column labeled "Weight Factor." Give each criterion a weight from 1 to 5 (where 5 is the best). For example, if you have two small chil-

Criteria
Safety
Price
Gas mileage
Trunk space
Reliability
Color

Figure 14.1

Criteria	Weight Factor
Safety	5
Price	3
Gas mileage	3
Trunk space	2
Reliability	5
Color	1

Figure 14.2

dren, *safety* might be the most important to you. Give it a weight of 5. *Gas mileage* may not be as significant because you will not be using this car for long-distance, gas-guzzling trips. Give it a 3. *Color* might be the least important. Give it a 1. Fill in the others in the same way as shown in Figure 14.2.

3. List the alternatives.

In column headings across the top of the board, list your choices. These are the columns where you will score each choice. The headings would be "Score (Volvo)" and "Score (Toyota)" as shown in Figure 14.3

Take the opportunity to ask the group to come up with other alternatives as well. Perhaps you can hold a short brainstorming session to encourage ideas. If you were dealing with more than two choices, they would continue in separate column headings across the top as shown in Figure 14.4.

Criteria	Weight Factor	Score (Volvo)	Score (Toyota)
Safety	5		
Price	3		
Gas mileage	3		
Trunk space	2		
Reliability	5		
Color	1		

Figure 14.3

Criteria	Weight Factor	Score (Volvo)	Score (Toyota)	Score (BMW)	Score (Mini-Van)

Figure 14.4

4. Evaluate the criteria for each alternative.

At this point, you have read consumer reports and have been to the car dealerships. You have taken the test drive, asked all the standard car-buying questions, and heard how the manager is going to give you the best deal in town. Now you are ready to evaluate how each car meets the criteria. As you do this, assign a score of 1 to 5 (again 5 is the best) and write it in the appropriate space in the grid.

Beginning with *safety,* you have determined through research that the Volvo has an excellent safety record. Give it a score of 5. Although the Toyota may not be at the very top, it does have a good safety record. Give it a 4. Moving on to *price,* the Toyota, being less expensive, gains the better score. Continue evaluating all criteria. When the columns are filled in, the chart looks like Figure 14.5.

5. Determine the weighted score.

Make two new columns on the right side of the chart labeled "Weighted Score (Volvo)" and "Weighted Score (Toyota)." Then by multiplying the weight factor by the score, you can determine the weighted score for each criterion. For example, to calculate *safety* for the Volvo, do the following:

Criteria	Weight Factor	Score (Volvo)	Score (Toyota)
Safety	5	5	4
Price	3	3	5
Gas mileage	3	3	5
Trunk space	2	5	4
Reliability	5	3	5
Color	1	4	5

Figure 14.5

5 (score)

x5 (weight factor)

25 (weighted score)

For Toyota safety, the calculation is:

4 (score)

x5 (weight factor)

20 (weighted score)

Continue calculating weighted scores for all the criteria. Fill the two columns with your calculations. The chart looks like Figure 14.6.

6. Total the scores.

Now you have only to total the scores in the "Weighted Score" column for each car. The highest score is the best choice based on the criteria you have set. Now you know which car to drive out of the showroom—in this case, the Toyota.

This method can be effectively used to resolve strategic business decisions. For example, where should we move our corporate headquarters? The choices are *San Diego* and *Los Angeles*. To make this decision, guide the group through the decision-making process. As before, make a grid with criteria, weights, and alternatives. It might look like Figure 14.7. Now determine the scores, the weighted scores, and the total scores which indicate the best choice.

Criteria	Weight Factor	Score (Volvo)	Score (Toyota)	Weighted Score (Volvo)	Weighted Score (Toyota)
Safety	5	5	4	25	20
Price	3	3	5	9	15
Gas mileage	3	3	5	9	15
Trunk space	2	5	4	10	8
Reliability	5	3	5	15	25
Color	1	4	5	4	5
Total Weighted Score				72	88

Figure 14.6

Criteria	Weight Factor	Score (San Diego)	Score (Los Angeles)
Lease or building costs	5		
Ease of commute	3		
Smog factor	2		
Proximity to customer base	5		
Impact on work force	4		
Golf courses for senior executives	1		

Figure 14.7

We have used this technique for helping groups make various kinds of decisions including selecting the following:

- A Reinsurance software package
- A PC-based client file system for the field force
- A Periodic Payments software package
- A LAN versus mainframe solution
- A DOS versus Windows platform

Before you know it, you'll be using this technique to help yourself and your friends decide all kinds of things like which VCR to buy, where (and if) to move, which of two job offers to take, or which day-care worker to hire.

ANALYZING THE NUMBERS

Remember that the results of this kind of analysis are not necessarily the "last word." This method uses numbers in an attempt to give rational weight to what might otherwise be subjective value judgments. But the numbers may be only approximations or "best guesses." If the outcome conflicts sharply with intuitive judgments, it could be you have not given appropriate weights to the criteria that truly reflect the group's opinions.

If your calculations indicate one choice, but the group's intuition leans toward another, listen to that intuition. You might end up throwing out the scores and buying the Volvo because you like the image it projects. This could mean that you overlooked certain criteria in the analysis. Maybe you should have added a criterion called "image factor."

Also, the final solution may entail a blend of two alternatives. For example, in a decision of whether to move the company to San Diego or Los Angeles, the team may decide to leave the corporate functions where they are and move the service center out of town. We used this blended solution in a package evaluation we recently facilitated. The total scores came out so close that in the end, the team decided to purchase 50 copies of one package and 100 copies of the other for its field force.

Even if your group rejects the solution with the best score, they will almost always find it valuable to have gone through the exercise. Sometimes, they will find out that their original first choice was really quite inferior to other alternatives. Often, they will be able to quickly rule out several alternatives, so they can concentrate on the best two. And they may determine that the differences between the preferred alternatives are so small that there will be little lost if they choose the "wrong" one. So they can move on, with a clear conscience, to the next issue.

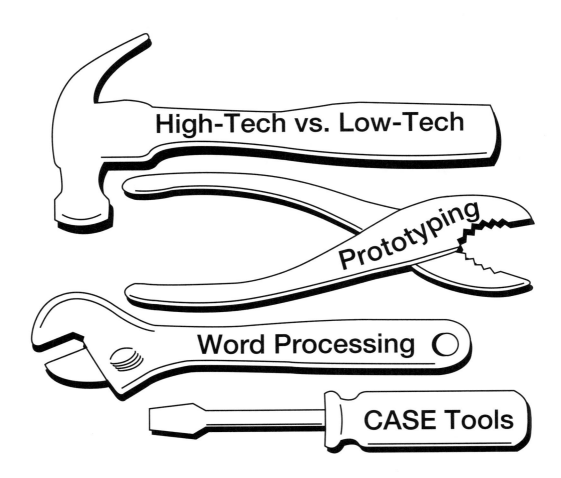

FIFTEEN ▷ ▶ ▶ ▶

USING TOOLS IN THE SESSION

How do you document your sessions? When you capture decisions, are you high-tech (use a CASE tool in the session), low-tech (use a word processor), or no tech at all (use flip charts and pens). Asking people, "What is the best way to document a facilitated session?" is like asking, "What's the best way to make chicken soup?" Answers cover the gamut. For example:

> "In sessions, I've used word processors, spreadsheets, planning tools, CASE tools, mainframe dictionaries, and graphics software. I also use printers to immediately print deliverables."
>
> —Larry Konopka
> Advanced Computing Techniques

> "Our scribes bring laptops to the workshops and take all notes in a word processor."
>
> —Marc Devlin
> American Airlines

> "I have occasionally used a Polaroid camera for highly graphical, pictorial sessions."
>
> —Dan Bartoes
> Nasdaq Stock Market Inc.

"Our favorite techniques are electronic white boards and Post-it notes. They are very useful. They allow the participants to interact and move around."

—Pat Edwards
Dome Software

In our survey to various facilitator groups, we asked, "How do you handle documenting your sessions?" Here are their answers. (Since people marked more than one item, percentages exceed 100 percent.)

64%   Someone else (for example, a scribe) takes notes by hand

62%   Use a PC word processor in the session

19%   Use a PC word processor in the session (*and* project it on a screen for the participants to view)

55%   Make notes on overhead transparencies

38%   Use a CASE tool in the session

11%   Use a CASE tool in the session (*and* project it on a screen for the participants to view)

38%   Write everything on flip charts (no other notes taken)

19%   Facilitator takes notes by hand

13%   Use scribe forms

 9%   Use meetingware (sometimes called "groupware" or "electronic meeting systems")

Other approaches that we did not ask about, but that people wrote in, include:

• Electronic board with a copier
• Magnetics
• Tape recorder (with participants' permission)

As you can see, there's more than one way to document a session. Most sessions are recorded by a scribe taking notes by hand or with a word processor. Overhead transparencies are popular. CASE tools and meetingware enjoy their successes, but have still not gained wide acceptance.

When you do use tools in the session, keep it simple. There's nothing worse than having the entire session wait in suspense while a scribe tries and tries again to move one part of the CASE diagram to somewhere else. Larry Konopka (of Advanced Computing Techniques in Glastonbury, Connecticut) says it well:

The key to a successful session is keeping the tools secondary to the process. Don't let the tools become the primary focus or driving force. Keep the process in tack using transparencies, flip charts, and so on.

That way, if the tool breaks, or if the scribe is slow on the tool, you can keep things moving.

Andrea Tannenbaum (of ITT Hartford in Hartford, Connecticut) concurs:

> There are amazing advantages when electronic tools such as word processing with an overhead projector are used correctly. But if used improperly, these tools can be so distracting as to disrupt the session and render it useless.

WORD PROCESSORS

When we first began doing JADs in the mid-1980s, we used a mainframe text editor to prepare JAD documents. But now that we have local area networks (LANs) and Windows, we have happily abandoned the mainframe text editor for a PC word processor. We use WordPerfect®. With the LAN, we can easily share and electronically transfer our WordPerfect JAD files. Furthermore, Windows allows us to work on multiple documents at one time and easily shift from one document to another.

More and more people are documenting the group's decisions online during the sessions using a regular PC or a laptop. Consequently, these people can easily turn around scribe notes and distribute them overnight. Donna Hoffman (from Health Care Service Corporation) says:

> I prefer to document the session online, using an overhead display for projection. When possible, we print changes at lunch or breaks and distribute them immediately. If this isn't possible and time frames are tight, we distribute documentation updates at the beginning of the next day's session, or hand deliver them if no session is scheduled. Yes, this means I might be typing at 3 AM and running around the company the following morning, but it reinforces the importance of the project.

Certainly this earnest approach is to be commended, but don't feel compelled to stay up until the wee hours to get the document out the next day. If you can distribute it in the next few days, you will be doing fine.

If you are selecting a word processing package for JAD use, choose one that automatically handles heading levels and tables of contents. And if you will use it *in the session,* use a word processor that is agile enough to quickly document and make changes without slowing the pace of the group.

Standard Templates

Standard templates are skeletal documents used to create other documents. Most people use standard templates for the Management Definition

Guide, the Working Document, and the generic sections of the final document (such as for open issues and data element definitions). You can also keep separate templates for memos to:

- Announce the pre-session meeting.
- Provide meeting information (date, time, location, and directions) for the session.
- Send with the Working Document.
- Send with the draft of the final document and to announce the review meeting.
- Send with the final JAD Document.

Using standard templates is obviously a great timesaver in the document creation process. Although you may spend time setting up templates in the beginning, once you have them, you can produce comprehensive final documents in a very short time. Preparing memos involves nothing more than copying the standard templates and replacing the variable information.

SCRIBE FORMS

Some people use no automated tools at all in the session. Some just take notes in their own format. Others use special scribe forms to record agreements made in the session.

Scribe forms can be either hardcopy pages or standard template files in your word processor (when you use a PC in the session). The information that goes on these forms is used to build the final document. Therefore, the forms are designed in the same format as the pages of the final document. For example, the Open Issue scribe form has space for the name of the open issue, whom it is assigned to, the date it will be resolved by, and the description. The Open Issues pages of the final document have exactly the same entries.

We used to use standard scribe forms more often than we do today. Our JAD projects have become so varied that the standard forms don't always apply. To supplement these, we often make one or two custom scribe forms.

Appendixes A and B show samples of several scribe forms we have used for the Management Definition Guide and for the JAD session.

CASE TOOLS

CASE (Computer Aided Software Engineering) refers to software tools (usually PC-based) that support various parts of the systems development life cycle. There are many CASE products on the market. For example, you often hear about:

- Intersolv's Excelerator®
- KnowledgeWare's IEW (Information Engineering Workbench)®
- Texas Instrument's IEF (Integrated Engineering Facility)®

There is front-end CASE (also called "upper CASE"), which addresses the planning, analysis, and design phases. There is back-end CASE ("lower CASE"), which addresses code generation and prototyping. Then there is I-CASE ("integrated CASE"), which handles the seamless integration of the entire systems development life cycle with a single tool set.

Opinions are mixed on whether CASE tools really increase productivity, but the majority view is that they do help when used appropriately.

How Are CASE Tools Used?

CASE tools support the following functions:

- *Graphics and Diagrams.* This feature allows you to draw data and process models, including data flow diagrams, entity relationship diagrams, structure charts, and decomposition diagrams (to name a few). Each CASE tool supports its own set of diagrams based on the methodology underlying the tool. For example, if the tool supports Information Engineering principles, then it produces the Information Engineering diagram set. Graphics are the most widely used component of CASE.

- *Central Repository.* The central repository (also known as the data dictionary) is the core of many CASE tools around which all other features revolve. It contains definitions for all entities in the system being described. For example, when you create data flow diagrams, you can define the data elements that make up the flows. This information is stored in the repository and the definitions remain connected with the data elements. Then, when you design screens using those same data elements, their definitions are reflected in the screen. If the data element is defined to the dictionary as 10 characters long, it displays as a 10-character field on the screen.

- *Prototyping.* This allows you to "paint" proposed screens, menus, and reports. Then you can simulate branching where, for example, you make a selection on the main menu and the next screen displays as it would in the final system. (There is no actual code behind the screens, just the screen images.) Some CASE tools support *full* prototyping. This means you can enter data into the screen fields, test the inputs and outputs, process transactions, and even make inquiries against a database.

- *Code generation.* This creates code based on detailed specifications that you have defined. For example, certain CASE tools can feed the data and process models, screen and report designs, and logic definitions directly into the repository. These tools then automatically generate Cobol, C, PL/1, and SQL statements. They can also reverse engineer, that is, create the design specs from the logic and data definitions.

- *Quality assurance.* This allows you to validate what you have created with the CASE tool by detecting errors in the design. For example, some packages analyze data flow diagrams for completeness (are all parts labeled?), syntax errors (do all processes have at least one data flow coming in and one going out?), and balancing (are the inputs and outputs of one data flow diagram equivalent to those on the next level?).

- *Other functions.* Some CASE tools support project management, project estimating, and word processing. These functions may be available within the CASE tool itself or through interfaces between the CASE tool and packages that perform these functions.

Crossing CASE with JAD

For people in search of another acronym, we now have AJAD. Take a guess: does the "A" stand for "accelerated," "advanced," or "action-packed"? Although any of these A-words aptly describe the process, AJAD actually stands for *Automated* Joint Application Development. This is what you get when you use CASE tools in JAD sessions.

We first observed the term in a 1989 *Computerworld* article written by James Kerr, president of Kerr Systems International, a management consulting firm. He describes how AJAD (integrating CASE tools with JAD techniques) combines the high quality of user-driven design with the exactness of CASE technology. Using a sophisticated CASE tool, you can automatically convert the design developed in the JAD workshop into a running prototype, which your business people can see.

A CASE Example

Let's look at how we might use a CASE tool in the session to create a data model for a training department that is designing a system to track employee training. The process is shown in four steps:

- In the first step, you diagram the employee and class data relationship.
- In the second step, you add the course entity.
- In the third step, you add the vendor information to the model.
- In the fourth step, you correct the model by moving the vendor entity.

Throughout the process, the facilitator drives the discussion with the users. IS translates the decisions into techno-terminology. And a scribe uses the CASE tool to document the results. The group observes the design evolve on a large screen. The scribe can interrupt the session at any time when the CASE tool shows an inconsistent design.

STEP 1:	
The group discusses this . . .	*Which translates into this . . .*
Facilitator: Can an employee take more than one class? User: Yes, depending on job need, an employee might take several classes such as project management or data base design. Facilitator: Do you track information about a particular class before an employee signs up for it? User: No.	We have a one-to-many relationship beween employee and class records. And we will create employee records before class records.

And the scribe creates the diagram as shown in Figure 15.1.

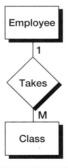

Figure 15.1

STEP 2:		Which translates into this . . .
The group discusses this . . .		
Facilitator:	What other information do you need to track?	We have a one-to-many relationship between course and class. We will create these records at the same time.
User:	We need specific course information such as the course description, duration, and cost.	
Facilitator:	How does that relate to the class?	
User:	We might hold several classes per year for a specific course such as "WordPerfect."	
Facilitator:	Does every course have a class associated with it?	
User:	Yes. But, we don't keep information about every WordPerfect course on the market. We only track course information for classes we will actually offer.	

And the scribe creates the diagram as shown in Figure 15.2.

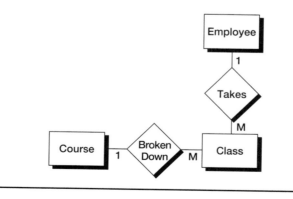

Figure 15.2

STEP 3:		Which translates into this . . .
The group discusses this . . .		
Facilitator:	What about the vendors offering these courses?	We have a one-to-many relationship between vendor and class. We will create these records at the same time.
User:	Yes, we track them as well. We need to know some basic information such as name, address, and phone number.	
Facilitator:	Can a vendor provide more than one class?	
User:	Definitely.	
Facilitator:	Do you track general vendor information?	
User:	Only for those classes we offer.	

And the scribe creates the diagram as shown in Figure 15.3.

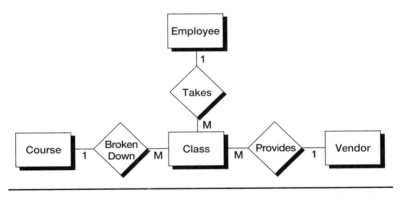

Figure 15.3

STEP 4:		Which translates into this . . .
The group discusses this . . .		
User:	I think the design is not quite right.	We need to correct the model to eliminate the vendor to class relationship and create a one-to-many vendor to course relationship. And we'll create the records at the same time.
Facilitator:	What's wrong with it?	
User:	We keep track of vendors by course, not by class.	
Facilitator:	Can a vendor provide more than one course?	
User:	Yes.	

And the scribe creates the diagram as shown in Figure 15.4.

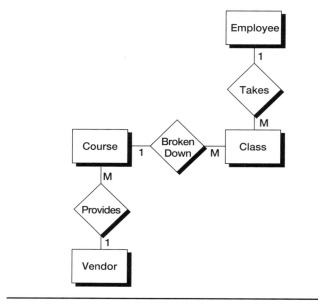

Figure 15.4

Data Modeling Training for Participants?

Should participants get trained in data modeling? There are a few schools of thought on this. Many JAD proponents believe that we should educate business area people in the specialized technical details of data modeling. In fact, prior to the workshop, some companies send their JAD participants to three-day courses with names like "Introduction to Enterprise Engineering," "Model-Driven Analysis and Development," and "Information and Analysis Modeling Workshop".

These advocates of participant training feel that the more the business users understand about data modeling, the more valuable their contributions will be.

Others believe that you can teach participants all they really need to know about data modeling in 15 minutes, *in* the session. We observed this in a seminar given by Gary Rush.

Still others believe that JADs should stick to standard English and business language. When people propose system solutions for business problems, they are better off expressing their models in a language that is immediately understood by the business community, without any special training. This philosophy relies on the facilitator's skill in translating technical vocabulary into a friendly format. Earl Brochu (a project methods consultant in Toronto) endorses this position. He writes:

> Sorry! Dataflow, entity-relationship and object-oriented diagrams don't work in joint client-provider efforts. Using a techno-centric model is like asking someone whose only language is English to do a crossword puzzle in Spanish using an English-Spanish dictionary . . . . They can probably do something. But it will be time consuming. They will not be confident that the result is correct. And next day they will not remember what they did. (Brochu 1992)

Brochu suggests modifying the technical models off to the side and bringing them into the session only to validate the information. The models do help the technical people ask business people the right questions. However, he suggests using the session only to update jointly the nontechnical models.

We recommend giving these techniques a go without necessarily sending the business area people to special training sessions. We have done process modeling in sessions without providing additional training beforehand. It works fine—though not in large sessions. Groups of five to eleven are ideal. For larger groups we come in with a proposed process model and revise it in the session.

Sometimes, however, you may find that the language of modeling just doesn't make it with a particular group. In those cases, let it go. Seek out the participants' own language and make it work. If you hear the group speaking very graphically, then use pictures instead. Turn the "things" they speak of into icons and draw them right on the board. You can transfer the outcome to data models later.

Scribing a CASE Session

If you use CASE in the session, find a scribe who is adept at the tools. For this task, you need a first-rate business analyst who knows how to capture what the business area people are saying and quickly translate these requirements into diagrams, screens, and prototypes.

For example, the facilitator sketches the data flow diagram on a white board. Once the team reaches consensus (two markers worth of changes later), the scribe enters the data flow diagram into the CASE tool. As the session progresses, the scribe steadily adds detail to the diagram. The scribe takes some time to clean it up and then projects the CASE output using a screen projection unit. Or, some facilitators prefer to build the diagram and periodically print parts of it for review in the session. Sounds great. So what's all the controversy among facilitators?

The Great CASE Controversy

"To CASE, or not to CASE?" that is the question. Opinions are widespread on this issue. Some die-hard advocates put CASE tools in the spotlight. They enter the participants' decisions directly into the CASE tool. Using this approach, you need the PC and screen projection unit in the room. The facilitator guides the participants along a structured path encouraging them to build data flow diagrams, entity-relationship diagrams, and screen designs. The group immediately sees the projected images and refines the models interactively. For some facilitators, this is the only way to go. Gary Rush (a recognized leader in using interactive design for requirements gathering) uses CASE tools in his workshops:

> When a Business Area Analysis workshop is over at four o'clock, you should be able to walk out with the CASE tool's output. There is absolutely no reason why you can't do that. (Rush 1993)

In contrast, many JAD proponents see CASE tools as counterproductive for effective JAD sessions. These people stress the importance of group dynamics in the session. They try to minimize technology in the workshop to keep it flexible and nonthreatening. They do not want the participants to become servants of a CASE tool. The following describes one interviewee's observations in a recent study:

> If the models and repositories become extensive, the tools are just not quick enough. The JAD workshops can quickly lose momentum by getting bogged down in CASE. (CSC PEP 1993)

Dorine Andrews and Naomi Leventhal (JAD consultants), hold a similar view:

> While it may be technically possible for the CASE/JAD specialist to enter information directly into the PC as the discussion proceeds, this is not a good idea. It does not provide an adequate amount of time for thinking and, more important, rethinking by participants . . . . CASE tools were not designed to support this type of "court reporting." (Andrews and Leventhal 1993)

Andrews and Leventhal, like most of the facilitators we surveyed, use paper and pencil forms, flip charts, or white boards to create an intermediary set of workshop results. The participants edit, refine and get consensus on these preliminary diagrams in the usual JAD way. Then, the scribe enters the information into the CASE tool *after* the session is over.

The CASE Bandwagon

What if you're not on the CASE bandwagon? James Martin has a view on this:

> Some *primitive* JAD workshops are conducted without automated tools. (Martin 1990)

Well, excuuuse me! If your company doesn't use CASE, does that mean you are running your JADs with a staff of neanderthals? Don't be intimidated by CASE enthusiasts. Flip charts and board pens still get the job done. Many a JAD is held without automated tools. You can still accomplish the same tasks.

Most companies haven't made up their minds about CASE. Many still attend the free vendor demos and read the waning supply of articles (less is written now than a few years ago). They talk to their colleagues about CASE, and wait for others to try it first. The fact is, the vast majority of companies have not yet taken the headlong plunge into the maze of CASE tools and vendors. With more than 300 vendors in the CASE arena, selecting among the peddlers is not an easy task. (Definitely a project for a JAD session!)

The Cold, Cruel CASE Facts

CASE has been around since the mid-1980s and most people consider companies that use it to be more "state of the art" than others. However, a study conducted by Andrews and Leventhal revealed that:

> Although 80% of all U.S. companies have purchased CASE tools, only 25% had used a tool at least once and only five percent were using the tool in a production environment. (Andrews and Leventhal 1993)

CASE results are mixed. Some companies have had great success, while others have left the expensive software collecting dust on a shelf. Here's a strongly negative opinion:

> It's time for someone to stand up and make a case against CASE. IS departments that sink millions of dollars into the myth of better computing with CASE are crazy. In most of today's business world, CASE has no place. It's expensive, cumbersome, requires a near lobotomy on the part of programmers, and usually results in a big waste of time. (Currid 1993)

In a 1992 survey of 430 chief information officers (CIOs), Deloitte & Touche's Information Technology Consulting Group found that "the importance CIOs attach to CASE has fallen sharply over the past two years". (Anthes 1992) According to the article, when the group conducted a similar survey in 1989, CIOs using CASE ranked it as the number one advanced application development technique. In the latest survey, CASE moved down to number five behind methodologies, prototyping, fourth-generation languages, and JAD.

So, despite all the press releases, industry hoopla from the software engineering gurus, and messianic claims from vendors, ("our CASE tool supports object-oriented technology and cures the common cold as well!"), CASE hasn't yet delivered.

But is CASE dead? In March, 1993, software engineering expert, Ed Yourdon, attended the CASE World conference in San Francisco to scope out the latest word on CASE. He actually heard "some sober, conservative, intelligent decision makers utter the phrase, 'CASE is dead.'" (Yourdon 1994) Yourdon concluded that it's really "old" CASE that died (or, as he puts it, "is comatose"). This refers to the CASE technology of the 1980s which focused on mainframe technology and third-generation programming languages. The "new" CASE (which is very much alive) supports fourth-generation languages, client-servers, GUIs, and object-oriented methods. He also pointed out that some vendors don't want to refer to their products as "CASE tools" anymore because of the stigma attached to CASE. Some now refer to them as "rapid application development tools." Oh no. From CASE tools to RAD tools. What's next?

Recommendation

In summary, some have tried CASE tools in the session and found they just do not work. "The tool is too cumbersome," they say. On the other hand, others bring CASE tools into the session to interactively build their models and project the images on a screen. And many of these people wouldn't have it any other way.

We use CASE tools, but not in the session. Here is our recommendation: If you do not have a methodology in place and you are not using CASE in your company, then don't focus on purchasing CASE tools just to support your sessions. Focus instead on tools that support the specific tasks you do in sessions. For example, if you build a lot of screens in the session, then look at interactive screen painters. If you do data models, then maybe a low-cost CASE tool with excellent graphics will meet your need. Don't get swept up into the full array of CASE tool functions that you have no use for now and that will only become shelfware later.

On the other hand, if you do have a methodology in place and you are using CASE for your systems development, then bring the tool into the session. It's part of the culture, people are familiar with the language, and it's your company's way of doing business. Give it a go. But before you do, make sure you bring into the session these three things: a strong methodologist, someone who is agile with the tool, and a tool that handles the task well. If you have all these things, then you just might become one of those people who "wouldn't have it any other way."

Assuring CASE Success

You may be among those companies looking at CASE from a broader perspective: to bring it in to support your systems development life cycle. For those situations, we thought we would include a few comments on assuring CASE success.

Don't overlook hidden costs

Justifying the cost properly is difficult. No one seems to be able to adequately document CASE benefits. The significant time required to become proficient in the tools makes productivity gains appear disappointing. CASE tools don't provide an instant payback. Initially, using CASE tools often slows down the project, especially since you devote even more time to the front end of the life cycle. What people often overlook, however, is that this effort shortens the back end of the cycle and the overall time required to complete the project.

Implementing CASE is a major investment, It is likely to cost about $10,000 per person. If you throw in structured methodology and advanced skills training and support, you could be up to $20,000 very quickly. CASE also costs money in project downtime while analysts develop their CASE knowledge and skill.

> 35% of the total cost for CASE can be attributed to software and hardware. Training, support, and many indirect costs raise the investment level. Forgetting this fact can lead to CASE failure. (Andrews and Leventhal 1993)

The methodology first, then the tools

Many companies purchased CASE tools simply because they were captivated with the technology. It was also fashionable to be rah-rah CASE. Make sure you adequately analyze the problem you want the tool to solve. Don't fall into "technology infatuation" and find at the end of the project that you have placed "a state-of-the-art technological wrapper around an essentially rotten core." (Nykamp and Maglitta 1991)

Lou Mazzuchelli, from Cadre Technologies Inc. (a CASE vendor) sums it up:

> A fool with a tool is still a fool. We say, choose a method, any method! Then choose a CASE tool for it . . . Any investment in CASE technology, no matter how small, can be squandered without that initial investment in learning appropriate structured analysis and design techniques. (Yourdon 1992)

The real CASE success stories come from companies that have had a structured methodology in place for years. Then, they invest in the tools. When you bring in the tools first, the tools will drive a methodology that may not be consistent with your original objectives. A tool that creates the most elegant data flow diagrams has no value if you don't use those kinds of diagrams.

To some degree, you can tailor the tool to your methodology. For example, you can select Yourdon diagramming techniques over Gane and Sarson. But you cannot tailor the tool to the overall way you develop systems.

Commit to training

Sometimes developers are not given enough time to acquire the software skills they need. Investing in the newest CASE technology is a waste of time and money unless you commit to staff training. You can't just plop down 45 copies of a popular CASE tool in your department and expect productivity gains. It takes a good six months to go through formal training and a pilot project. You need to carefully select the tools, formally introduce them, and prepare a detailed plan on how to integrate them into the organization. In other words, companies need to actually redesign the way they work.

In Summary of CASE

If you can successfully capture the results of a JAD workshop with a CASE tool (whether during the session or afterwards) and manage not to alienate anyone in the process, so much the better. Why make those bubble charts with a green plastic template if you can do it faster with an automated tool?

However, to put the matter in perspective, Norman Kashdan (founder of a software engineering firm specializing in software methodologies) observed through work with his clients that the choice of CASE tools or structured methodology does not have as great an impact on the project's results as does the ability of the participants to work together as a group. He says:

> In project after project, the real breakthroughs in getting things done involve the improvement of communication and cooperation among developers . . . . Those processes, methods, and tools that improve the

collaboration among individuals and meld them into teams seem to have the most impact on success." (Kashdan 1991)

As Kashdan implies, JAD is still the key to project success, with or without the tools.

PROTOTYPING

Prototypes are working models of a system. IS developers work interactively with the business area experts to build prototypes before constructing the real system. Prototyping allows you to turn conceptual business requirements into actual screen and report designs through trial and error. In this way, you can see the design early in the life cycle, rework it, modify it, refine it, and enhance it again to your heart's content. In the end, the prototyped model more accurately reflects the business needs than if the system were designed from hardcopy specs or, worse yet, from the programmers' vague memories of conversations with users.

James Wetherbe (professor of Management Information Systems at the University of Minnesota) compares this trial-and-error technique of prototyping to activities in our everyday lives. You try on sneakers before you buy them, drive the mini-van around the block before you lay down $20,000, and date lots of people before you get married. Life is a series of trials and errors. (Wetherbe 1991)

Unfortunately, our traditional systems development life cycle does not include time for trial and error in the up-front design process. We wait until the testing phase to catch errors in design. This is not very efficient! Furthermore, we impose budgets and target dates for projects before we have a working prototype. Consequently, to meet these prematurely defined mandates, we eliminate useful system functions. Wetherbe feels this is unrealistic:

> Have you ever moved to a new city where you had to purchase a new home? Did you have a price in mind and a desired date to move in before you began your search? Were you able to keep to the original price and schedule or did you need to adjust to meet your requirements? Often you looked at houses (prototypes) and saw the ones you really wanted. What would have happened had you forced someone to meet your housing requirements within the original price and schedule you started with? (Wetherbe 1991)

Wetherbe advocates interviewing users, developing an initial prototype quickly, and then working with the users to revise it until it's right. That way, management can set more realistic schedules and budgets based on something more tangible. In situations where users do not know exactly what they want, prototyping stimulates creative ideas for system solutions.

Prototyping and code generation tools are powerful and easy to use. With the fourth-generation languages of today, users are able to interactively and quickly design their systems and add layers of changes on the spot. Interactive screen painters and report generators allow users to be creatively involved in the design process. These tools have become so good that once users are exposed to this way of prototyping, they will not be satisfied going back to the old way of designing systems. Prototyping will become the predominate means of building interactive systems.

JAD and Prototyping

So how does prototyping fit into the JAD process? JAD and prototyping are a perfect pair. After you define screens, menus, and dialogs in a JAD session, for example, you can ask the IS developer to build the prototype. Using a fourth-generation language, application generator, or other prototyping tool, the developer can translate the requirements into a working model. Depending on how complex the system is, it can all be done in a week or two. You can then hold another session to refine the prototype and reach consensus. In this way, users form a good idea of how the system will work. Users can then expect the final production system to look like the one they built together in the prototype. Sounds great. But are there any drawbacks?

Cautions on Prototyping

We absolutely recommend prototyping. However, remember the following:

- *Don't cut corners on systems analysis and design.* Make sure you complete the prior life-cycle phases in your usual comprehensive way (documentation included!) If your logical design is incomplete or incorrect, your prototype will be the same. It's the ol' rule of GIGO (garbage in, garbage out).

    Even with prototyping, some system design is still needed. For example, an automobile engineer would not build a prototype car without sufficient analysis and some documented specifications. Engineers realize that basic design decisions must be made before any prototype can be built. (Weinberg 1991)

- *Prototypes are not finished systems.* Because prototypes give the illusion of a completed system, they may bring false expectations to the users, making them think that they can have the new system in a couple of weeks. Remind your users that there is no programming code behind that prototype. There is still a major effort ahead.

- *Know when to stop.* Prototypes encourage users to change their minds. This is good, up to a point. But you don't want to fall into a never-ending cycle of changes that prevent you from ever seeing the real system.

Prototyping a Field System

We used prototyping for a policy information system developed for our field force. Once the screen requirements were defined in hardcopy, we created a prototype. First, individual screens were produced using a screen painter. Then the screens were tied together via their various navigation routes. Of course, there was no programming behind the screens and there was no live data. For any particular screen, no matter what policy number people entered, they would always see the same name and information display on that particular screen. The prototype was simply pictures of screens that we could see on the terminal.

The beauty of the prototype was being able to view and change the screens right on the spot. We asked Bob (the one who created the prototype) to move this field, highlight that prompt, and alter the title. He made the changes in a flash, and we saw the new version instantly. Sometimes we changed things several times to get them just right. These are the kinds of back-and-forth adjustments that drive programmers mad. But with prototyping, the process was smooth and no doubt saved numerous maintenance requests down the line.

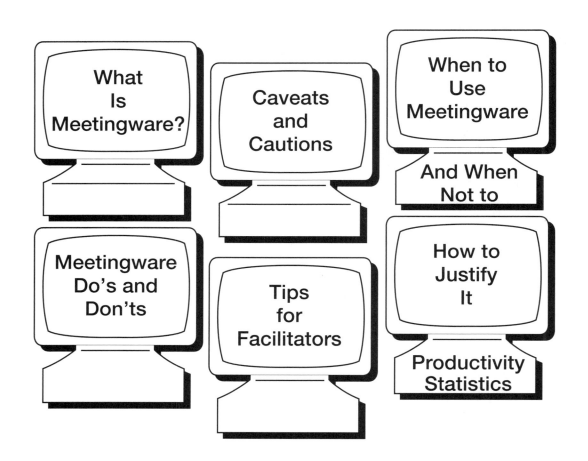

SIXTEEN ▷ ▶ ▶ ▶

MEETINGWARE

In a previous chapter, we talked about promoting creative thinking by asking the group to imagine how they would change their business if they had no constraints. Let's try some of that medicine on ourselves. Consider our own business of running facilitated sessions. If we were leading the ultimate session, what would it be like?

Well, in our ideal session, we would certainly like to stifle the problem-makers—the dominators, the grumblers, and the endless digressors. At the same time, we would like to hear more from the quiet participants who keep all their valuable knowledge and ideas locked tight in their heads. In fact, wouldn't we prefer to hear from everyone equally? And for the sake of time, could we hear from everyone *at once,* while the scribe accurately documents this simultaneous group contribution? And how about the participation list? At times, wouldn't we fancy having more people from other locations?

As wild and crazy as all this may sound, there is a technology designed to fulfill this fantasy description. It's called *meetingware.*

WHAT IS MEETINGWARE?

Let's talk about the distinction between "meetingware" and "groupware." Groupware in its broadest sense encompasses an array of software and hardware tools that help people share information and work together. This includes everything from flip charts, chalkboards, and overhead projectors to electronic bulletin boards, electronic mail, voice mail, calendaring systems, teleconferencing, audio-conferencing, video-conferencing, team rooms, and any other technology that helps dissolve the constraints of time and space. The 1993 Groupware trade show displayed more than 400 products from more than 250 companies. Sales for 1993 were projected to reach almost $2 billion worldwide. (Hsu and Lockwood 1993)

In other words, in its most liberal sense, groupware is anything that helps groups communicate. But when you say "groupware" in the facilitators' arena, most people assume you are talking about the wave of computer software designed to help groups create, organize, and evaluate ideas.

Some other familiar aliases for meetingware are "electronic meetings systems"(EMS) and "electronic JAD (E-JAD)." These specifically refer to using computers and associated software in facilitated sessions. This is exactly what we will be referring to from now on, when we talk about "meetingware."

A Typical Meetingware Session

In a typical session using electronic meetingware, all participants have a PC on the table in front of them. As the session progresses, participants type their comments into their PCs. The system automatically compiles everyone's typed responses and displays them on a large screen for everyone to see. In this way, all participants speak at once, but remain anonymous. Using meetingware, groups can build agendas, brainstorm ideas, generate and sort those ideas, vote for and rank them, make decisions, and document the group's progress. A facilitator guides the group as in any facilitated session. Open discussion continues to interweave throughout.

For example, we attended a meetingware session facilitated by Len Bezar of Team Dynamics Associates (an IBM business partner) in their Philadelphia facility. Nine people attended, none of whom had participated in this kind of session before. The goal of the afternoon meeting was to create action plans to solve problems occurring in a particular business area. To do this, Len guided us through the following agenda:

- We began with a short brainstorming session where the group entered (into our computers) what we considered to be the main obstacles to productivity. Twenty-three problems were identified and displayed immediately on a large screen at the front of the room.

- The group reduced the 23 problems to 15 by eliminating redundancies.

- We each prioritized the problems (again, via our computers) by sorting each one sequentially—1 through 15.

- The facilitator used the meetingware system to create one list of prioritized problems that reflected an average of everyone's ranking. This displayed on the large screen, as a list of items and as a graph. (Note how this resembles the nominal group technique with Post-it notes described in Chapter 13.)

- Finally, we all entered our comments about what should be included in the action plan for each of the top five problems.

In the end, we had complete action plans to address the top five problems that the group had identified. Also, we had a list of ten other problems to handle in the future. All this was printed in a report that we took along with us at the end of the meeting.

Meetingware's Brief History

Meetingware was pioneered at the University of Arizona in the early 1980s. It was first used for business in a manufacturing and development facility in Owego, New York. The company was IBM. Other corporate pioneers include Boeing, Dell Computer, GM Europe, Marriott, MCI Communications, J.P. Morgan, Pacific Gas & Electric, Price Waterhouse, Southern New England Telecommunications, and Texaco. Now, many meetingware products are available. To name just a few:

- GroupSystems V® (from Ventana Corp. in Tucson, Arizona)
- MeetingWorks for Windows® (from Enterprise Solutions in Seattle, Washington)
- VisionQuest® (from Intellect Corp. in Dallas, Texas)

Other companies offer established meetingware rooms as well as facilitators with expertise in various business areas. So you can simply show up with your people and your meeting objectives, and the company does the rest. One such organization is the Group Productivity Center in Windsor Locks, Connecticut. Another is Team Dynamics Associates in Wayne, Pennsylvania.

HOW MEETINGWARE CAN HELP

Meetingware is not a panacea (what is?), but it offers many benefits. Here are a few:

Anonymity Encourages Everyone to Participate

They say that at an average cocktail party, 5 percent of the people eat 95 percent of the peanuts. In the same way, at an average facilitated session, 20 percent of the people do 80 percent of the talking (Kirkpatrick 1992). And for those who do speak, it's sometimes a case of tossing an idea on the table and waiting to see how the boss reacts.

Why do some people refrain from speaking in the first place? Perhaps they are uncertain about expressing opinions in front of a group or in front of a boss. Maybe they aren't sure their idea is a good one or they just can't get a word in edgewise. Meetingware allows everyone to speak without the potential of even the slightest ridicule. Everyone contributes anonymously.

Now, let's say in a regular facilitated session, you could overcome the challenge of getting everyone to talk. What happens when opinions are given? Often ideas are judged by who says them. When the one with power (or high status) speaks, everyone listens and gives careful consideration. Sometimes this is done in a fateful kind of way, where people behave as though this idea was etched in stone even before it's evaluated. On the other hand, when somebody's clerical assistant speaks, people offer the obligatory consideration (at most) and then move on to the people that matter. Consequently, many valuable ideas are filtered out and not truly heard.

With meetingware, ideas are leveled. Because all responses are anonymously "spoken" through the keyboard, no one knows who said what. The silent majority has voice. The quiet secretary has the same say as the boisterous vice president. You can throw out that wild idea that might get totally ridiculed and you can blatantly disagree with your boss without his knowing.

In meetingware circles, you often hear the story about the session held to gather ideas for a new product:

> The idea selected by participants turned out to come from a department secretary. The secretary waited several days, however, before stepping forward to claim ownership of the winning idea, saying she had feared her idea would have been discounted if everyone else knew it came from a secretary. Had she not been able to make her suggestion anonymously, she might not have made it at all. (Employee Benefit News 1992)

In this way, meetingware encourages cultural diversity. Separating people from their ideas instantly weeds out discrimination. You don't know if the idea is coming from the dominating, six-foot department head or from the shy, soft-spoken clerk in the corner.

Different Times and Places

Meetingware does not limit you to a single session meeting room. Meetingware can network people together in a single room, between offices, or around the world. It can link off-site colleagues, departments, and entire corporations.

Likewise, people's contributions need not be simultaneous. Group members can type in their ideas over a period of time. Then the meetingware compiles the results and sends them back to the participants. This is ideal when group members are scattered across the country—that is, when travel is not practical, but participation is essential. In the same way, sessions can span global time zones without being limited by the reality that while some participants are having lunch, others are deep in sleep.

Sessions Move Faster

Can you imagine a session where everyone talks at once? Do you envision total chaos, a session gone totally out of control? With meetingware, everyone *can* talk at once, without the chaos. As one vendor points out, "In a typical hour-long meeting of 15 people, everyone has an average of only four minutes of air time. With computer support, everyone has the potential to talk for 60 minutes." Of course, this doesn't account for silences or for the facilitator's time. But you can see, with everyone speaking through the keyboard simultaneously, people have far more time to talk.

Another reason sessions move faster is that most people read faster than they listen. Therefore, with meetingware, they can deal with more material than before.

Furthermore, creativity is enhanced. Ideas are handled very quickly. In a matter of moments, the entire group's contributions can be sorted, viewed, and voted on. This speed alone is enough to inspire new ideas. After all, one person's idea sparks another idea, and so on. Creativity is contagious.

No More Trips to Abilene

With everyone anonymously contributing and viewing ideas at the same time, certain detrimental tendencies of groups are neutralized—for example, the "Abilene paradox." This group dysfunction was named for an episode where a group of people, unable to decide where to go for lunch, ended up driving 50 miles to Abilene. They realized afterwards that no one, not even the one who suggested it, had any real desire to drive all that distance. In this way, groups can fall into bad decisions because everyone figures everyone else likes an idea, so they go along, just like sheep. Using meetingware, anonymity defuses our propensity to follow along with the others.

No Hasty Conclusions

Like the wild plays made in the last five minutes of a football game, sometimes meetings can draw to a hasty close. In this case, the group tends to make grand conclusions that have little connection to the meeting objectives. Meetingware's demand for total participation discourages these kinds of careless conclusions.

Sense of Accomplishment

Meetingware also helps motivate participants by allowing them to see all ideas immediately displayed. The resulting sense of accomplishment tends to amplify creativity and team productivity.

Stronger Consensus

Using meetingware, any one person probably contributes more than usual. This is a key element to consensus. With more of everyone's ideas being woven into the solution, consensus is stronger. Consequently, overall commitment to success is likely to be higher.

Leveled Participation

As you can imagine, having to enter ideas into a keyboard tends to stifle aggressive and dominating participants. With meetingware, everyone's contributions are brought in at the same level. Consequently, people can evaluate all ideas objectively without being influenced by personal likes and dislikes. (At the same time, however, you still need to deal with these loudmouth types, who often resent the meetingware approach.)

Immediate Documentation

Meetingware provides an instant record of the session proceedings. You can capture ideas and sort them in realtime. At the end of the session, you can distribute the documentation on disk or hard copy. Furthermore, your documentation is more likely to be accurate and complete. Participants record ideas in their own words without the scribe's interpretation.

CAVEATS AND CAUTIONS

With the entire previous section espousing the benefits of meetingware, you might be considering installing it in every conference room in your company. Certainly the meetingware vendors would not mind if you did. But don't throw away the flip charts yet. There are some caveats, shortcomings, and pitfalls to consider.

Be Wary of Statistics

When we first looked into meetingware, we did what many people have done—we read the marketing material. We called all the vendors, pored over their glossy brochures and accompanying articles, and were absolutely wowed by the productivity statistics, the case studies, and the potential of this burgeoning technology. Then we looked further.

We called a popular columnist who writes on hot topics in our industry. We asked him about meetingware. "Between you and me," he said, "it's all crap." 'Twas then we realized that opinions vary somewhat.

Yes, meetingware can increase participation and shorten meetings. We often hear statements like this: "Meetingware increased our productivity by 60 percent" and "With meetingware, we accomplished our objectives in half the time." But what do these numbers really mean?

When certain vendors say meetingware shortens meetings by 40 percent, they are comparing the meeting time to traditional nonfacilitated meetings. Facilitated meetings also yield such productivity gains. For example, "Using JAD, we reduced the requirements definition time by 40 percent." So is it the *meetingware* that saved the 40 percent or is it the fact that the meeting was *facilitated?* In other words, how much time savings is due to participants entering their comments via a keyboard and how much can be attributed to a good facilitator and a structured agenda?

Another common meetingware claim is that it increases productivity. People make comments like, "We produced more than twice as many ideas using meetingware!" Just because a session produced 50 ideas instead of 20 doesn't mean the session was better or that they saved time. Quantity does not necessarily yield quality.

You can do a lot with meetingware. But you can't do it all. To counter the zealous claims you hear from time to time, the following sections describe some things that meetingware does *not* do.

Meetingware Does Not Heal a Dysfunctional Group

A group that can't converse together and make decisions together will not be saved by meetingware. If they can't "form, storm, norm, and perform" together, they're going to be equally lost trying to participate through a keyboard. Despite meetingware promises of chilling out and leveling the dominator, this person will still be the source of the group's discontent. What you need here is not a keyboard, but a good facilitator.

Meetingware Does Not Level the Power Field

Yes, meetingware does make people equal in terms of being heard. (Although some people will continue to holler out their contributions, just like before.) But meetingware does not level people's power entirely. The VP is still the VP. No matter what the meetingware results, the VP might say, "I disagree with that conclusion. We'll do it my way." You still need to manage power abusers through group psychology and good facilitation.

A good facilitator does not need meetingware to draw out ideas from everyone. The facilitator can create a nonjudgmental atmosphere by querying the group in certain ways. Then, by getting those ideas on a board or entering them into a word processor or CASE tool (and projecting them on a screen), the facilitator can separate ideas from the people who offered them.

Meetingware is Not the Only Way to Anonymity

We hear so much about the element of anonymous contributions in meetingware, as if this technology is the only ticket to real anonymity. On the contrary, for years facilitators have used various techniques to allow groups to contribute ideas anonymously. For example, in the "Harvesting Ideas" section of Chapter 13, one facilitator describes a way to have participants write their ideas on index cards, while someone posts them on the board in front of the room to categorize and evaluate. This approach may not be as flashy as red and green bar charts projected on a big screen, but it works. The point is, although meetingware can help in this area, it is but one of many approaches.

Meetingware Does Not Replace the Need for Conversation

Even with the most sophisticated comment-capturing system, groups still need to talk, just like before. (And thank goodness! Wouldn't it be boring to make group decisions without talking with one another?)

It's best to combine meetingware with facilitated conversation. For example, during a brainstorming session, you can use meetingware to capture ideas and sort them into groups. Then you can talk about them as you would in any facilitated session. Some say it's best to talk at least 50 percent of the time. But many sessions require much more nonmeetingware interaction.

Meetingware Will Not Replace a Good Facilitator

Meetingware sessions do not run themselves. Even though the system automatically collects responses, all the usual group dynamics remain and operate in the session. For example:

> We have one guy—a very strong personality—who tends to dominate traditional meetings. Because he can't do that using [meetingware], he isn't terribly inclined to participate or use this tool. Instead of typing his comments on the keyboard . . . the backslider calls things out, starts a discussion, changes the topic and leads everyone down a different path. (LaPlante 1993)

You still need a good facilitator to keep the session on track, guide the discussion and the meetingware functions, as well as handle all the people problems that arise in the usual ways.

Research Finds Mixed Results with Meetingware

The University of Arizona and American University collaborated on a study to determine how JAD can benefit from meetingware. (Carmel et al 1992) They studied 11 JAD sessions (six that used meetingware and five that did not). The organizations they studied covered three U.S. states. They were diverse (both public and private) and represented a range of products and services. The sessions involved development projects under various settings and conditions.

Here is a summary of their findings. As it turned out, meetingware sessions fared worse in all but one of the four areas studied. Meetingware sessions had:

- *Less discipline.* In fact three of the meetingware sessions "bordered between informal and chaotic."

- *Less success resolving conflicts.* There were problems with closure. The study says that meetingware may "dilute the powerful techniques of a JAD session by losing the conflicts in a mountain of electronic text."

- *Less overall session management.* Meetingware facilitators had little involvement and rarely interrupted the sessions.

- *More participation.* Contributions were more equally distributed among the group.

Now, before drawing hasty conclusions about this study, here is a question to consider: Is it the meetingware that stifled the sessions or is it the lack of good facilitation? In this study, the meetingware facilitators:

- Were not accountable for the outcome.

- Prepared for the session in several hours (as opposed to several days for the nonmeetingware sessions).

- Rarely interrupted conversations in the session.

In any JAD session, if the facilitator skimps on planning and rarely interrupts the session, won't that session fare badly as well?

Perhaps the key point of this study is not that meetingware has weak areas, but that when you skimp on facilitation, the session suffers. The most valuable lesson of this research is: Sessions using meetingware usually *do* skimp on facilitation and they degenerate accordingly. As the study concludes:

> The principle weakness in electronic JAD may be the under-emphasis on facilitation. (Carmel et al. 1992)

In summary, meetingware can help and it can hinder. Much of this depends on how the facilitator handles the session. Here are some comments about the pros and cons of meetingware:

> One reason the group can be helped by computers is that they [computers] do not have many of the qualities that can be destructive of group life: they do not fight, take sides, dominate the conversation, bully or provoke. They can, however, distract, allowing a group to flee from the task at hand, or to be diverted from the real issues. They can also intrude on the group life, or even destroy it, by isolating individuals from face-to-face contact. (Phillips and Phillips 1993)

WHEN TO USE MEETINGWARE (AND WHEN NOT TO)

Meetingware works best in groups of between 7 and 15 people. It tends to be more successful in sessions lasting more than an hour and in groups with lower to middle management. People who are not used to using computers (which often includes upper management) are likely to resist the technology. Consequently, meetingware may not be as successful for executive meetings.

Also, be wary of using meetingware with old-style managers who worship hierarchy. They will be very uncomfortable when their voice is made equivalent to people three levels lower in the reporting chain. If you do hold sessions with these folks (and sometimes you must), be wary of the traditional management override. Entering ideas via a keyboard will not stop old-fashioned managers from rolling over the majority.

Companies most successful with meetingware are those that work in teams where information sharing is part of the culture. The following describes the observations of Bernard DeKoven, a management consultant who has worked with companies using meetingware:

> DeKoven has worked with several companies that have successfully integrated [meetingware] into their environments. Mostly, they've been companies that have adopted flat organizational structures, where everyone has access to information, and high-tech companies, where workgroups are the norm. In more traditional companies, [meetingware] systems succeed best when they spread above and below from middle management. (Hsu and Lockwood 1993)

What Meetingware Can Do

The following describes what you can actually do using a typical meetingware system:

- *Brainstorm.* Groups can generate new ideas in a free-form, unstructured way by responding to questions or to comments from others in the group. For example, you could ask members of a strategic planning team, "If you had no constraints, how would you change the organization?" Or you could have the group compile a complete set of requirements (including the blue-sky ones) about a particular facet of business.

- *Enhance ideas.* People in the group can type comments about existing ideas, then anonymously send their commentary to the electronic file folder for that idea.

- *Organize ideas.* Groups can refine, rearrange, consolidate, and categorize ideas. For example, a group might create a list of 50 ideas through brainstorming, then use this feature to organize them into seven categories. Or they could create a list of data element names, then sort them into groups for various screens.

- *Create outlines.* This is like brainstorming, except it's structured. Groups can develop a tree or outline of their ideas or of any kind of information. For example, a group might plan the contents of a report, gather ideas about a project, describe a business process, or develop the outline for a strategic plan. Or they could use it to decompose processes.

- *Vote.* You can poll groups using several voting methods including agree/disagree, yes/no, and true/false. For example, a group could vote on whether to buy the CEO a new leather office chair (agree/disagree) or compare a prototype against a list of predetermined requirements to see if they are met (yes/no).

- *Rank items.* Groups can rank a list of items in order of importance or desirability. Then the system displays the list in order of group preference. Groups can use this to prioritize a series of tasks. They could rank a list of 40 brainstormed ideas, select the top 10 and discuss them in detail, or rank the importance of various system enhancements.

- *Rate ideas.* Groups can rate a list of items, for example, on a scale of 1 to 10. Then the system displays the average rating for each item.

- *Allocate resources.* Groups can allocate a finite number of resources among a list of items. For example they can allocate budgeted funds among various projects.

- *Evaluate alternatives.* Groups can rate a list of alternatives against a list of criteria. Then they can view the results in various formats, like the voting feature. Groups can test "what if" conditions by adjusting the weights of the criteria. This might help, for example, when deciding between two alternatives for purchasing a software package.

- *Create lists.* In JAD sessions, groups create lists for such things as open issues, assumptions, and constraints. Instead of using flip charts, they can maintain these lists in separate text files.

- *Perform surveys.* People can be surveyed with a series of questions that group members respond to anonymously. For example, you can query groups for performance reviews, formal management surveys, or questionnaires for suppliers and customers. The resulting information can be compiled in one report.

- *Write reports.* Groups can create, review, and revise reports together. For example, they can develop corporate policies, strategic plans, action plans, requirements documents, presentations, or session summaries. Or they can simply gather ideas and opinions. After the session, the scribe can synthesize the text and produce the formal document. Participants can then add their changes and even sign off online.

- *Create graphics.* People in the group can draw at their station, then have everyone see what they created. For example, groups can work on data models together.

- *Create agendas.* Groups can plan a future meeting, building an agenda as they develop the plan.

- *Create matrixes.* Groups can build information in a matrix format of rows and columns. They can add values to the cells and evaluate the degree of consensus for each cell. The matrix can be used to group data elements into functional groups, map processes to data elements, or assign issues to participants.

- *Pass information.* Within the group, people can pass along information such as word processing documents, spreadsheets, and graphics.

For some features such as ranking, rating, allocating, and scoring, some systems allow you to view results in various graphic formats such as scatter plots, bar charts, and text reports. You can see how these features might help in some of the tasks you do in facilitated sessions.

Meetingware offers opportunities to include more than these standard features. Erran Carmel, Joey G. George, and Jay F. Nunamaker, Jr. (experts on electronic meeting systems) suggest that the following two features would "round out" the meetingware tool set for JAD sessions:

- *GroupCASE.* The entire group accesses the same CASE tool at the same time to create data models and build repositories.

- *Screen Design Tool.* The entire group accesses a screen-painter-like tool. Participants either see the prototype and make comments or evaluate screens (for example, the screen is fine, needs improvement, or should be nixed). (Carmel et al. 1992)

MEETINGWARE DO'S AND DON'TS

If you decide to use meetingware in your sessions, here are some tips to help assure that the technology works *for* you and not *against* you.

Don't Let the Technology Impede Communication

Don't let the technology disrupt the flow of conversation. For example:

> Only three times during the work session did we use the machine on our desks—once to enter the initial points on the questions being asked, another to personally rank the list of ideas the group collectively generated, and third, if you chose, to key-in personal comments at the end of the session. The rest of the time the machine sat in front of us, physically impeding group communication and causing us to crane our heads to see and hear others speak. [It was] an excessive use of technology. (Brochu 1994)

The point is, be careful not to overuse meetingware. If only 10 percent of a session agenda calls for the tool, consider not using it. And no matter what the format, good ol' conversation is still the primary form of getting things done.

Don't Assume Everyone Will Love Meetingware

Some people do not take to meetingware. Extroverts, for example, are often not comfortable typing their ideas; they would rather talk about them:

> Extroverts tend to "drop out" of electronic meetings because they are so dismayed with their inability to use their strong verbal skills. You tend to get much more input from shyer people, but you also lose others . . . . Balanced use of these tools is the answer. In most Hewlett Packard meetings . . . the electronic portion represents between only 25 and 50 percent of the meeting. (LaPlante 1993)

Do Be Wary of Data Manipulators

Can one person manipulate the data in a meetingware session? Here's one way:

> One meeting participant—a fast typist—pretended to be more than one person when he vehemently agreed or disagreed with an idea being discussed. He'd type "Oh, I agree," and then "Ditto, ditto" or "What a great idea" all in quick succession, using different variations of upper-case and lower-case letters and punctuation . . . . He tried to make it seem like a lot of people were concurring, but it was just him." (LaPlante 1993)

Meetingware is not foolproof. Watch for people who try to "beat the system" by manipulating entries for other intentions.

Don't Take Your Meetingware Results As Gospel

Whatever results your meetingware process yields, do not blindly translate them into solid conclusions. Whether you are using meetingware to vote, rank, brainstorm, or whatever, consider the results as a tally of responses for all to see. Then, discuss those results. Question them and modify where necessary. Keep the strength and vigor with the group.

Don't Use Meetingware for Information Sharing

Meetingware is not for disseminating and sharing information. For example, it would never do for a status meeting. It's better suited to help in activities where you are asking questions and making decisions. In the same way, it has no use in meetings with a lecture format.

TIPS FOR FACILITATORS

Facilitating meetingware sessions carries all the challenges of running other facilitated sessions. In a presentation on meetingware, Paul Collins (President of Jordan-Webb Information Systems, Ltd.) talked about how the facilitator's role changes as the meetingware session progresses. First the facilitator acts as *director* (explaining what will be done in the session). Then the facilitator becomes a *salesperson* (selling the group on the process and gaining commitment and trust). As the session continues and the group matures, the facilitator becomes the *enabler* (guiding the group through tasks), and finally, the *delegator* (assigning tasks to the now more-seasoned group). (Collins 1993)

As your facilitating role changes through the course of a meetingware session, here are some tips that can help:

- *Work with a technology specialist.* When you first begin using meetingware, it is essential to include a technology specialist who knows the system well. For example, when people need help entering their comments, the specialist can assist while you are free to continue facilitating. In time the need for a technology specialist will lessen. However, certain sessions may still require a second person.

  In any session, remember that facilitation is a full-time role. Even when the group is absorbed in entering their comments, you continue to "read the room."

- *Don't push people.* As with any new technology, certain people will resist. With meetingware, resistance comes more likely from the extroverts (who would rather chat than key) and from those higher in the organization (who might feel threatened by not being in command).

  For those you suspect may have a hard time with this medium, take your time. Give them the opportunity to become comfortable with this way of communicating. When they protest openly in the session, don't confront their resistance. Instead, acknowledge it, help them get through what they are working on, and carry on.

- *Define your queries carefully.* A major part of your facilitation role is to guide the group through various questions and discussions. Take time before the session to determine exactly how you will state the questions. You need to phrase them simply and with clarity. Your meetingware responses will not have much value if participants have interpreted your questions in different ways.

- *Set time limits.* When asking the group to respond, set time limits and let the group know what those limits are. That way, participants know how much detail to provide. And they will not feel that at any moment, you could halt their air time right in the middle of a good idea.

  Find the timing balance. Every group has its pace. Stay aware of how long it takes the group to respond to various queries, then adjust your time limits accordingly. Find the balance between cutting them off too soon (and losing good ideas) and letting them dawdle too long (resulting in flippant and superficial responses).

- *Accept silence.* As opposed to other facilitated sessions, meetingware sessions contain longer periods of silence while people ponder ideas and type them into the system. Although these sessions vitally depend on conversation, don't insist on constant deliberation. Better to leave a comfortable backdrop of silence while the group thinks and types together.

- *Keep the technology in its place.* Meetingware is just a supporting tool. Don't let it take over the session, especially in the beginning when you are enthused about what it can do. Never let meetingware consume more than half your session time. Even 25 percent of tool time is fine.

- *Give more breaks.* Offer more breaks than other facilitated sessions. Working at a computer screen can be stifling without frequent short recesses. Even five minutes can do wonders.

- *As always, prepare!* Last and foremost, don't skimp on good planning before the session. This is as vital to success as in all facilitated sessions.

A Creative Icebreaker

Here is an exercise you can use to help people become familiar with meetingware and with each other as well. Give each person a number (passing the hat will do). Have each person type three characteristics about themselves. For example, someone might say, "I play tennis, read mystery novels, and do bungy-jumping." That person enters this information along with the number already given. Then, have the group enter (for each number) who they think the person is. The group views all the responses. This loosens up the participants and familiarizes them with the system.

Training Facilitators

Everything covered in "Training Facilitators" (see Chapter 23) applies to meetingware as well. However, now that you are dealing with a purchased technology, you will hear certain meetingware vendors promising you all the facilitator training you need to get your sessions up and running. *Do not rely solely on vendor training!* No vendor can provide sufficient training for a facilitator to effectively run a session. You may get training on using the software, but not on handling the group dynamics. Be prepared to supplement vendor training either within your own company (via other seasoned facilitators) or from a company who offers facilitator training. Here are some comments from The Boeing Company:

> Vendor training provided to each facilitator as they joined the team was *not* sufficient. New facilitators would return from their initial training eager to begin work leading sessions, but were ill equipped to do so . . . . Facilitator trainees did not experience full size group dynamics. Also, the vendor training was not "real" enough as it relied too often on insignifi-

cant test problems and issues—nothing like the complex and dense issue areas which our facilitators faced in the actual sessions. (Post 1992)

Here is how Boeing handled their own training:

Seasoned "lead" facilitators were given direct responsibility for giving each new facilitator a graduated series of apprenticeship lessons and experiences. New facilitators were asked to conduct mock sessions and lead them using volunteers [as participants]. (Post 1992)

Boeing estimates the learning curve for meetingware facilitators is up to two years. This gives them time to become competent with the technology as well as to learn to handle various kinds of sessions.

HOW COMPANIES ARE USING MEETINGWARE

Companies have used meetingware for all kinds of projects. Here are some examples:

- One company used JAD, meetingware, and CASE to revise screen formats. They displayed screen prototypes via the CASE tool. The group typed their comments into the meetingware system. The group viewed these comments and revised the screens accordingly.

- In the past, when Dell Computer endeavored to name a new product, they called for suggestions from their employees. People submitted ideas via electronic mail. Then managers held meetings to evaluate the suggestions. The names were displayed on flip charts, opinions were kicked around, and consensus was long in coming. Using meetingware, a group of marketing and sales managers was able to rate 75 product names and, in a matter of moments, select five finalists.

- EDS created a meetingware facility called The Capture Center. Here is a description:

  The Capture Center was created six years ago to develop artificial intelligence applications with our biggest customer, General Motors . . . . We use Apple Macintosh computers. The Macintoshes are imbedded in the tabletop, so that participants can see each other without obstruction. (Spates and Grou 1993)

  Now the Capture Center is used with various clients primarily for brainstorming, creating strategic and tactical business plans, planning projects, generating documentation in groups, creating presentations, and for process and data modeling.

- Marriott used meetingware to find new ways to improve guest satisfaction. The group generated 139 ideas in 25 minutes. Then they rated them on a scale of one to five, first according to how the idea would impact the guest, then according to cost. As a result, the group decided to step up training for hotel employees in certain areas.

- Proctor and Gamble used meetingware to generate product names and to do qualitative research with customers and consumers. They also used it to prepare strategic plans, develop new ideas, and design products and packages.

- Southern New England Telecommunications used meetingware to develop a customer relations strategy. The technology replaced the previous use of focus groups and surveys.

- J.P. Morgan has used their 13-seat meetingware room for various meetings about strategic planning, organizational changes, auditing, and employee surveys.

Meetingware and Downsizing

In an article called *Trying groupware on for (down)size,* Michael Schrage gave a less cheery perspective on why companies are going for "groupware":

> The recent GroupWare conference in San Jose, California, was no Groupware Woodstock, where people grooved on the concept that computer-mediated cooperation is "where it's at, man." . . . The big motivator was downsizing. (Schrage 1993)

Schrage feels that most companies are interested in groupware, not to position themselves for growth (the motivation "espoused by its most ardent advocates"), but rather to help them become smaller. He continues:

> After downsizings, organizations have fewer people trying to do more work. The brittle infrastructure that remains just doesn't cut it anymore, and managers are grasping for whatever tools they can to handle the added burdens. (Schrage 1993)

SOME STATISTICS ON PRODUCTIVITY

We'd like to pass along some statistics on how meetingware has helped some companies. One must consider the sources, the motivation behind preparing the various statistics, and how much guestimating might have been involved in developing the numbers. At the very least, though, these statistics show there are some downright satisfied meetingware users. For example, any company that uses meetingware for 150 sessions (as both Marriott and Proctor and Gamble did) must be feeling some sort of satisfaction. Here are some comments. (Many use the more general "groupware" term, although they are referring to electronic meetingware.):

Boeing studied the use of groupware in decision-making. They had 64 sessions, with a total of 654 persons over nine months. They . . . showed a 91% increase in efficiency or about $6,754 savings per session. They calculated a return on investment of 170%. (Collins 1993)

At Metropolitan Life Insurance Co. in New York, a recent brainstorming session ran for 14 minutes before we cut it off, and we got 287 ideas. (Hamilton 1992)

At Boeing a group of engineers, designers, machinists, and manufacturing managers used [meetingware] to design a standardized control system for complex machine tools in several plants. Managers say such a job normally would take more than a year. With 15 electronic meetings, it was done in 35 days. (Kirkpatrick 1992)

Proctor and Gamble used groupware in 150 sessions with 1,500 people over 18 months . . . . When benchmarked against regular meetings, the meetings using groupware showed from 2 to 10 times improvement in effectiveness. (Collins 1993)

Marriott used groupware for 150 sessions with 1,480 people over six months. They generated 15,200 ideas, 95% of which were rated as valuable. (Collins 1993)

At Marriott, the electronic meetings take an average of one-tenth of the time of traditional meetings . . . . This has saved Marriott about $1 million in worker productivity. (Eckerson 1992)

HOW TO JUSTIFY PURCHASING MEETINGWARE

To determine if meetingware will help your organization, you need to consider such questions as the following. Using meetingware:

- How much faster can the group make decisions?
- How much better are these decisions?
- What is your return on investment?

How do you answer these kinds of questions without bringing in the technology to make the comparisons? As in most new purchase justifications, you have to estimate. To help in this endeavor, we'd like to summarize a study at The Boeing Company. (Post 1992) The study involved 654 participants (including upper, middle, and lower management) over the course of 64 meetingware sessions. The sessions, which averaged almost five hours with 10 participants, covered the kinds of work found in Figure 16.1. Boeing found that meetingware:

Kinds of Work	*No. of Sessions*
Requirements definition	18
Planning	16
Surveys	14
Consensus	7
Information systems planning	7
Management strategy	2

Figure 16.1

- Saved 1,773 days (or 91 percent)
- Showed 170 percent return on investment
- Saved $432,260 in labor

And how did the participants feel about meetingware? All 654 people were surveyed at the end of their meetingware sessions. They were asked to rate several potential benefits on a scale of 1 (no benefit) to 5 (great benefit). Figure 16.2 shows the benefits along with their mean responses:

Meetingware Benefits	*Mean Responses*
Improved communications	3.92
Provided insightful information	3.90
Provided more complete decision-making	3.69
Helped set clear objectives	3.63
Improved teamwork and morale	3.62
Increased commitment to the session results	3.54

Figure 16.2

Several weeks after the sessions, follow-up surveys yielded similar positive responses. Almost everyone was willing to participate in other meetingware sessions.

Jadding with Icosahedrons

A Multiple JAD Marathon

Planning JADs

SEVENTEEN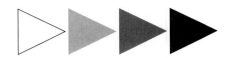

HANDLING LARGE PROJECTS

Large projects involve a series of related JAD projects, usually scheduled one after the other. They include a succession of interviews, sessions, more interviews, and more sessions. If you are working under tight time constraints, the phases of one JAD project can overlap the phases of the next. Often they must. In the same week, you might be interviewing for one JAD and preparing the final document for another.

Why overlap your projects if they are more complex and, as you can imagine, a bit intense? Why not just schedule the JADs concurrently, using separate facilitators? These JADs are usually held consecutively for the following reasons:

- You need the output of one session to use in the next.
- The same participants are required for several sessions. Some may even be required for all of them.

And why not spread the project over a longer period? The answer lies in the facts of the real world: When upper management says the system must be running by January 1, it *must be running* by January 1.

Some examples of our large JAD projects include:

- Defining requirements for a new insurance product introduction that affected processing for underwriting and policy issue, policy administration, the agency network, commissions, and dividends.

- Building a new field compensation system from scratch to support such business processes as agency managers' compensation, payment and accounting, recruiting and retention, and information tracking.

- Revising five systems to handle the new tax laws passed by Congress.

To handle such projects, we plan separate sessions for each business area involved. People attend only the sessions that affect their area. Each JAD has its own cast of characters, visual aids, and agenda.

A MULTIPLE JAD MARATHON

Of all the projects we have done, none was larger or had a tighter time constraint than this one:

The project involved defining requirements for a new insurance product that allowed policyholders to customize an insurance plan by combining the features of whole life and term insurance in one policy. This product also allowed policyholders to change or add to their existing coverage (without having to buy a separate policy) as their needs changed over time. To support such a flexible product, complex requirements needed to be defined affecting five separate computer systems.

To meet the time crunch, we ran 25 back-to-back sessions—not half-day, but *full-day* sessions. That's a lot of Danish!

The Time Constraint

In December, the Business Systems Engineering (BSE) group of our company was asked to become involved in this project. To meet the deadlines, the programming staff needed all the JAD documents by March of the following year. Thus, we had four months to do all the JAD work. Somehow, between Christmas and the Ides of March, we had to become familiar with the new insurance product and its effect on five computer systems, prepare for the sessions, conduct the sessions, and produce the final JAD documents. Ultimately this involved making 30 flip charts, 90 overheads, 150 magnetics, completing hundreds of pages of scribe notes, and generating 748 pages that made up the six final documents.

The People

Our resources included two facilitators, a business systems analyst, and an administrative assistant for such tasks as copying handouts, preparing overhead transparencies, and assembling the final documents.

The Approach

We divided the project into six JADs, one for each of the five business areas and one to define the data elements for the data base. Each of the six sessions lasted three to five full days and each had its own list of participants. We could not run any sessions concurrently because some participants were directly affected by the work in more than one business area. Therefore, they needed to attend several JADs. In fact, some people attended every session of every JAD.

For each separate JAD, we assigned a facilitator and the business system analyst to follow through from the first interviews to the creation of the final document. Both facilitators actually participated to some degree in each JAD project. This "cross-familiarization" was necessary so that one facilitator could fill in for another, if necessary. In fact, during one JAD session, the facilitator could not make it into work because of a major snowstorm. The second facilitator filled in.

To handle this project, we made adjustments to our standard JAD practices. The following sections describe them.

Phase 1: JAD Project Definition

- *Interviewing management.* The challenge was scheduling. The people we wanted to meet with for the upcoming JAD were often attending the current session. We arranged evening and weekend interviews.

- *Selecting the JAD team.* We developed one master participation list that we updated regularly. It included a running total of participants for each JAD as well as a grand total. We used this list to see at a glance who was attending what sessions, to determine room size and seating, and for distribution of memos and the final document.

- *Management Definition Guide.* This project had such priority that a high-level "Working Committee," run by the business area, met regularly to plan and track its progress. They maintained a project plan and had already determined the purpose, scope, and objectives of the project. Therefore, we did not prepare a Management Definition Guide.

- *Scheduling the Sessions.* We kept one master schedule to track meeting-room locations. We held all six sessions in one off-site facility, although many times we had to change rooms from one day to the next.

Phase 2: Research

- *Familiarization interviews.* We shortened the time for observing the existing business processes. Such comprehensive familiarization was a luxury that the time constraint did not allow. Instead, we held brief interviews, then focused on understanding the preliminary product requirements that the actuaries and the IS project managers had prepared for the new insurance product.

- *Documenting business processes.* We created some overview data-flow diagrams and analyzed the work performed in the business areas. But we did not document work flow to the detailed level as in other JADs.

- *Gathering preliminary information.* We handled this as usual, gathering as much as we could on data elements, screens, reports, and processing requirements.

- *Preparing the session agenda.* As always, we prepared the agenda before each session. Normally this is done as early as two weeks before the session. For this project, however, the agenda was sometimes not finalized until the day before (or sometimes minutes before!) the session.

Phase 3: Preparation

- *The Working Document.* Here is where we completely changed procedures. Since the BSE staff did not have time to prepare an official Working Document before each of the six sessions, we relied on the project managers to compile preliminary information.

- *Training the scribe.* We had a different scribe for each of the six sessions. This meant the facilitators had to spend more time training each scribe. We needed to cover not only the scribing process, but also how to use the standard templates and the word processor.

- *Visual aids.* We never skimp on these.

- *The pre-session meeting.* These were not held.

- *Setting up the meeting room.* Since the sessions for all six JADs ran back-to-back, we transferred the supplies to the facility in one move and stored them in a locked closet throughout the 25 days. Our presence at the facility became so consistent that we were soon "promoted" to residency status (which means we received our own keys to the storage closet and rest rooms).

Phase 4: The Session

The main difference in these sessions was that they were full days instead of half. While one facilitator ran a session, the other worked with the scribe of the previous session to prepare the final document, as well as interview participants for the next session.

Phase 5: The Final Document

- *Producing the final document.* The challenge here was contending with the snowball effect. After the first JAD, we produced the document right away. After the second JAD, we spent a little longer completing it because we also had to prepare for the next JAD. Since preparing for the session was the number one priority (you have to be ready to walk on stage), the final documents could easily be slighted or put on the back burner. To avoid this trap, we worked overtime to keep up with the documents.

- *Assembling the final document.* Rather than use separate binders for each JAD document, we combined the documents into one larger binder, using tabs to separate each project. People attending four of the six JADs, for example, received a 2-inch binder containing the documentation for all four projects.

- *Tracking distribution.* Tracking distribution was more critical for this project than any other. One participant might receive one final document, while another might receive all six. Since documents were being sent out every week or so, we had to track who already had binders, what size binders they had (1-inch, 1.5-inch, or 2-inch), and how many documents they received. This major tracking effort would have been impossible without documenting who received what and when.

- *The review meeting.* Because the sessions for one JAD began as soon as another one ended, we could not hold review meetings. Some of the people who would have attended those reviews were participating in the next session, so we could not have scheduled everyone together. Instead, we selected two or three key participants from each JAD to review the document for accuracy prior to distribution.

- *Approving the document.* With so many sessions going on, it was difficult getting all the approvals. However, for each of the six sessions, the user project manager and IS manager signed the document.

The Wilt Chamberlain Syndrome

Perhaps the biggest challenge of doing a project with tight time constraints occurs long after the project is done. If you succeed in pulling it off, some people assume you can work at that pace on an ongoing basis. Therefore, they might expect the same from you again.

In a basketball game in 1962 between the Philadelphia Warriors (now the 76ers) and the New York Knicks, Wilt Chamberlain scored 100 points. His fans, of course, wanted to see this extraordinary feat again. Some felt that when Wilt had a 50-point game, he was doing only half of what he could. Even if they forgot about the 100-point game, there was still his average to consider: 50 points per game for a whole year. As he said in his book, *Wilt,* "That meant any time I hit 30 points in a game, it was a 'bad' night: I'd have to get 70 the next night just to make up for it and stay even."

Although you can't quite compare a JAD session to a basketball game with "Wilt the Stilt," the resulting syndrome is the same. Try not to be pressured by other people's expectations that were set during a successful but overly intensive round of JADs.

We recommend spreading out the schedule quite a bit more. Even adding a few days between sessions would have made a world of difference. Nevertheless, we have summarized this crunch-mode project for the sake of those who may fall into such a situation when upper management says, "We need this project done by January 1."

PLANNING JADS

Now that we've dragged you through this war story, we will describe a couple additional ways to help handle large projects. When you embark on a major project that will necessarily require several series of sessions, you can hold a planning JAD to identify how the project will be organized. Some major projects are clearly delineated by the business area. Others are organized in the old traditional way of looking at things—by system. If you can, organize your projects by line of business. For example, the design effort for an Order Processing project might be organized into the following JAD projects:

- Customer order servicing
- Inventory management
- Shipping
- Receiving
- Accounts payable and accounts receivable

You need to assemble the key people from the business areas along with someone from IS who understands the general impact the project will have on all systems involved. Objectives of the planning JAD might include:

- Define the overall project objectives, scope, and benefits.
- Divide the project into a series of separate, manageable JADs.
- Identify problems with the current environment.
- Create preliminary participation lists for each JAD.

- Set a preliminary JAD schedule.
- Identify open issues that must be resolved before the JADs begin.

It's not easy to determine the number of JAD workshops required for a particular project. Dorine Andrews and Naomi Leventhal (JAD consultants), offer the following parameters to determine how many workshops you need:

- Organization size and politics (How many business units, job levels, and people are impacted by the project? Is there much hostility among the users?)
- Number and complexity of business functions (Are there 10 business functions or 25? How complex is each?)
- Level and type of detail required (Do you need a high-level data model or one in third normal form?)

For example:

> A retail company with over 200 stores identified eighteen participants to define the [design] for a point of sale inventory and accounting application. It was determined that two four-day workshops would be required here, one to define [process] and data models, and one to complete [data flow diagrams] and screen design. A two-day workshop was also tentatively planned to allow users to evaluate a prototype of the application. (Andrews and Leventhal 1993)

A seasoned facilitator uses past experience as a guide for knowing how many workshops are needed to produce the deliverables.

JADDING WITH ICOSAHEDRONS

Here is an excellent technique to help organize the various sessions of a large JAD project. It's based on a shape called the *icosahedron*. As you may remember from geometry class, an icosahedron is a three-dimensional shape with 20 surfaces. Such a shape embodies 30 struts (straight lines) that connect at 12 nodes.

So what do big projects have to do with icosahedrons? Well, let's say the 30 struts represent 30 team members (a typical size for a group working on a large project). And the 12 nodes (where the struts come together) represent the major topics to cover. You can see in Figure 17.1 how each team member (that is, each strut) connects to two separate topics (nodes) and is likewise in the vicinity of several other topics as well. In this way, each person communicates directly with all the people in the two sessions, who in turn communicate with several other people, and so on.

struts
(team
members)

nodes
(JAD
topics)

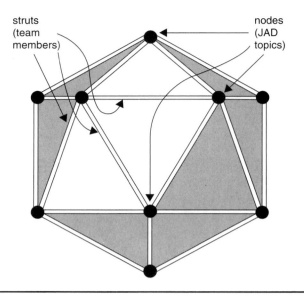

Figure 17.1 Icosahedron for planning JAD projects.

Using this approach, you optimize communications. After all, you can't ask all 30 people to attend all 12 sessions, with each session lasting three to five days. But you *can* use this structured approach to plan the topics and sessions. Earl Brochu (a project methods consultant) explains how to do this:

> To deploy the human icosahedron, the team initially convenes as a whole and composes the 12-item list of significant topics. Once the topic list is set, 12 JAD sessions are held in a predetermined sequence to reverberate knowledge and ideas. Each workshop is conducted in the usual manner with a subset of the 30-member team. (Brochu 1993)

However, when Stafford Beer (the acclaimed founder of management cybernetics) conceived of this concept, he probably didn't expect us to take it literally. You can't expect every large project to involve exactly 30 team members over 12 sessions. Nevertheless, the metaphor is a good one. This icosahedron approach to planning sessions for large projects helps you get the most out of the expertise available to you. People can stay in touch with as much of the project as possible without burning out.

PART
5

JAD AND BEYOND

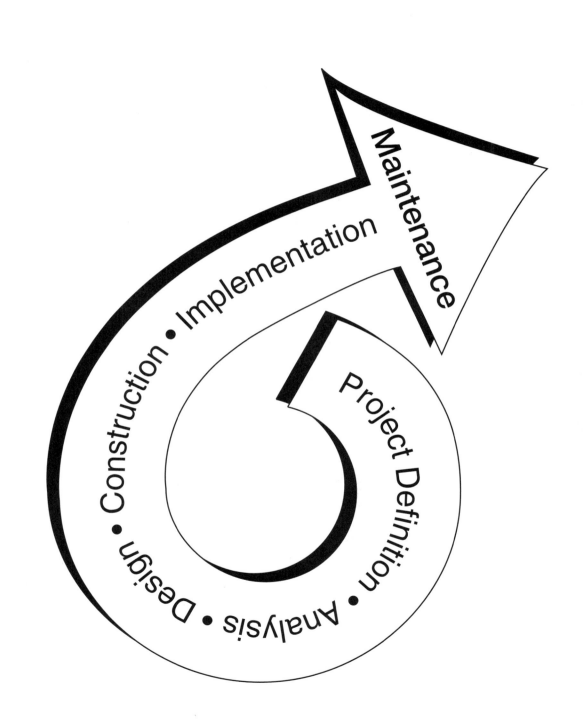

EIGHTEEN

JAD ACROSS THE LIFE CYCLE

In the past, JAD has been used mostly for defining requirements and designing systems. But this chapter deals with running sessions in other parts of the systems development life cycle (SDLC). In Chapter 19, we discuss how you can diversify your services and use JAD techniques for projects that have nothing at all to do with systems or any part of the SDLC.

TYPICAL JAD TOPICS

What are people doing in JADs? In our survey to several facilitator groups we asked, "How often do you do the following activities in your sessions?" Figure 18.1 shows the outcome. As you see, percentages add up to more than 100 percent because, of course, people do more than one activity.

We also asked, "What were the topics of your last five sessions?" The responses ran the gamut. People are doing JADs for everything from enterprise modeling to GUI screen design, from defining business processes to creating test plans. Industries of every kind are using JAD. Facilitators have run sessions for every business application you can think of. To name just a few:

Activity	*How Often Done* *
Define business requirements	98%
Define business processes	79%
Define data elements	79%
Do data modeling	90%
Design reports	52%
Design screens	52%
Data base design	24%
* This shows the percentage of people doing this activity.	

Figure 18.1 Activities done in facilitated sessions.

Accounts payable

Agricultural loan accounting

Asset management

Bank cards

Career planning

Claims processing

Customer orders

Customer service

Document management

Freight dispatching

Health care

Investment portfolio management

Manufacturing operations

New insurance products

Sales compensation

Speech recognition

Telemarketing

Time and attendance

Transportation

FACILITATING ACROSS THE LIFE CYCLE

You can use the JAD process in virtually every phase of the systems development life cycle. This does not mean that you should try using JAD for every systems development task that comes across your path. Not all tasks are best accomplished in group sessions. Typically organizations use JAD in the earlier phases of the life cycle, such as analysis and design. But as time goes on, JADs eventually work their way into some "not so common" applications. Users see that JAD works well for many purposes beyond its original intent. For example:

> TWA has expanded the original JAD concept to span the systems development life cycle from strategic planning and problem definition

through requirements definition and external design. So far, nearly 300 JAD sessions have been conducted for thirty automated systems.

—Trans World Airlines
(Guide International Corp. 1989)

It takes some JAD "maturity" (both successes and failures) to know when to apply it and when to hold a "regular old meeting" instead. (Although, couldn't most meetings benefit from structure, an unbiased facilitator, and good tools?)

From 1987 to 1989, "Guide," the IBM User Group, studied JAD across the life cycle. Their findings include the experiences and practices of many seasoned JAD facilitators from various companies including Levi Strauss & Co., TWA, General Electric Co., Fina Oil and Chemical, and The Church of Jesus Christ of Latter-Day Saints. The study describes how to apply JAD techniques to the following kinds of sessions within the life cycle:

Project definition

Requirements

Software package evaluation

External design

Internal design

Code and test validation

Post implementation evaluation

Maintenance

Now let's take a little journey through these areas of the systems development life cycle and explore how JAD can be used. Much of this information is based on the Guide study. (Guide International Corp. 1989)

Project Definition

In this type of JAD session, your goal is to reach consensus on the contents of the Management Definition Guide. The session sets the stage for the rest of the project phases and gets consensus on the project's purpose, scope, objectives, and constraints. Other deliverables from the session may include high-level business processes, cost benefit analyses, and a project plan.

Requirements

This type of JAD focuses on either the data or processing requirements or both. Here's where having a facilitator well-versed in data modeling techniques pays off. The JAD team builds the models together in the session.

The facilitator extracts from the participants all the information needs of the business and identifies how people use the data to do their jobs on a typical work day. The level of detail required depends on the particular project. You might simply define all entities and their relationships or actually get down to the individual data element (attribute) level. Some skilled facilitators may even introduce the concept of data normalization (up to third normal form!).

Susan Burk (of American Management Systems) participated in a JAD for an insurance company that focused solely on data modeling. The group created a 3-foot by 5-foot data model with 250 entities and 3500 data dictionary elements. The session ran four hours a day for three and a half months. Based on this data model, 120 people worked for two years to develop the application and data base and put it into production. Five years later, the system is still meeting the users' needs.

A Requirements JAD session identifies processes—that is, what users do with the information. This can be described in data flow diagrams or as a list of processes with short descriptions.

These JADs also identify what information goes in and out of the business areas. In the Design phase of the life cycle, these requirements will dictate what system interfaces to build.

JADs for Estimating Projects

Some companies, such as New York Life, hold JADs that focus on estimating the cost of software development. After defining requirements, but before jumping into designing a major system, the people in the business area gauge the cost and value of a project:

> An Estimating JAD . . . can last anywhere from 1 to 2 days depending on the complexity of the request. . . . Business functions are identified as well as inputs and outputs of those business functions. If the project impacts existing systems, then those systems are discussed as well to determine the scope of the enhancements needed. Certain technical issues are addressed at this time; for example, security, projected growth of the system and hardware requirements. (New York Life 1986)

The final document of an Estimating JAD can also be used by IS to determine the resources needed for the project.

Software Package Evaluation

More than ever, companies are choosing to buy, rather than build, their applications:

Buying ready-made systems to reduce backlog is increasingly popular. Blue Cross/Blue Shield of Kansas City, Mo., typifies this attitude.

"In the past," explains Judy Bond, Assistant Vice President of IS, "the company built systems because it feared no one would understand its business as the in-house programmers could."

"Now," she says, "we take advantage of software that is already built and tested. If we really need a new system, we'll go out and buy it." (Nykamp and Maglitta 1991)

JAD is invaluable for helping select among various software packages. In the last two years, we've used this type of JAD to evaluate packages for reinsurance, PC-client file systems, periodic payments, and agent sales concepts tools. This kind of session generally occurs once you have defined requirements.

To evaluate software packages, we use the following steps:

1. *Prioritize the criteria.* Hold a JAD to identify the criteria of the software packages that you are evaluating. These criteria align with the user requirements; for example, cost, ease of use, and training support. Next, prioritize the criteria by assigning weights to them (for example, one to five). If *cost* is a major issue, give that criteria a weight of five. If the *quality of reports* is not important, give that criteria a weight of one. Identify any "must have" criteria that would cause you to immediately eliminate a particular package. For example, if the package must run in the UNIX environment and it doesn't, it's definitely out. For details on how to assign weights to the criteria, see Chapter 14.

   Keep the detailed Requirements document at your side during this first session. The list of evaluation criteria usually jumps out at you from the document's pages. But on a few projects (do we dare admit this?) we let the scope of what the package can do help us determine the business requirements. Although this may seem backwards, your users may not have a clue as to what some of these packages are capable of doing. (Especially if they've been doing the process manually for the last 25 years!)

   For example, in evaluating PC-client file systems for our field force, we realized that many agents did not know that these packages offered such capabilities as automatic speed dialing and importing target lists from companies like Dun and Bradstreet. So, they naturally did not include these as requirements. Once they discovered the "cadillac characteristics" that were available, they immediately proclaimed, "We definitely need the system to do that. Give it a weight of four!." What we now do for these projects is summarize and explain the system features ahead of time so users are somewhat educated on what the package can do.

2. *Gather preliminary information.* Send for those glossy vendor brochures, demo diskettes, and the all-important customer reference list. Do some networking. Call your friends. Call that second cousin of your

tennis partner who once worked for a company that used that software package. And go ahead and call a few names on the vendor reference list. (However, don't trust these references entirely. It seems the users on those lists have nothing but nice things to say, when you are really more interested in hearing the dirt.)

At this point, narrow the field to two or three vendor packages. The entire JAD team will later evaluate the "finalists."

3. *Send out the RFP.* Send out the Request for Proposal (RFP) to your candidate vendors. Ask them to send you their system documentation, user manuals, sample contracts, financial statement, and detailed pricing list.

4. *Hold product demos.* Arranging for the vendors to come in to "show off" their packages is a great way to start to see the differences. (That is, if you can endure 15 slides about the virtues of the company before you get to the "beef"). We've also found that where possible, a more "hands-on" approach works best. Many vendors have demo diskettes or complete systems on a 3.5-inch diskette. We install the system in our model office and let the JAD team sit at a terminal and evaluate the package against our predetermined criteria (defined in step 1).

5. *Select the best alternative.* Again, this is where using a JAD session is valuable. Based on the RFP responses and other information gathered, evaluate each product's performance against the established criteria (how does each vendor meet the criteria?). At the end of the session, the group is able to recommend a final action, which could include a buy now, buy later, or "build in-house" decision. The session deliverables include the scoring matrix. (For an example, see Figure 18.3 later in this chapter.)

External Design

This kind of JAD defines the "user view" of the new application. Sometimes people refer to this view as the "logical" design to distinguish the user's view of the business and information from the programmer's "physical" view. The logical design comes first. The session focuses on what the users care about most. And as you know, users are fixated on forms, procedures, and "what will my screens and reports look like?" They care about the training program, the conversion plan, the acceptance test plans, and the user guide. They want to know who will have access to their system and how the error messages are worded. This type of session lends itself well to prototyping techniques that help users define and fine-tune their requirements.

Screen Design

Screen design used to be one of the most popular JAD session activities. We spent a large part of one chapter in the first edition of this book discussing how to effectively design screens. Although the focus on screen design has shifted, in our survey to several facilitator groups, we found that still half (52 percent) use JADs for screen design. Other companies don't want to spend the time designing screens with 15 people in a room. Instead they may use screen-painters and build the screen prototypes interactively with users in smaller groups.

Test Plans

It makes sense to define a project's test plan as early in the life cycle as possible. If you can get everyone to buy into building the test plan during the Design phase, you will save yourself headaches later on. In essence, you use a facilitated workshop to go back and revisit the requirements. In this way, you are saying to the participants:

> Here is the list of how this plan should work, based on the facilitated workshop that we had [several] months ago. Now we want to test the system, to see that it works correctly. (Edwards 1993)

Other Items

External design sessions can also identify what is needed for:

- Reports (What management reports do we need? And how will they look?)
- Application interfaces (Should we provide a direct feed to the accounting system?)
- Calculations, edits, validation rules, error messages (How exactly will the error messages be worded?)
- Hardware (How many more PCs do we need in the business areas?)
- Communications (How will we handle file transfers to the field?)
- Control, audit, and security rules (Who has access to the system?)
- Forms (What manual forms must be created?)

For more examples of JADs we have done for the Design phase, see Chapter 22.

Internal Design

For all you "tekkie-machos" out there, this is the JAD for you! This kind of session is not commonly done, but when it is, it goes like this: In the confines of a three- to five-day session you can wow everyone in the room with your knowledge of file structures, program languages, and database calls.

You can decide between batch and online functions, hardware configurations, and your favorite teleprocessing monitor. You can quibble over architecture and physical design, reusable code and capacity planning, as well as choose the most efficient access method or operating system. You can get excited about response time, transaction logs, and drivers. And you can create your very own backup and recovery plan. You can even talk in pseudocode if you want to. Why? Because there aren't any users in the room! (Or if there are, there'll only be a few.) The output from the session is an Internal Design Specifications document. From it, programmers can start program design and coding.

Code and Test Validation

Coding and testing are not typically "team" activities. However, some companies use JAD techniques to review and validate the accuracy of a program, module, or the test data. This JAD resembles the traditional "structured walkthroughs" that have been popular in the past. In a JAD-like session, the participants look for possible defects in the code or data and usually document the defects in terms of metrics. According to the Guide paper (we've never done one of these ourselves):

> One of the reviewers in the session will "read" the code, interpreting the logic and flow of the program. The reviewers will ensure that the code will deliver the function described in the requirements documents, that the code has been prepared in accordance with the shop standards, and will meet the requirements established in the architectural documents. The facilitator keeps track of the comments and metrics, and ensures that the tone of the session stays positive and constructive, and that the group remains a peer group. (Guide International Corp. 1989)

Code reviews? Metrics? Now that's impressive. However, we consider this type of JAD to be overkill at our shop. There is no time for holding JADs to review Cobol code here. We have five more systems to build, 20 more to enhance, we've just lost three programmers, and senior management moved the target date up six months—maybe in another lifetime!

Post Implementation Evaluation

JAD is also an excellent forum for post implementation review. This is the JAD we'd really love to do, but alas, no one seems to have the time to do this type either. In this kind of session, a post implementation review takes place *after* the system has been in production. The session measures the success of the new system from the point of view of both business and IS people. In other words, are they touting the system as the greatest thing since sliced bread or are they "trashing" it every chance they get?

In these reviews, the group rates various aspects of the system. For example, they might analyze (on a scale of 1 to 5) the following types of questions:

- How well were the management objectives realized (or not realized)?
- How well did the project meet each of its milestone dates and resource allocations?
- To what extent does the system provide each of the business functions?
- Are the interfaces in place and fully functional?
- Are backup procedures adequate?
- How well does the security comply with shop guidelines?
- How well were people trained? (This includes training for developers, operations staff, and users.)
- How productive were the developers (function points per work month)?
- How well does the system perform (average CPU utilization, run time, elapsed time, and response time)?
- How would you rate the quality of the system (number of defects per function point)?
- How complete is the documentation (for users, operations staff, and the system)?
- How confident are the users with the reliability and accuracy of the system?

Based on the responses to these questions, the user manager determines whether to accept the system into a maintenance state.

Maintenance

Can you use JAD for maintenance projects? You eventually change, fix, or enhance almost every system you build. Some of the changes are small and easy to implement, while others are complicated and time-consuming. You can hold a JAD for those changes that fit your JAD criteria; for example, projects across user areas, complex projects, or those with high visibility.

JAD sessions can especially help in maintenance projects because existing systems often lack sufficient documentation. To understand how the proposed enhancements impact the system, you need to gather information from many people. A JAD session with system experts can accomplish this by providing a forum for piecing together what the system is currently doing and determining how the changes can be made.

Furthermore, JAD helps ensure that the impacts of modifications are carefully analyzed before they are integrated into the existing system. A maintenance JAD project can reap the same benefits as a new development project. It also includes the same life cycle phases for project definition, analysis, design, and so on. Therefore, the standard JAD sessions used for the multimillion dollar project may be just as effective when applied to system modifications in a $250,000 effort.

Keep Your Phases Separate

As projects develop through the life cycle phases, it's not always clear which tasks go with which phases. It's easy to let parts of one phase crop up in another. For each session, try to keep your phases separate. This is especially true with the Analysis (Requirements) and Design phases. While in the midst of an analysis session, don't let the IS people launch into defining the data base calls. The tasks and techniques involved for each of these phases are completely different. Analysis deals with the *business*. Design deals with the *system*.

> If you separate analysis (the *what*) from design (the *how*), facilitators can [capture] the *what* fairly quickly. (Rush 1993)

Furthermore, these phase differences affect who is in the session. Analysis sessions require different people than design sessions do. So, remember to customize the participation list from one phase to the next.

Does It Matter Which Methodology You Use?

The most popular methodologies today are structured analysis and design, information engineering, and object-oriented systems analysis. Each has its own structure, vocabulary, diagrams, and rules. You can adapt JAD to any of these approaches. If your company adheres to a strict systems development methodology, then align your JADs accordingly. For example, if you adopt James Martin's Information Engineering (IE) methodology, your JAD sessions might support the IE components of information strategy planning, business area analysis, and business system design.

Where Should You Focus Your JAD Efforts?

As you've seen, JAD techniques benefit many areas of the life cycle. You can use them for high-level corporate planning as well as for detailed data and process modeling. But beware of the pitfalls of trying to do too much too soon. Depending on the expertise of your JAD staff, you may not be able to lead sessions that do everything from process decomposition to detailed data modeling. Don't be too ambitious and then wind up with a bad model because of an inexperienced facilitator. It's hard to recover your reputation after a JAD failure. Gain some success with the more traditional JADS (such as defining screens and data element definitions) and then extend JADs into other life-cycle phases later on.

JAD supports many different types of projects. For example, if you want to improve the competitive market position of your business, the project lies within strategic planning. If the purpose of the project is to give users more access to business information, the project lies within requirements. If you want to build an integrated application system, the project scope is in design and code and test validation. However, focus less on which category the project falls into and more on meeting your project objectives and deliverables. Your job is to figure out where JAD can be used anywhere in the life cycle to produce a higher quality deliverable in less time.

A JAD OF MANY PHASES

In this section, we describe a project that covers several phases of the systems development life cycle. It begins in the Project Definition phase and extends into Requirements. It also includes a package evaluation (using the Kepner-Tregoe technique).

The Problems

In our business (life insurance), we administer ongoing periodic payments (to our customers) resulting from settlement options on life insurance contracts, annuity contracts, and pension contracts. Provident Mutual and its subsidiaries issue numerous checks and electronic fund transfers.

Periodic payments was a decentralized process, which impacted five areas of the company in two geographic locations. To handle these repetitive payments, we had an old periodic payments system (running on an IBM mainframe), written in the 1970s. This system calculated benefits; processed payments upon deaths and surrenders; and handled reserves, disbursements, correspondence, and management reports. We also had a user-written PC system for our individual annuity products and an old Wang system for our subsidiary company in Delaware.

Various problems existed in processing periodic payments. When analyzing the business processes, we found a lot of pieces of paper taking some rather complex routes. Also, the existing system had no online capabilities. Consequently, replying to customer inquiries often took up to 24 hours because people had to search through many file cabinets filled with payment cards. Our objective was to centralize and automate the entire periodic payments process.

This was an ideal project to facilitate because it impacted so many areas of the company. The impacted areas were:

- Benefit Payments (in Philadelphia)
- Benefit Payments (in Delaware)
- Group Pensions
- Individual Qualified Plans
- Individual Annuities

The project was organized into two separate JAD sessions: one session to define the project and the requirements, and a second to select the software package. The following describes each session.

Session 1: Project Definition and Requirements

The ingredients for this session were:

12   users (ranging from managers to clerical) representing the five business areas involved in periodic payments
 3   IS project managers
 1   facilitator
 1   scribe
 5   observers

To prepare for the session, the facilitator, Alan, sat with each of the five areas doing periodic payments. He observed work flow and documented the processes. For example, for the Benefit Payments area, he identified processes for:

- Disbursements
- New business
- Partial surrenders
- Voided checks
- Stopped payments
- Death (yes, he even analyzed the *death process*)

Alan used a graphical technique for documenting work flow. Several years ago, our Human Resources department brought in a Towers Perrin consultant to help with our first business process reengineering project. They taught us this method for documenting work flow that identifies

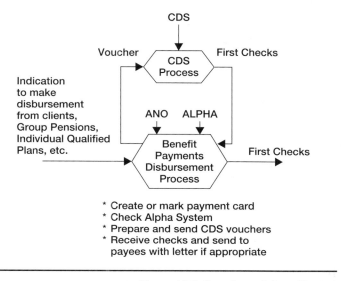

Figure 18.2 Sample work flow diagram.

processes and breaks them into tasks. The users have found these easy to understand. Figure 18.2 shows a sample of one business process diagram from this project.

Alan compiled all these business processes into the Working Document, along with the purpose, scope, objectives, high-level business functions, open issues, and various assumptions.

In the session, Alan guided the group through finalizing the business processes. The best part was that each of the five business areas could see how the other areas handled periodic payments. This helped merge views and created a common perspective that would help when the time came to plan for centralization.

At times, keeping everyone focused was a challenge. When the actuaries started talking about the subtle details of valuation and reserve calculations, the session plummeted into momentary breakdowns, since actuaries are the only living beings who thrive on these details.

Centralization became a big issue. One of the five business areas already handled periodic payments on a PC. This area is run by a tekkie manager who is free-spirited, competent, and had no interest in paying the cost of purchasing a centralized package. He already managed quite well with his own homegrown PC system. Having not resolved the issue in this session, the group carried it through the next session. In the end, however, the cost benefit analysis showed that the expense of adding this additional area to the centralized system was minimal compared to the increased control that centralization would yield. Even with that, the issue was resolved only via a mandate from senior management.

Another controversial issue was, who would own this system? There weren't a lot of volunteers claiming ownership for a system that crossed five major departments. This migrated into another issue: How would cost for the centralized system be allocated across user areas?

By the end of the session, the 17 participants had reached consensus on the requirements.

Session 2: Package Evaluation

With requirements defined, we were now ready to select a package to meet all these needs. This session involved the same group as the first session along with some additional micro support people.

Here are the steps we performed to select the package. The first four steps involved various members of the group, then the final one was in a formal JAD session.

1. *Prioritize the criteria.* We were able to sort out the criteria based on the requirements gathered in the first JAD session. We did not assign weights to them until the final session (step 5). A major issue arising early on was whether the package would run on a mainframe or a PC. This debate continued through all aspects of our package evaluation.

2. *Gather preliminary information.* Alan probed the periodic payment market through various software digests. He pored over vendor literature. He called one of the VP's contacts who had just been through a similar evaluation. Alan's analysis reduced the package selection to two alternatives. The other packages were eliminated for various reasons. For example, one was nixed because it was a full administration system with a periodic payments component that could not be separated out.

   Next, Alan made conference calls to several names on the vendors' reference lists. Some were with IS managers who had recently implemented the packages. Others were with companies who had been using the packages for years. Each conference call lasted a good hour. (Alan had three pages of detailed questions to ask.) After each one we felt "Yes, that iced the cake, this is the vendor to go with." Our certainty lasted until the next phone call when we contacted a user of the other package. Then, the pendulum swung and we felt that the second package was now the best choice. Although these conference calls were useful, they mostly brought to light how vendors only give you the names of their most satisfied customers.

3. *Send out the RFP.* Alan and members of the group prepared an 80-question Request for Proposal (RFP) and sent it to the two vendors.

4. *Hold product demos.* To explore the look and feel of the packages, Alan set up a model office environment to simulate how the business units could handle periodic payments in the real world. He set up some test data and let the users loose. We were somewhat set back when one of the vendors refused to send us the software without their over-the-shoulder supervision. So we resorted to having that vendor present a two-day demo and work session. It wasn't quite the same, but it had to do.

5. *Select the best alternative.* Everything that we researched, compiled, and evaluated came together for the JAD session. Alan compiled a fact sheet that showed at a glance some statistics for each package. This spreadsheet included such items as the packages' programming languages, the size of the vendors' support teams and customer bases, and license and maintenance fees. In our session, we dealt with two questions:

- Which package would we purchase?
- And would it run in a mainframe or PC LAN environment?

We did a Kepner-Tregoe (KT) evaluation. For each question, we used the white board to list criteria, assign weights and score these criteria, add up the scores, and make the decisions. For details on the KT process, see Chapter 14. Meanwhile the following sections describe how the group handled these decisions.

The Package

For the package decision, there was a significant spread between the two choices. The winner came out on top because the system:

- Was easier to use.
- Had more vendor support.
- Had been around longer and served a broader marketplace.
- Handled payment and pension administration better.
- Had company-level security.
- Had better archival capabilities.
- Had better online help.

The Platform

For the mainframe-versus-PC LAN decision, the results were close (only a 10-point spread). In the end, we went with the LAN because:

- LAN applications tend to be easier to use, offering a GUI interface and easy-to-create ad hoc reports.

Criteria	Weight	Vendor 1 Mainframe (Score)	Vendor 1 LAN (Score)	Vendor 2 LAN (Score)	Vendor 1 Mainframe (Weighted)	Vendor 1 LAN (Weighted)	Vendor 2 LAN (Weighted)
Ease of use	5	4	3	2	20	15	10
GUI interface	3	0	4	2	0	12	6
Online help and screen error correction	4	4	3	1	16	12	4
Ad hoc reporting	3	2	4	5	6	12	15
Company level security	4	5	5	1	20	20	4

Various business functions

Criteria	Weight	Vendor 1 Mainframe (Score)	Vendor 1 LAN (Score)	Vendor 2 LAN (Score)	Vendor 1 Mainframe (Weighted)	Vendor 1 LAN (Weighted)	Vendor 2 LAN (Weighted)
Ease of maintenance	4	4	4	4	16	16	16
Screen tailoring	3	5	5	1	15	15	3
Scope of customization	4	3	3	3	12	12	12
IS learning curve	1	5	2	3	5	2	3
Productivity gain (PC tools, multi-tasking)	3	0	5	3	0	15	9
Short-term risk	3	5	2	3	15	6	9
Long-term risk	4	3	4	2	12	16	8
Cost	3	2	3	4	6	9	12
Total					280	293	225

Figure 18.3 Deciding between two software packages.

- The long-term risks were less. The market is moving in the PC LAN direction and vendor support of mainframe packages is diminishing.

- LAN applications allow people to work in multiple applications at the same time, thus increasing productivity.

Figure 18.3 shows the "boardtalk" that evolved as the group analyzed this decision.

So how did this project turn out? Just when we were ready to sign on the dotted line with the vendor of choice, a new candidate product entered the mix. This new package used the latest state-of-the-art, object-oriented, GUI-based, LAN-based architecture and appeared (at first) to be less costly. The JAD team re-evaluated the alternatives and documented the new costs and benefits. The final decision was to go with the original choice.

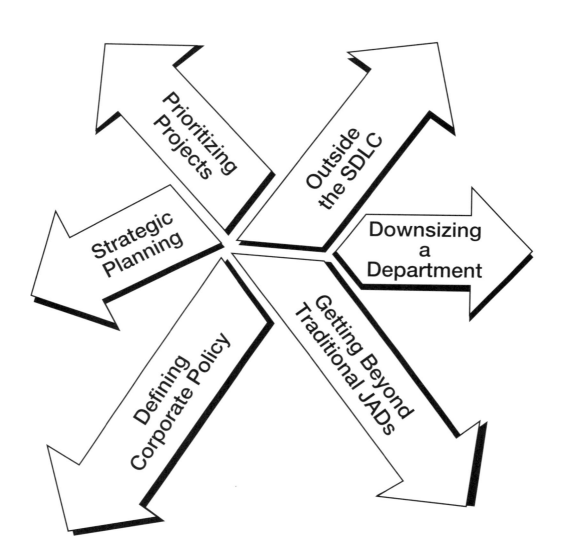

NINETEEN ▷▶▶▶

BREAKING OUT OF THE LIFE CYCLE

Traditionally, JAD supports the up-front part of the systems development life cycle. And it has served well in that role. But as JAD has matured, companies have made productivity gains by escaping the boundaries of the life cycle, and using JAD methods for other endeavors as well.

In our survey to several facilitators' groups, we asked, "What do you use facilitated sessions for (besides application development)?" Here are some of the replies:

- Ad campaign evaluations
- Brainstorming
- Defining company policy
- Developing corporate goals
- Employee evaluations
- Mergers
- Morale survey feedback sessions
- Planning for disaster recovery

- Planning technology strategy
- Preparing mission statements
- Preparing standards and guidelines
- Prioritizing projects
- Resolving conflict and settling disputes
- Restructuring organizations

In other words, you can facilitate just about anything that involves a group of people with an objective. Nor are there any constraints on the type of business your session can address. Facilitation cuts across all endeavors. One facilitator, for example, described a session that designed a community model for dealing with drinking and driving.

STRATEGIC PLANNING

Facilitated sessions provide an excellent forum for establishing a company's mission, vision, and strategic direction. You can guide groups in defining corporate, business unit, and department strategic plans. In this type of session, you ask those probing questions like: "What will our business look like in five years?", "What information do we need to make strategic decisions?", and "What does this company really want to be when it grows up?"

Depending on the level of the audience, the session may define the company's global architecture, identify directions that will give the company that "competitive edge," and rescope business-area boundaries. Based on the results of the session, senior management determines which projects (including systems development projects) belong in the work queue. For example, suppose an insurance company's mission is to provide "state-of-the-art" service to its customers. How can they do this? If the group agrees to give the customers 24-hour dial-up phone access to policy information, then as a result of the session, a project may appear to define requirements for a voice-activated information system for customer queries.

Good strategic planning sessions can also reduce IS backlogs. These sessions force senior management to reexamine priorities and objectives and identify those applications most necessary to meet business goals. Andrews and Leventhal (JAD consultants) describe one organization that held a two-day JAD workshop and "was able to cut its application maintenance backlog forty percent and dismantle an application maintenance group of ten people and reassign these individuals to new development projects." (Andrews and Leventhal 1993).

Good techniques to use in strategic planning sessions include brainstorming, nominal group technique, out-of-the-box thinking, affinity analysis, force field analysis—all described in Chapter 13—as well as the Kepner-Tregoe technique described in Chapter 14.

Deliverables of strategic planning sessions can include such things as an enterprise or business model; a document that defines the organization's goals and objectives for expenses, revenue, product lines, and marketing; or a list of prioritized projects. This type of session usually includes senior executives from the business area you are addressing. Because of the far-reaching and significant implications of the session outcome, the pressure is on to accomplish the objectives.

Now for some examples of using JAD in nonsystem development projects. Here are three stories.

DOWNSIZING A DEPARTMENT

Downsizing has been an all too familiar reality these years. One corporation faced the challenge of having to downsize a Human Resources department from 400 people to 150. That's not an easy task. So what did they do? They called a facilitator.

Carol is the facilitator they brought in for the job. Her mission was to guide the group through determining which 150 people would remain in the department and, consequently, which 250 would go. She was to do this with a group of 15 newly-appointed managers who had never before worked together as a team.

The Tools

Before the session, the 400 employees filled out a short resume. At the same time, the new management team defined the "target" positions, functions, and skills required. (Some of these positions were new.) Carol compiled these loosely defined functions on an Excel® spreadsheet. She gave every participant a copy and also projected it via a screen projection unit so everyone could see it. Figure 19.1 shows how Carol set up the spreadsheet.

In the session, the group focused particularly on the "New Team" column. For clarity, Carol sorted the data on this column. Excel sorts by numbers first, then text, and finally blanks. To make this sorting work for the task at hand, the group used certain conventions when adding information to this column. Figure 19.2 shows these conventions.

The Session

The group met every morning for two weeks. For each business unit, Carol guided the managers through the evolving process of matching people's skills with the new positions. At the end of each session, Carol re-sorted the spreadsheet by the "New Team" column so that managers could see who

Name	Current Dept	Old Grade	New Team	New Grade	New Unit	Notes
Sara Balderston	Staffing	6	1		Line Support	
Rita Cinelli	Payroll	12	1		Corporate Support	
Meredith Gail	Staffing	10	1		Corporate support	
Angie Goida	Benefits	15	2		Flex Benefits	Team manager
Judy Inslicht	Benefits	12	2		Flex Benefits	
Melissa Lynn	Benefits	10	2		401K	
Dulcie Schmidt	Payroll	8	3		Payroll	
Marilyn Segal	Payroll	10	3		Payroll	
Jean Willis	Education	10	4		Compensation	
George Hoag	Compensation	14	4		Compensation	
Marjory Spencer	Education	12	5		Education	
Anne Barnett	Payroll	10	*			Candidate for 3
Lynn Hervey	Education	15	*			Candidate for 1, 5
Karen Leweke	Benefits	12	P			Placed
Susan Huish	Benefits	8	R			Retired
Chris Barusic	Compensation	15	T			Transferred
Carolyn Moore	Payroll	10	T			Transferred
Cathy Kluckholn	Education	12				

Figure 19.1 Spreadsheet for a downsizing project.

This entry . . .	Designated . . .
Numbers	The unit the person was assigned to in Human Resources. For example, Unit 5.
*	Units are considering the person. (The interested unit shows in the "Notes" column.)
Letters	The person has been placed outside the department. For example: R—Retired T—Transferred P—Placed
Blank	The person has not yet been placed, and no one has expressed interest.

Figure 19.2 Adding information to the "New Team" column.

was assigned to their units so far. This way they could evaluate how their units were coming along, which skill sets were met, and who was still available to fill the open spots.

The Issues

The thrust of the session was matching job functions with people's skills. At first glance, this might seem like a competitive endeavor of seeing who can grab the best people first. But that's not how it turned out. Sometimes managers selected people for their well-known talents, only to find upon further analysis that their skills were best utilized somewhere else.

We asked Carol how she dealt with conflicts between managers contending for the same people. She said:

> When these conflicts arose, we discussed which match would be best for the company and the person. Also, sometimes managers interviewed people who had opportunities for more than one placement. The process was very fact-based. Conclusions were logically drawn.

As the session drew to a close, only a few open positions remained. The group methodically considered every unmatched person. Those familiar with the person being discussed described how the skills of that person might apply to the open spot or where they might have skills critical for a specific unit.

The Conclusion

Have you ever looked at an organization chart and asked, "How did these people ever end up there?" Consider how jobs are often filled. Sometimes the decision is made with haste and without really taking to heart if a particular person's skill set matches the functions required. Carol's approach, on the other hand, offered a structured and objective way of resolving a very difficult situation.

DEFINING A CORPORATE POLICY

One financial company needed to come up with a new corporate policy and procedures for Purchasing and Accounts Payable (see Figure 19.3).

What were the problems that led to this project? Well, to put it bluntly, people were breaking the rules! For example, managers ordered PCs on their own and agents ordered furniture for their offices from whomever they pleased. Therefore, the company did not always benefit from the quantity and corpo-

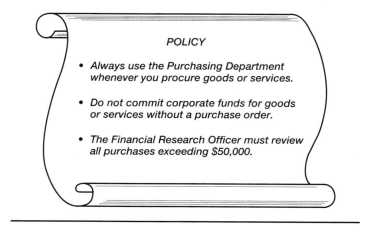

POLICY

- *Always use the Purchasing Department whenever you procure goods or services.*

- *Do not commit corporate funds for goods or services without a purchase order.*

- *The Financial Research Officer must review all purchases exceeding $50,000.*

Figure 19.3

rate discounts that the Purchasing department could obtain. People were not getting the most for their money. This applied to everything from purchasing cardboard boxes, to leasing vehicles, to acquiring consultants' time.

Because of a lack of centralization, people had a tough time figuring out the status of pending requisitions and purchase orders. Managers often went over their authorization limits. And the lack of controls created the potential for paying bills twice.

A project emerged to centralize all purchasing and accounts payable activities. The goal was to automate the tracking of everything from requisitioning the goods and services to paying the vendors. The company needed to look at the entire process from filling out the "red req" for a box of pencils to paying the vendor for those pencils, and all the steps in between. This involved not only the requisitions, but also purchase orders, vouchers, invoices, and receiving documents.

The project scope was broad. It included the parent company and all its subsidiaries. Furthermore, it dealt with an issue upon which the whole project pivoted. That is, would senior management support the centralization (without exception) that the JAD group recommended? This is a case where management commitment was critical.

The People

The session included:

10 Users

5 Users on call

2 Co-leaders (while one facilitated, the other scribed)

There were absolutely no participants from IS. After all, the JAD team was designing a *policy* not a *system*. (One IS person attended, but he was really a *user* representing the purchasing needs of IS.)

Because this project affected both Purchasing and Accounts Payable, there were two executive sponsors (the Executive VP of Corporate and the VP of Finance).

Defining the Procedures

Going into the session, the JAD team had a Working Document filled with 10 pages of already defined procedures in flow-chart form provided by the auditors. There were procedures for ordering goods and services, for handling standing purchase orders, and for ordering supplies from Boise Cascade. (The facilitator had to explain to one participant that Boise Cascade was an office supplier, not a dishwashing detergent from Idaho). The document also had 24 open issues.

The users who attended this session did not feel comfortable with flow charts (an example of a group being oriented more verbally than graphically). Consequently, the scribe converted the flow-charted procedures into a playscript. This "stage-play" format involves describing procedures in terms of *who does what when*. It brought life to an otherwise convoluted work flow. (Systemation 1986)

Figure 19.4 shows the before and after of a small segment of the procedures. These procedures and the open issues drove the session. By looking at the procedures, the team could see where they needed to apply some strong rules. And the issues evolved into policy statements.

Turning Issues into Policies

To begin with, there were the obvious issues like:

- How do you handle purchases from the field? For example, how will Agency 99 go about ordering a calculator and paying for it?
- How do you handle differing prices? For example, what if the invoice says $90, and the purchase order says $85?
- How should invoices be coordinated for payment of cross-departmental publications such as the *Wall Street Journal?*
- What do you do when you order 25 staplers and you only receive 22?
- And of course, what would be the destinations for the green, white, pink, yellow, and goldenrod copies of the purchase orders?

Also, there were complex issues to resolve. For example, a big issue (which actually turned into a controversy) arose: Will IS have a separate

BEFORE:

AFTER:

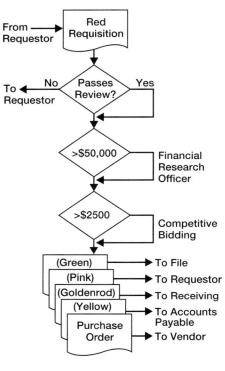

Who	Does What
Requestor	1. Sends an authorized red requisition to the Purchasing department.
Purchasing	1. Reviews the request for completeness, accuracy, and validity. 2. Contacts the requestor if there are any questions. 3. Refers purchases of $50,000 or more to the Financial Research Officer. 4. Gets competitive bids, when appropriate. 5. Creates the purchase order. 6. Sends the PO (the original white copy to the vendor, the goldenrod copy to Receiving, the yellow copy to Accounts Payable, and the pink copy to the requestor.) 7. Files the green copy of the PO.

Figure 19.4 From flow chart to playscript.

purchasing policy? IS felt that no one else had the expertise to deal with purchasing such things as mainframe equipment and LAN software. (Is this a case of the "electronic priesthood"?) At any rate, IS had always made their own purchasing decisions in this arena and they wanted to keep it that way.

With a little bit of negotiating (and a lot of mandating), the issue was resolved: IS would still decide which mainframe to buy and they would still review and approve all invoices, but all the paperwork would now go through Purchasing. And so the policy was written.

Another issue related to enforcement. How do you punish the guilty? For example, what does the Finance department do when they receive an invoice for a CD player and they have no record of the order? The outcome was a policy of strict enforcement. The group decided that for policy infractions, Purchasing would "tattletale" to a department administrator or a division head, depending on the violator's rank in the company and the amount of the infraction. And again, the policy was written.

The Climactic Finale

In the end, the participants talked about rolling out the policy (as opposed to rolling out the system). Classes were planned to train people how to initiate orders, set up standing POs, and authorize expenses. And people were told what would happen if they tried to circumvent the policies.

To show the company's commitment to the policy, the users turned the final JAD document into an official booklet. This was prepared using a desktop publishing tool with fancy fonts, prominent heading levels, and bold highlighting to emphasize the most stringent rules. This policy booklet was distributed to all supervisors and higher (in other words, to anyone who makes purchases).

Two years later it was reissued with very few changes. It seems the JAD process helped to create a good policy the first time.

PRIORITIZING PROJECTS

In this endeavor, we assisted the head of Business Systems Planning in prioritizing all the systems development projects for the coming year. We sent out a questionnaire to the key users who submit projects to IS. To help them identify their projects, we included such mind-jogging questions as:

- Which systems produce incorrect information?
- What information is not available to you online?
- How can we improve the quality of your reports or statements?
- Which systems should we replace or reengineer?
- Which business processes do you wish you had more control over?
- Do you know of any business functions in your area that other insurance companies perform more effectively due to automation?
- What do you wish you were able to do in your area that you cannot do now?

After we received the completed questionnaires, we sorted the responses by project theme. For example, there were projects for tax laws, agent correspondence, and online policy changes. (We even had a category for blue-sky projects.) Then we eliminated the redundancies by combining similar requests and we assigned a unique number to each project.

Most of the user areas had less than 10 projects each. The Operations department, on the other hand, submitted almost 50 projects. There was no way IS could do all that work in one year. Therefore, we held two JAD sessions to define and prioritize the projects for this area. The sessions included all the user managers from Operations; the executive sponsor attended to provide a broader company perspective. In the first session, the JAD team:

- Described each project.
- Defined the benefits (both financial and nonfinancial) of each project, as well as the consequences of not doing them.
- Identified the key players impacted by each project.
- Nixed the out-of-the-question projects.
- Determined which projects depended on other projects.

Eileen (the analyst and scribe) captured this information on forms designed specifically for this session. She then spent a month gathering additional information that would be required by the IS Steering Committee later on. Eileen compiled all this information on the standard corporate planning forms.

Then Eileen sent each manager a list of all the projects and asked them to rank these projects consecutively, 1 through 45. The votes were tabulated and, based on the average of all responses, Eileen produced a preliminary list of the projects in priority order. To prepare for the second JAD session, Eileen created magnetics with all the project names and put them on the board in the same priority order.

In the second JAD session, the team reviewed the planning forms for accuracy and completeness. They tweaked them where necessary. Then came the fun part. The facilitator unveiled the results of the project rankings (which had been hidden on the white board behind the projection screen until this moment). Seeing all the projects ranked in their totality, the team now bargained and bickered until everybody was happy with the priority order. They made those critical, final switches that would affect which projects got done the next year.

The session produced a list of projects ranked in order of priority. This list was merged with the projects from other departments and submitted to the IS Steering Committee for approval.

Rapid
Application
Development

Participatory
Design

Empowering
Groups

TWENTY ▷ ▶ ▶ ▶

SON OF JAD: RELATED METHODOLOGIES

As they say, "Success has many fathers, while failure is an orphan." So it is with JAD. Over the past several years, many related processes have come into use. Some *refer* to JAD, some *derive* from JAD, while others make JAD a part of them. For example, we now have RAD, PD, AJAD, and E-JAD (E-Gad!). Both AJAD and E-JAD have already been covered. This chapter covers some of JAD's other relatives.

RAPID APPLICATION DEVELOPMENT

Question: What can blow away your backlogs, bring back credibility to your IS department, create satisfied users, and happens to rhyme with JAD? Some say the answer to this question is RAD™. Others say that RAD is just another fad, passing in the night like hula hoops, fondue pots, and S & L takeovers.

Before passing judgment on the status of RAD, let's investigate a bit. Rapid Application Development, or RAD, is a life-cycle process first formalized at

I saw a lad.
His name was Brad.
He carried a book.
The book said "JAD".

I took the book
and read a tad.
The book said RAD
was just a fad

I told this to Brad
and he got mad.
And I asked the lad,
"Why are you sad?"

"If RAD's a fad,
then we've been had!"
said Brad.
Too bad.
—Bruce Schwartz

DuPont in the mid-1980s under the name RIPP (Rapid Iterative Production Prototyping). (Kerr and Hunter, 1994) It was popularized by software engineering guru, James Martin. In the 1990s, it became known as a method for developing applications better, faster, and cheaper. As Martin says:

> A top criteria for IS must be that it never interferes with business's ability to seize a competitive opportunity. *Speed is essential.* (Martin 1990)

To accomplish this goal, RAD combines five popular application development techniques, each of which improves productivity in its own right. To truly realize the full benefits of RAD, you use these techniques in concert:

Rapid Prototyping. Prototyping is at the core of RAD. Users can immediately navigate the proposed menus, try out screens, simulate interfaces, and examine reports. They can then feed back their critiques into the prototype builder and create a revised prototype. This iterative process (which usually continues three or four times) enables users to see the results of their efforts as the application develops. They are no longer in the shadows during the project's Design and Construction phases. The prototype becomes the final system.

Integrated CASE Tools (I-CASE). RAD works best with the most powerful I-CASE tools you can buy. These tools must be able to detect errors and inconsistencies in the design specifications and generate bug-free code automatically from the data models, process models, and business rules. It is also important that the CASE tool and code generator be able to accept the final code from the prototype and reverse engineer it back into the CASE tool. The central repository stores all source code, data bases, and documentation.

SWAT (Specialists With Advanced Tools) Teams. RAD focuses on training small teams of highly motivated analysts in the use of I-CASE tools. These teams analyze the design, generate code, test, and continuously improve the system.

Martin suggests putting the SWAT team in their own private area close to real users. He even suggests depriving them of access to the telephone (although E-mail is acceptable). After all, "when highly creative people doing complex work are interrupted by a phone call, it takes them at least 15 minutes to return to productive work afterwards." (Martin 1990)

Interactive JAD. Rather than using the traditional white board and scribe approach, RAD captures requirements and specifications using the I-CASE tool *in the session*. Users provide design specifications, which skilled analysts enter into the tool. Then the group works together in an iterative process to finalize the design. The design stored in the repository is the basis for the Construction phase.

Timeboxing. To prevent "scope creep," RAD imposes strict limits on how much time to spend on defining requirements, building prototypes, and generating code. Getting something into production fast is the primary RAD goal. The RAD approach focuses on results, not process. The speed of delivery is more important than technical excellence. "Fail fast, win fast" is the RAD motto. It's better to have a system with the basic functions *today*, than to wait two and a half years for a system with all the bells and whistles. Therefore, a typical fixed period, or "timebox," (anywhere from the preferred 60 days to 120 days) is imposed on the team to complete an application. To accomplish this, users must prioritize requirements and agree to incorporate changes into later releases. If the scope of the system cannot be implemented within the timebox, the project is rescoped.

Should all projects use RAD? Actually, RAD is best suited for quick applications where seeing a short-term benefit is important. For example, a typical project might be "one with no more than 15 entity types, 25 business processes, 20 application screens, 10 users, and most important, a stable, well-defined business area." (Martin 1990) However, RAD has seen success in larger projects as well.

Phases of the RAD Life Cycle

RAD has four phases: Requirements Planning, User Design, Construction, and Cutover. The following sections describe each phase.

Phase 1. Requirements Planning

In this phase, selected high-level IS people and top corporate managers attend a three-day Joint Requirements Planning (JRP) workshop to brainstorm the system requirements. These business executives examine their problems, goals, critical success factors, and strategic opportunities. The session identifies the business functions and their priorities, the benefits of each function, and the system scope. It may deliver high-level data and process models using the I-CASE tool.

Phase 2. User design

Using I-CASE tools and prototyping, the RAD team completes the detailed Analysis and Design phases in the following two JAD workshop sessions:

- In a five-day session, the RAD team defines detailed entity-relationship diagrams, process decomposition diagrams, and screen and report layouts for each business function. The team also develops and refines working prototypes for each critical system component. Before this session, the users should, if possible, receive training on understanding CASE diagrams. In this way, they can add value to the process.
- Then, in a two-day session, the RAD team finalizes the design.

After these sessions, the SWAT team measures the complexity of each prototyped business function and estimates how long it will take to build. Then the team determines the number of functions they can complete in the remaining timebox.

Phase 3. Construction

The SWAT team completes the detailed design, generates the program code and data bases, and tests the system. The team makes extensive use of

CASE tools, code generators, and the repository. The SWAT team must complete the application within the timebox. However, if near the end of the Construction phase this seems unlikely, the team defers the low-priority functions. The target date does not move!

Phase 4. Cutover

In this phase, you complete the testing, prepare the documentation, train the users, and prepare for the typical culture shock of adapting to a new application.

RAD Roles

As you can see in the description of its phases, RAD requires the same participants as does its close cousin, JAD, along with a few more. The following summarizes the "few more":

- *User review board.* This team of user experts tests and critiques the system after construction and sends back modifications to the SWAT team for rework. This cycle repeats until the prototype is acceptable. In the end, the user review board decides whether the system meets the users' needs and whether it should be moved into production. They sign off on an actual I-CASE design rather than 200 pages of hardcopy documentation.
- *Scribe.* You train the RAD scribe to use the I-CASE tool to capture design specifications. This person is usually an IS analyst.
- *SWAT team.* The small team of three or four IS developers is highly trained in the use of I-CASE tools and the RAD methodology. Large projects may require several teams to work concurrently.
- *Data modeling expert.* Each RAD project has a data modeling guru assigned to it. This expert consults on all data models across the project.

Other IS analysts may participate in the RAD process as well. For example, these might include human factors experts or even repository managers, depending on the size of the project.

Some Measurements of RAD Success

IS organizations today achieve only about eight function points per person-month using the traditional life cycle. (See Figure 20.1.) If you can believe this chart, RAD proponents are realizing from 100 to 200 function points per person-month during the Construction phase. (Mimno 1991)

	Productivity	*Cost*
Some large government projects	2	$1500
Average for traditional COBOL life cycle	8	800
3GL life cycle with productivity aids	13	500
Well-managed 4GL CASE life cycle	35	250
Reasonable target for RAD life cycle	100	100
Some of the best examples of RAD	200	50

Note: Productivity in function points per person-month. Cost in dollars per function point.

Reprinted with permission from the January 1991 issue of the *American Programmer* journal, published by Cutter Information Corp., Arlington, MA 02174-5539

Figure 20.1 Productivity comparisons among development techniques.

Imperial's Esso Petroleum Canada division used RAD to develop a mission-critical system for its retail outlets. They deployed the system in three phases. In Phase 1, they completed the business area analysis and developed a working prototype in less than 120 days. In Phase 2, they completed external and internal design in 150 days. In Phase 3 they built, tested, and moved the system into production—all in only 70 days!

> When done, the system consisted of 500,000 lines of Cobol II, 45 user procedures, and 19 screens. (Martin 1990)

James Kerr and Richard Hunter (RAD experts) believe:

> RAD is not magic, and—like any major organizational change—it's not cheap or especially easy. *The great advantage of RAD is that it works.* It has been measured in dozens of organizations, with hundreds of teams, and it has consistently produced order-of-magnitude improvements in quality and productivity time after time. (Kerr and Hunter 1994)

Why Isn't Everyone Radding?

If RAD is as good as they say, then why aren't more companies using it? It is because most companies that try RAD do not see an improvement in development time. As W. Burry Foss (Senior Associate at the management consulting practice of International Systems Services Corp.) declares:

> Rapid application development methods can speed systems delivery by as much as 1,300%. But most companies get 0% improvement because they talk about changing tools, not techniques . . . . RAD isn't about fancy automated tools but about significantly rethinking development methodologies and management techniques. (Foss 1993)

To make RAD work, companies must be willing to shake up their existing culture. They must reexamine and restructure their work processes. In particular, they must endorse the following.

Incremental Delivery of System Components

Introducing the RAD life cycle to IS professionals accustomed to doing things the older and slower ways is a little scary. RAD is revolutionary. First of all, you must accept piecemeal delivery of your application system. The first component may come out in three to four months and the rest of the system in three-to six-month intervals.

The traditional approach of delivering every system module at the same time has its drawbacks. You can probably recall several projects in your own company that failed to meet target dates. Perhaps some were as much as 18 months overdue before final delivery, right? And probably many of the original specs (established at the project's outset) were obsolete by then. RAD tries to deliver a system that meets user requirements as best as possible at the time the system goes into production. It's just that the delivery is likely to be in pieces.

Intensive Training for IS Developers

Why does training always seem to work its way out of the IS budget? Does management really think that spending millions of dollars on hardware and sophisticated software tools will automatically guarantee a faster development cycle?

Contrary to what you might expect, using state-of-the-art tools can actually delay a project's delivery time. The developers have to get over an initial learning curve before they can be productive. So, if it's RAD you're endorsing, you can't skimp on training dollars here. (Especially since you probably don't have the right experts on board to make RAD work.) The developers need training in I-CASE, data modeling, prototyping, information engineering methodologies, and JAD. And your management must be willing to accept that productivity improvements may not necessarily come in the short term. RAD results are long-term.

JAD is at the Core of RAD

RAD success stories have one thing in common: The JAD process is instrumental in the project's success. Here are two examples:

A Houston division of a $104 billion energy company completed the Construction phase for a 12-month project in seven months using RAD. The Houston company did not even use all of the RAD components on this project. In fact, they did not use any leading-edge CASE tools. They used Cobol technology with some assistance from an application generator and concentrated most of their efforts on making the JAD process work.

Travelers Insurance Company had a similar experience. Before using RAD, their average application took 18 months to get into production. Their IS department turned to RAD to solve these delivery problems. Although they used some automated development tools, in the end, the tools were secondary to the productivity gains realized through the team-based JAD decision-making approach. As Foss concludes:

> Face it: Old habits die hard. But RAD can help to significantly increase development productivity, as long as IS groups approach it as a new way to manage development, concentrating on teamwork . . . . Otherwise, no software tool, no matter how advanced, is going to make any difference. (Foss 1993)

Bob Spurgeon (Director of CASE Enablement Services at Andersen Consulting in Chicago) also takes a more cautious view of RAD. He says:

> RAD is being sold as the latest silver bullet. But most people would be better off seeing it as just one more tool to pull out of their bag. (Baum 1992)

PARTICIPATORY DESIGN

Participatory Design (PD) comes to us from Scandinavia. This systems development methodology encourages even stronger user involvement than JAD, emphasizes mutual learning (between users and designers), and is much less structured.

A Typical PD Session

Let's peek in on a typical PD workshop. The session is oddly devoid of managers. The participants are mostly workers, that is, the people who will actually use the system. (Some sessions include managers; others do not include them at all! Sometimes the managers meet later in separate sessions.) Instead of a "facilitator," a "designer" guides the activities. The designer not only leads the session but also gives technical advice. To prepare for the session, the designer has immersed himself in the job functions by working as a clerk in the department where the new system will be.

Prototyping is the main session event. But unlike the prototyping we are used to, the participants actively use the prototype in a PD session. They "play" with the system, fumble with it, rework it, and learn from it. In the same way that children use props to simulate various environments, a PD session uses cardboard props and mock-ups to further simulate the workplace. As industrial designers have put it, "the artifact is more tangible than the idea."

What about visual aids? Blackboards are filled with writing, while index cards and Post-it notes cover the walls. As with many facilitators, most PD leaders find automated design tools work okay outside the session, but find them not agile enough to use in the session.

The group continues with these hands-on, learn-by-doing activities. They critique work flow, create what-if scenarios, and discuss the resources needed to implement various alternatives. They might also use storyboarding, video, and brainstorming. All the while, they keep their focus on the workplace, not the system.

Less Structure, More Creativity

In place of structure, improvising and creativity are stressed. And what about deadlines for this project? Well, when it's done, it's done. The focus is on goals, not time frames.

Can you imagine the luxury of having no deadlines? Or even being able to say, "Well Mr. Vice President, you see we can't really tell you how long this project will take, it all depends on when we finish our tasks." More than likely we'd be given the boot, right along with our approach.

What Can We Learn from PD?

In this country PD is not often used, confining itself mostly to academic circles. As it is, companies find it too idealistic and not structured enough.

But can we learn from PD? Yes. Perhaps we can benefit by shifting our focus more from designing the *system* to designing the *workplace*. If we adjust some of the PD principles to accommodate the realities of our resource-limited, time-critical environments, we can learn much from this creative, innovative process.

EMPOWERING GROUPS

We've all heard about the rewards of group empowerment—that is, having teams take responsibility for their own destiny. This involves giving people the power to make decisions about their day-to-day work such as planning, staffing, and exactly how to get the work done.

Most of us are familiar with "quality teams." Some companies, for example, have a network of quality teams that come up with ideas and innovations to increase quality and save money. These kinds of teams, however, operate separately from the standard reporting structure. They are not necessarily *empowered* to make ongoing business decisions.

Many companies do empower their working units. For example, Corning Inc.'s Information Services Division has enjoyed the following results by giving more power directly to groups:

- 48 percent fewer operations personnel than the industry average and 29 percent fewer total data center personnel than the industry average
- An increase in the percentage of help desk calls resolved immediately—from 75 percent to over 90 percent, with customer satisfaction increasing from 78 percent to 100 percent
- Operations services staff reduced by 20 percent while errors decreased 70 percent
- Cost savings over $500,000 annually (Kettelhut 1993)

So how does this all relate to facilitated sessions? Michael C. Kettelhut (of Alcon Laboratories in Fort Worth, Texas) has made some interesting observations. First of all, he noticed the similarity between empowered groups and facilitated sessions. Figure 20.2 shows the key success factors that Corning, Inc. uses for their empowered groups (described by Kettelhut). Then we added a column that compares these factors with those of facilitated sessions. It's interesting how closely they align.

But this analogy is not completely parallel, is it? There's one difference. Empowered groups are ongoing, while facilitated groups are not. Empowered groups enjoy whatever life span the corporate structure allows (in other words, until the next reorganization). On the other hand, the longevity of facilitated groups depends on the length of the project. However, can this be changed? Can facilitated groups become ongoing entities, continuing long after the first project is complete?

Kettelhut answers these questions in the affirmative. He suggests creating JAD teams around business functions:

> When many organizations use JAD, they establish new teams for each new project, and team membership usually changes. Suppose we created "functional JAD teams" responsible for the ongoing development, implementation, and maintenance of applications in a given organizational function. We would be moving toward creation of empowered development groups. (Kettelhut, 1993)

These success factors for empowered groups . . .	*Correspond to these principles for facilitated sessions . . .*
Start with a vision and clear goals.	Set a clear agenda and define your objectives.
Ensure management commitment, visible support, and a willingness to take risks.	Management commitment is key to success.
Pay particular attention to middle managers and supervisors.	Involve the users.
Involve staff in all phases of the project.	Full-time participants must attend the entire session. All participants are equal.
Communicate!	Yes! That's what facilitated sessions are all about.
Keep your eye on the ball.	Keep the session on course.
Educate all those involved.	Use a trained facilitator.
Develop a reward system that promotes success.	User involvement means better results.

Figure 20.2 Comparing empowered groups with facilitated sessions.

That's an interesting concept! Would it work? In our company, the participants vary for every session. Even when projects are along the same business lines, the uniqueness of the projects may call for different user areas to attend. At the same time, however, core groups do tend to continually represent the various business lines. For variable life insurance products, for example, we always count on a common nucleus of five people to participate. In that sense then, part of the group carries on through the various projects. Perhaps this core group could become a distinct "functional JAD team" as Kettelhut describes.

Who Are You
Selling To?

Know Thy Customer

Want to
Buy a JAD?

Expanding
Your
Business

Benefits of Facilitated Sessions

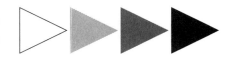
MARKETING YOUR SERVICES

How do you get the word out about your JAD services? Do you work really hard to produce quality results and know that virtue is its own reward? Oh, if it were only true! But not in this cutthroat, dog-eat-dog world. As much as we are facilitators at heart, we must use some of that energy for selling our services as well. We must spread the word and, at times, even do the commercials.

This chapter has several quotes from Sue Leonard of Amoco Oil Company. At a Midwest JAD Facilitators' User Group, she gave an excellent presentation on how to market facilitated meetings.

WHO ARE YOU SELLING TO?

First of all, who are your potential customers? Who will reap the benefits of your services? Here are some aspects to consider when identifying your market.

Who Runs the Projects?

You need to determine who actually makes the major decisions on development projects. Is it the users or IS? Although we like to think the users make these decisions, it really depends on the organization. And sometimes it can vary within the organization. In some areas, the users let IS decide whether to use JAD. So do not overlook the IS project managers. However, a common mistake in marketing JAD is to focus only on IS:

> I can give you a personal example of a misdirected marketing effort. When I first started facilitating, I assumed that my best customer would be Systems Development. My promotional efforts were aimed at systems managers and supervisors, and emphasized the advantages of compressing data-gathering time, and so on. I soon found out I was fishing for little fish, like smelt in a lake full of salmon. The biggest buyer of facilitated meetings in our company was the user! (Leonard 1993)

You need to look at your market carefully, so you avoid targeting the wrong people. Do not hastily cast your marketing probes in all directions at once. Instead, learn who has the authority to decide about bringing in your services and focus your marketing there.

Who Needs the Help?

Seek out the people who have the large work loads—the ones with projects too big and staffs too small. These are the ones who can really use your help. This may seem obvious, but this marketing focus is often overlooked.

Who Are the Innovators?

If you are introducing JAD into your organization, begin by targeting the innovators. You know who these folks are. As Leonard describes:

> These are the people who were the first to get an ATM card, the first to try grocery ordering on their terminals at home, the first in your company to adopt structured programming, Information Engineering and quality. (Leonard 1993)

These people are more likely to be open to a new approach and will put more into making it succeed. As JAD becomes used and accepted, you can expand your target market to those who respond more conservatively to new ideas.

KNOW THY CUSTOMER

The first priority is getting to know the people who can use your services. Explore their needs. What are their problems? You need to identify the "ouch" in their work—that is, the corporate pain that bugs them daily. What problems are on their minds? What do they complain about at the lunch table? You *don't* often hear people lament, "Oh, I'm so concerned about increasing our productivity." More likely they grumble about having too much work and too little time, or particular departmental conflicts that plague them every day.

If you already work with these people, this research is easier to accomplish. If not, then your challenge is greater, but certainly not impossible. Here are some ways you can get to know the concerns of your potential customers.

Talk with Them

Of course, this is the most direct way to link to the right people. Although the ultimate goal is to sell your services, this initial discussion focuses on exploring their needs, so that later you can intelligently show how JAD can help.

Depending on your relationship with the person, you can do this either formally (in a meeting) or informally over lunch, for example. Naturally, each of these approaches assumes a completely different nature. Informally, your queries are spontaneous, meandering between "how's your family?" and "have you seen any good movies lately?" to the real business matters at hand. A conference-room meeting, on the other hand, calls for more structured questions.

Following are some sample questions you might ask. Remember, these questions are not an inflexible tally of what to ask verbatim. They are simply expressions of what you would like to get out of the conversation. Phrase your questions on the basis of the relationship you have with the person you are talking with.

- *Scope.* What exactly is the nature of your work? What services do you provide? Who uses these services? What other departments do you work with?

- *Goals.* What are your department goals? (If possible, have the person quantify these goals.) Do you have to produce a certain number of items? Service so many clients? Or is the goal less quantifiable? (For example, keeping the customers "happy.")

- *Obstacles.* What are the biggest obstacles to these goals? In other words, what has prevented you from reaching these goals in the past? What makes your job difficult?

- *Wish you could've.* What would you like to accomplish in your department that you haven't been able to?

- *Meetings.* Do you frequently hold meetings to make decisions or do planning of any sort? How do these meetings go? Do they take place over several sessions? What keeps the meetings from being effective?
- *Issues and conflicts.* Do you have any impending issues that have gone unresolved? Are there conflicts within your department (or with other departments) that you would like to settle?

Once again, remember to take care in this line of questioning. You don't need to uncover the nitty-gritty details of perennial rifts within the department. They may not want to give you that kind of information anyway. You don't need the details. You only need to know that issues exist that could be resolved.

All this information provides the foundation for your return visit later when you show them how your facilitation services can help solve their dilemmas.

Read What They Read

Here is something you can easily do. Find out the publications that your potential customers read. What magazines and journals do they subscribe to? What reading material do you see on their desks or book shelves? You might be wondering, who has time to read what somebody else reads, when we barely have time to read what *we're* supposed to read? Nevertheless, this is a good way to find out what's hot in their line of business, what problems they face, and which buzzwords they use.

Hold a Focus Group

Have you ever been to a focus group where people gather in a room to answer questions posed by an interviewer? Sometimes the room has a one-way mirror where the interviewer and the group answering questions remain on the mirrored side, while the curious onlookers hide on the other side to observe the session through the transparent glass. Although holding a focus group may be extravagant for some (in tight times, we've had trouble justifying coffee and Danish, let alone focus groups), you could gain much from this kind of research. Sue Leonard recommends this as one way to do your "customer detective" work. She says:

> A focus group is a market research technique used to determine customers' attitudes, values and beliefs. You can invite current customers to a focus group to find out why they used JADs. You can have another session with people who aren't using JADs to understand their issues and problems. (Leonard 1993)

You could hold the focus group on various levels of formality. For example, you could go all out and hire a market research firm to administer the questioning (in the room with the one way mirror). Or you could simply hold such a meeting yourself, taking an hour or two to ask questions to seasoned JAD users or potential new customers. This veers away from the true focus group concept, but it may be all you need.

WANT TO BUY A JAD?

Now that you have gathered information about people who can use your services, it's time to turn those *potential* customers into *your* customers, into bona fide JAD users. Here are some approaches to getting the word out about JAD and your other facilitation services.

Prepare a White Paper

Create a summary of the JAD process for *senior management*. Describe how it works, list the benefits, identify the projects that could use JAD, suggest a proposed pilot project, and provide testimonials from satisfied JAD users. The purpose of this first step is to get senior management behind the effort to bring JAD into the company.

Produce a Brochure

You can assemble a small booklet about your services. We did this years ago when we first brought JAD into the organization. We sent it to all the officers of the company and any other managers involved in making decisions about how projects get done.

This booklet was part informative and part marketing. The information part described how JAD works because, at that time, no one in our company had ever heard of it. And the marketing part showed how JAD could help them.

The contents of your brochure or booklet depend on your audience and the nature of your services. Here are some ideas.

- *What is JAD?* Explain the technique, but be brief. You want to get to the next part very quickly.
- *How JAD Can Help.* Yes, it's the WIFM (What's In It For Me) that people want to hear. How is JAD going to solve their problems?
- *JAD Roles.* This describes who does what during a JAD.
- *Who Uses JAD?* If you are introducing JAD for the first time in your company, include testimonials and success stories of other companies using JAD. Include quotes from these other companies about how JAD worked for them. Quote this book! (See the quotations in the

"Benefits of Facilitated Sessions" section in this chapter.) One of the easiest parts of our research has been finding success stories from JAD users. You can find them in various journals and publications as well.

If you have used JAD for a while, and want to expand your services to other parts of the company, you can use quotes and success stories from your own organization. Your own customers can be your strongest supporters. Certainly the most convincing testimonials come from people your audience knows and respects. There's nothing like a good quote from the same person who rides the elevator with your potential customers.

- *Kinds of JADs.* Give examples of how JAD can be used. Although JAD is often used for defining requirements and designing systems, explain how the same techniques can be used for other projects as well, such as strategic planning and deciding between alternatives. And, of course, include other services you offer as well. (More about this later.)

Our contacts from the facilitators' group in Europe passed along a couple of sample publications from companies in the United Kingdom. For example, National Westminster Bank produced an 8.5-by-11, 20-page booklet that includes some nifty graphics and a page of endorsements from satisfied customers. National Power produced a 6"-by-8", canary yellow, spiral-bound handbook that includes the do's and don'ts of JAD, a glossary of terms, and a flow chart of the JAD phases. British Telecom produced two separate 3.5"-by-6" quick reference guides—one for the clients and one for the facilitators. These include workshop critical success factors, the pros and cons of various presentation aids, and a centerfold of . . . yes, the JAD room.

Give a Presentation

Here's a way to reach a lot of people in one session. Your challenge, however, is to include enough substance to satisfy an audience with a wide range of needs and problems.

What is the best audiovisual format? There are several possibilities. You can use overhead transparencies, some board talk, or even a video if you have the resources to create one. We prepared a JAD presentation using slides. We called it "The Power of JAD." We covered the grim statistics (quotes revealing the immensity of IS backlogs and the price we pay for waiting until after the system is designed to identify errors), how JAD can help, the JAD roles, the kinds of JAD projects (showing its diversity), and some spicy JAD success stories. The slide medium allowed us to bring JAD to life with photos of various executive sponsors (familiar faces to those in the audience), JAD sessions in progress (with more familiar participant faces), various room setups including our off-site location, visual aids including a board full of magnetics and a flip chart with a typical agenda, and even a photo of our CASE tool in action.

Around the presentation room, we hung typical flip charts used in sessions. We also brought along some magnetics which we used as we guided the group through a typical JAD task of deciding between two alternatives. Specifically, the group had to decide which family vehicle to buy—a station wagon or a mini-van. By participating in this mock example, they experienced the flavor of team participation in a workshop environment.

Your presentation can be very effective in any medium from overhead transparencies, to slides, to sophisticated multimedia software. Or you can simply talk to them straight. But we suspect that if you are doing JADs, you are quite comfortable with using visual aids to enhance your presentation.

Hold a Seminar

Another way to reach your potential customers is to hold a seminar. Craig Peters (of United Technologies Hamilton Standard in Windsor Locks, Connecticut) is among 12 facilitators who support 7500 employees. As part of their marketing program, they offer sessions that help empower people and add value to teams throughout the company. Their impressive list of course offerings includes benchmarking, creative problem-solving, conflict management, presentation skills, and team facilitator training. These sessions give the facilitators visibility, and consequently, more requests for services.

In seminars, people will get to know you and your staff. As you weave in vignettes about your work, they will understand more about the services you provide.

Write Articles in Company Newsletters

If you have an internal IS or company newsletter, write articles on JAD. Describe some of the success stories in your organization. Include people's names and details on a project or two. Announce a schedule of upcoming sessions.

Collect JAD Success Stories

In addition to summarizing and quoting success stories in your brochure, presentation, or seminar, keep a collection of articles on how companies are using JAD. You never know when you can pass one along. For example, after you meet with someone about your services, you can follow up by sending an article or two about other companies using JAD.

Here's a good tip: If you send an article as it is, copied and stapled, chances are that most people will observe its length (three or four full pages, for example). Then considering their busy schedule, they will likely set it aside with the best of intentions to read it when they get the time. (Don't we all have one of those read-later piles, which unfortunately often turns into a two-foot, read-never pile?) Instead, highlight the strong points of the article. This way, you dramatically increase the chances of it getting read. Simply use a colored marker to box off a paragraph or two. As they say, underline the good parts.

You can find examples of articles containing success stories in the bibliography of this book. Or you can do a computer search at your local library. "JAD" is an official entry in the Computer Literature Index used by libraries across the country. The ABI/INFORM index is also another good source.

Close the Sale

Now that you have met with your potential customers, perhaps chatted with them in the hall, maybe gave a presentation, or sent them brochures and articles, you're ready for the final step. Your marketing is not complete until you've made them your customer. In other words, it's not over until you close the sale.

This is the part, as Sue Leonard describes, where you hand them your business card and invite them to try your services. Here is an example of how you might express this invitation:

> Weren't you interested in IE projects? We have an interactive IE design session set for next Tuesday. Why don't you drop by and observe the session between 1:00 and 2:00? I'll call you to firm up the arrangements. (Leonard 1993)

Or for other kinds of services, you could say something like this:

> Didn't I hear that your group wanted to improve your documentation on the next system? I'll send you a copy of our meeting documentation, so you can see if that's closer to what you want. (Leonard 1993)

EXPANDING YOUR BUSINESS

We talked about how you can reach out, probe the territory, and identify new potential customers. All this leads you to more business. And once you are providing your services throughout the company, then all you need to do is keep up with the good work, right? Well, perhaps that will work in the beginning. But any good business owner knows that to keep pace, you need to continually stay aware of your customers' changing needs and adjust your services accordingly. The more narrow your services, the more vulnerable you are to inevitable changes. But if you have diversified your services, you can easily adjust when those changes come.

You can break down the services you already provide and repackage them into smaller parcels for your customers. We all know that for a customer to first use JAD requires an element of risk. It's quite a commitment to bring in outside people (who your customer has not worked with) and actually allow them to take over tasks that have traditionally been handled by the project managers, analysts, and programmers.

Well, an old standard marketing strategy for this obstacle is to begin working with a new customer on a platform of low commitment. For example, there's the builder who advertises "No Job Too Small." Or the landscaper who sells you a nice bush in hopes some day to get a contract to landscape the whole development. Consider IBM. You can purchase one PC for your desk or you can bring in a bank of mainframes for millions of dollars. You probably wouldn't do the latter without having some success with the former. The small stuff leads to the big stuff.

So what is your "small stuff"? Break down your services. You:

- Facilitate meetings.
- Provide decision support.
- Analyze requirements.
- Improve business processes.
- Create documentation.
- Design and prepare visual aids, and so on.

Can you add these service segments to your inventory?

In our company, we have been called upon to do such services as analyze the data for a field compensation system and help set up a data dictionary, moderate nonJAD meetings for any number of subjects, create a "how to" guide for a homegrown project tracking system, resolve a problem between two people with a persistent conflict, and revise an insurance product training guide. We have even been asked to do such "sophisticated" tasks as creating flip charts for other peoples' meetings!

Getting your foot in the door with small-scale tasks makes your customers all the more likely to consider you when the big projects come along. Here is an example from Sue Leonard:

> I was asked to take notes in a meeting that a client decided to facilitate himself. While I never got business from that person, two of the people in the meeting were so happy with my documentation (and were dissatisfied with the amateur facilitator) that they asked me to facilitate a

meeting for them. This helped me expand my business into a new organization. (Leonard 1993)

Another good reason to segment your services is to make sure you have work to carry you through the slower times. Most businesses have their peaks and valleys. During the valleys, how do you allocate the staff that you hired for the peaks? Perhaps these smaller services can carry you through until the next season when the JAD job jar is overflowing once again.

BENEFITS OF FACILITATED SESSIONS

There is somebody wiser than any of us, and that is all of us.

—Napoleon Bonaparte

Understanding the benefits of facilitated sessions can help in your marketing. Keep in mind, though, the point is not to offer your customers a generic list of benefits. You need to find which ones apply to them, then focus on those items that you know relate directly to their weak spots.

The benefits of JAD were highlighted in Chapters 1 and 2. This section brings them all together and offers some comments from other companies using JAD. This information can help in your own efforts to gain management support in bringing the process into your organization.

Many companies using JAD have recorded productivity gains from 20 to 60 percent in the Analysis and Design phases of the life cycle. These companies include American Airlines, IBM, Mutual of New York, CNA Insurance, Carrier Corporation, and Bell Canada. (Rush 1985) CNA Insurance of Chicago began using JAD in the early 1980s. A joint productivity study conducted from December 1982 to March 1983 with IBM showed the JAD process had boosted productivity at CNA by more than 50 percent. (Gill 1987)

These companies, as well as our own, have found that the JAD process can do the following:

- Accelerate systems development.
- Increase the quality of the final product.
- Improve project estimates.
- Improve user relations.

The following sections describe each of these benefits.

Accelerate Systems Development

As our industry confronts the challenge of our burgeoning application backlog, we also feel the pressure to build systems faster.

> "The tendency to have systems take 2 to 2–1/2 years to develop is long gone," says Hugh Nickel, director of systems services at Midas International Corp. in Chicago. *"You've got to provide a business system for a user in three to six months in order to be effective."* (Nykamp and Maglitta 1991)

JAD shortens the systems development time. It can reduce months of meetings to one workshop attended by everyone involved in the project. Agreements are finalized because everyone affected is there. This group consensus short-circuits the traditional approval process, where draft documents sit on reviewers' desks for days or weeks. Also, by defining more about the business in the beginning, you spend less time later having to gather additional specifications or clarifications from users to fix what was not coded correctly in the first place. The result of this up-front group consensus is earlier implementation.

Exactly how much time you can save with JAD varies. Companies using JAD typically experience a 40 percent reduction (and sometimes more) in project design time.

Increase the Quality of the Final Product

JAD brings all the right people together to accomplish objectives. An impartial facilitator guides the participants through a formal agenda. These ingredients produce a final product that is more complete and accurate than could be attained using traditional methods.

> We've probably held 60 JAD sessions in the last year alone, and there hasn't been a single session in which we haven't been able to make improvements to the business process before we even talked about automating anything.
>
> —Carl Wilson
> Senior VP, Management Information Systems
> Grand Met/Pillsbury
> (Freedman 1991)

After using JAD for two years, Wilson mandated that all new systems development projects use JAD.

Improve Project Estimates

For many companies, JAD has dramatically improved their project estimates. The best way to describe this benefit is to cite a recent study. Two researchers (Lederer and Prasad 1993) polled 115 randomly selected computing managers, analysts, and programmers. The average number of employees in each company was 9,950. Sales for these firms ranged from $200,000 to $22 billion, with a mean of almost $2 billion. The study revealed the following four most common causes of inaccurate project estimates:

- Frequent requests for changes by users
- Overlooked tasks
- Users not understanding their own requirements
- Insufficient communication between users and analysts

Certainly numerous techniques can help address these problems (for example, using a structured systems development methodology). However, JAD is especially made to tackle these dilemmas.

This study found that the greatest cause of inaccurate estimates is "frequent requests for changes by users." The unending river of user requests is the epitome of traditional systems development. This does not belittle the validity of these requests. After all, users are telling us exactly what they need. Rather it is the way these requests continue to dribble in via a series of phone calls, forms, and loosely structured meetings.

The second cause of inaccurate project estimates is "overlooked tasks." Tasks are much less likely to be overlooked when everyone comes together in the same room and views the totality of what needs to be accomplished. The third cause, "users not understanding their own requirements," is squelched in the process of group discussion, consensus, and documenting the decisions. And the fourth cause, "insufficient communication between users and analysts," leads directly into the next JAD benefit.

Improve User Relations

A good system design does not guarantee user satisfaction; you can win the battle but lose the war. You can design the best system of your career, but still find that the users are alienated and the programmers won't talk to you.

JAD helps close the traditional communications gap between IS and users. It creates an atmosphere of problem-solving and cooperation among participants. And it generates group identity. At the beginning of the session, people are reserved, cautious, and even skeptical, especially if JAD has not yet been used in the company. By the end of the session, a spirit of creative enthusiasm has developed and people have relaxed to the point where, even in the midst of intense technical endeavors, jokes and laughter often punctuate the proceedings. For example, FINA Oil and Chemical said:

> JAD was established at FINA to give our users a "say" in designing their computer systems. At that time, the relationship between [IS] and the users was a very poor one . . . . Our major benefits include improved

working relationships between [IS] and the users, a more structured way of collecting user requirements, and our users actually taking ownership of their systems. (Guide International Corp. 1989)

After participating in a session, participants are generally convinced that JAD is the best way to get the job done and they often request that it be used for their next project. They are satisfied with the system because *they designed it*. It is their system. Being committed to its success, they are more willing to participate in system testing and implementation.

The benefits of JAD are not limited to only these. Your services may have other byproducts as well, some totally unexpected. For example:

- *Increase awareness.* In facilitated sessions, everyone learns about other people's perspectives. Technical people gain an understanding about how the business runs. For example, they might for the first time see clearly the users' business processes. At the same time, users learn what technology can do for them. For example, they might understand more about LAN technology or GUI screen design. During the sessions, users also gain an appreciation for the work done by IS. We often hear comments from user participants like, "no wonder it takes so long to make changes to the data base."

- *Identify unworthy projects.* Consider this scenario: A group of participants assemble in a JAD session to define requirements for a new software package. The *expected* outcome: a final requirements document and a signed contract with the vendor of choice. But instead, the outcome is: "This new package is too expensive. Cancel the project." Certainly money is saved in cases like this.

  Do not overlook the value of JAD in determining that a project should not be done. Sometimes you need the group dynamics to get a clear picture of the project and realize it's not worth doing.

PART
6

*IN
CLOSING*

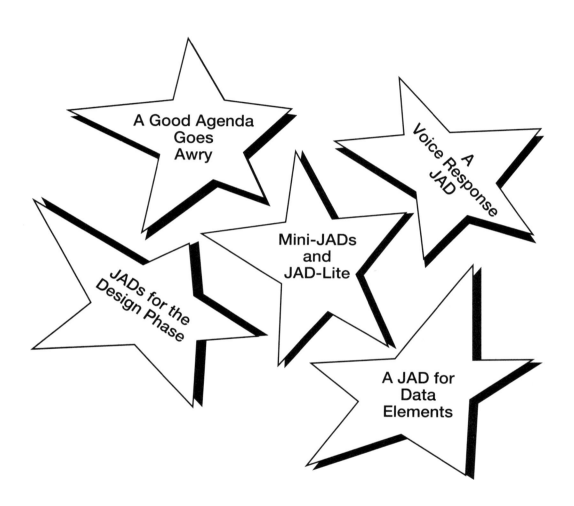

TWENTY TWO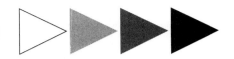

JAD ANECDOTES

In closing, we would like to describe some high points (and low points!) from our JAD projects as well as some tales from other companies. Among them is a project that people called a JAD but it was not, a project where someone tried to completely change the agenda in the session, and a project that addressed nothing but data elements.

A REVIEW MEETING DOES NOT A JAD MAKE

When JAD becomes successful in an organization, people often want to align themselves with the process. For example, one facilitator in the midwest described the following experience:

> We had been doing JADs for years. Everyone in our group had been trained in the process and had numerous JAD stories under their belts. Last year, a rather intense project was evolving to become what would be the biggest endeavor to come down the company pike in 10 years. The IS managers of the project preferred to work independently, not using our JAD resources, but using traditional methods and hiring mostly consultants for defining requirements.
>
> Then we heard that this group was planning a JAD session. We inquired about the agenda and found that they planned a three-week

round of meetings to review 10 requirements documents that had already been prepared, and in some cases, were considered by the analysts to be virtually complete.

We felt that this series of meetings was worthy in its own right, but to call them JADs was unspeakable! When we requested that these meetings not be referred to as JADs, their reply was, "What does it matter what we call them? How can you be concerned about such a minor detail?"

The IS project manager figured if they called these meetings *JADs,* they could get management's commitment to free up people to participate in three-weeks worth of full-day sessions. So that was that. With our six-year track record of productive JAD sessions, management had no problem mandating all the invitees to attend.

Well, we figured that was the beginning of the end for JAD as we knew it, and now anyone could call any kind of meeting a JAD. And it probably would have been the case, had not the project team become so overwhelmed. They had to deal with the enormous scope of requirements and the business area's lack of acceptance towards these already documented assumptions. The IS project team realized that much work needed to be done to complete and get consensus on the business requirements. In the end, they called in our JAD group to renovate the planned review meetings into full-blown requirements-gathering, features-defining, consensus-building JAD sessions.

On such short notice, we were just barely able to prepare. It wasn't the best JAD we ever held, but it worked out. The requirements were agreed upon, and the users were satisfied. But we still have not solved the problem of what to do when someone wants to call their review meeting a JAD session!

What's in a Name?

Indeed, this concern is valid. When JAD becomes successful, there is a natural inclination to share in its success. And why not? The more people that use it the merrier. But unfortunately some people connect with JAD only as far as using its name, and then end up using techniques that vary from (or are contrary to) the JAD approach.

The problem is, if the name "JAD" is misused, the perception of JAD will decline. Here is an example: A facilitator described to us how he had diligently prepared for a three-day session involving 14 participants. The JAD process was new to the company, so most were not familiar with it. The morning of the session, the Executive Vice President stopped by the facilitator's office to inform him that he had invited 28 more people to the session because he thought their exposure to this critical project would be educational.

You can imagine the result. What had begun as a carefully planned session of 14 people, mushroomed into a chaotic collection of more than 40. The session was a total flop. And the word went out that JAD was a disaster.

So what is the answer to this dilemma? Do you tell the Executive Vice President that this is not a party and to uninvite the 28 people? Here is one way to handle the situation.

MINI-JADS AND JAD-LITE

How do you handle situations where people in the company refer to ordinary meetings as "JADs"? Dan Bartoes (an independent facilitation and Information Engineering consultant in Newington, Connecticut) offers this approach:

> The best way to handle this problem is to set clear guidelines on when JADs can be held and who can and cannot participate. For example, at one company, we set up guidelines that say JADs are held only when a certified facilitator is involved. This facilitator must have attended Gary Rush's six-day FAST course, and must use the prescribed methods including preparing properly, gaining executive sponsorship, doing interviews, and so on. Furthermore, no one invites additional people to the session without prior arrangement with the facilitator.
>
> Of course, enforcing this is a challenge. For example, one area of the company got around the guideline by saying their sessions weren't real JADs, but rather were more like "mini-JADs". So we also needed a way to control the proliferation of these JAD lookalikes.
>
> To handle this situation, we identified two distinct types of sessions: "FAST Sessions," which adhered to the rigorous standards of JAD, and "Facilitated Meetings", which may or may not be run by a certified facilitator, and do not necessarily involve as much preparation.

We can relate to Dan's experience. These "mini-JADs" seem benign enough, but they can easily catch on as new acceptable terms. When it comes to undermining the adherence to JAD principles, these references are just as insidious as referring to a review meeting as a JAD session.

In summary, beware of people figuring, "All we have to do is call it a JAD and we can get all the people we want to come to our meetings." It's important to not let anyone confuse JAD with the traditional meeting mania that we have fought to overcome. A mini-JAD does not a JAD make. And JAD-lite won't even help you lose weight.

A GOOD AGENDA GOES AWRY

Here is an episode about a facilitator who met with all the right people before the session, developed a well-planned agenda that everyone agreed upon, then in the session, found an assertive participant attempt to revise the whole agenda. Susan Burk (of American Management Systems in Manchester, Connecticut) describes this episode:

A well-planned agenda can be the difference between horror and success. I once facilitated a group that was doing a fact-finding mission with subject matter experts. The group developed and agreed upon the agenda. However, the Project Manager, who was also a team member, had some other issues on his mind.

During the session, the Project Manager sprang some major scheduling and resources issues on the unsuspecting participants. I'm sure he thought he was being efficient, and that addressing these issues would really help. But it was the wrong time and place. The group resisted but the Project Manager used his higher position to back the participants into a corner.

Before things got any more out of hand, I asked the group if they would like to change the agenda. I told them that we could certainly do so, as long as we all agreed to it. Furthermore, I explained that if we did make these changes, we would need to decide when to reschedule the original agenda.

The reality of rescheduling convinced the group that the original agenda was the current priority, and that the scheduling and resource issues could be deferred. This preserved the original agenda and defused the Project Manager without embarrassing him.

A VOICE RESPONSE JAD

In this project we designed the script for a voice response system. Our mission was to design an easy-to-use system for employees to enroll in (or change) their benefit plans by phone. For example, employees wanting to change from a traditional health plan to an HMO would call on the phone to make the change in the same way they use their phone at home to pay bills. In this way, they could make changes to their medical, dental, life, or disability plans.

Our company already had voice response technology in place for agents in the field. They can call for up-to-the-minute information about their clients' policies (such items as cash values, loan amounts, and paid-to dates).

About the Session

For this session, we brought together:

- Five people from Human Resources representing the various benefits areas
- Two IS people
- A facilitator and a scribe

The goal of the session was to write the script for the voice. This script would be like the typical, friendly (but somewhat robotic) voices you

encounter when calling certain organizations. For example, when you call the art museum, the voice might say, "Press 1 for membership information, press 2 for upcoming events, and press 3 to speak to a real person." In the same way, we needed scripting for employees to select and update various benefit plans.

A Voice-Driven Review Session

For the review session, we focused on the script. This is where we had some fun. As opposed to just documenting the script on paper, we presented the script as it would exist in its final form—that is, in voice. We used the services of the scribe's husband, Bruce, who is known for his smooth, radio-announcer voice. We taped Bruce reading the script.

To get this review session going, we first presented a humorous version of the script, using the voices of Mark (a programmer analyst) and Dave (the key programmer analyst on the project and also a part-time actor). They read various parts of the script using German, Chinese, and French accents. They used the voices of Katharine Hepburn, Jack Nicholson, Elmer Fudd, Ronald Reagan, and Bert and Ernie to satirize parts of the script. And Dave impersonated the distinctive voice of the company CEO. Being used to hearing the CEO give quarterly status reports and other lofty messages, people enjoyed hearing that same voice enrolling people in dental plans.

After that, we proceeded through the recording of the real script. Using this voice prototype, people were able to envision the final product, not just as words on a page, but in its true form, in voice. Consequently, many errors in flow that would otherwise not have surfaced were identified early on. When people did not like the wording, we stopped the tape and noted the revisions on hard copy. Sometimes people asked us to rewind the tape and listen again. We weren't sure how all this would fly, but in the end, it worked well. The key element was that the output mirrored the medium in which it would finally be delivered.

Some Issues We Dealt With

The process we followed was very much like designing screen flow, including the error messages. All the same human factors pertained, such as the tone of the text and user friendliness. The only difference, really, was that we were dealing with voice instead of words on a screen. For example, just as with screens, we dealt with what to do when the caller:

- Forgets the choices
- Selects a choice that's not on the list
- Wants to undo what he just did
- Wants to exit the system

For this system, branching was complex and quite nested. For example, we dealt with branches that depended on:

- Which of the available HMOs the caller selected
- Whether the request was within or outside the open enrollment period
- Whether the caller was from the field or the home office

One peripheral issue was: What would this benefits voice response system be called? Some suggestions were Ben-a-phone, ABE (Automated Benefits Exchange), and BEN (Benefits Exchange Network). We chose the latter because of the link to Ben Franklin, a famous Philadelphian. It also supported the mission of administering "BEN"efits.

The Gender Controversy

Probably the biggest debate of the session was whether the real voice should be male or female. Some argued that since our other voice response system was male, the only politically correct approach was to make this one female. Some felt that a man's voice is more authoritative. Others felt that a woman's voice is more comforting. And still others were offended by both assumptions.

The group decided on the male voice, but not for any profound or ideological reasons. As it turned out, using the male voice that we had used for our other voice response system was a better deal. Since we already had digitized his voice for numbers, dates, and common messages, we wouldn't have to pay as much in recording charges.

The Conclusion

The programmer analyst turned the script into code for the voice response system. He sent all the script modules to the professional narrator for recording. Then a small pilot group tested the system with the real voice before going live.

In the end, BEN got a real workout. Soon after we went live, the company replaced all its health insurance providers with one company. Consequently, in a two-week period, over 1000 employees enrolled in their new plans by talking with BEN, the touch-tone administrator who never sleeps.

So what is in BEN's future? We plan to add more responsibilities to BEN's repertoire. Down the road, he will handle:

- 401K plans (including balances and loans)
- Payroll (People can request changes in deductions for such things as United Way contributions.)
- Vacations (People can call BEN to find out how many vacation days, personal days, and sick days they have used.)

SLEEPER JADS

We're *not* talking about great JADs that gained little visibility (as in "that JAD was a real sleeper"). On the contrary, these are JADs where it's easy to doze off. Following are several episodes of JAD sessions used for the traditional Design phase activities. As you will see, the tasks in these sessions tend to be repetitive and tedious, indeed.

JAD 1: Another Hundred Data Elements

This session had one objective—to define all the data elements for a new insurance product. In other words, what should the data base contain to support this new product? We also handled some data base design and open issues. But the main focus was on data elements.

By the end of the four-day session, the group had added five new records and 45 new data elements to the policy administration data base and modified 15 existing elements. For each data element, we identified the name, format (alphabetic, numeric, or alphanumeric), and length. We provided definitions that ranged from half a page to two full pages. All this information went into the final document, which was a prerequisite for several JAD projects to follow.

In this session, we developed several customized scribe forms to handle record definitions. For example, we had forms that identified which data elements would be contained in each record type as well as expected record volumes.

JAD 2: Another Eighty Transactions

The company wanted to produce a consolidated monthly statement for its clients. This statement would allow clients to review at a glance a summary of all their policy information and recent transactions. The business requirements had already been done. This JAD dealt with identifying all the existing transactions from the policy administration system that would feed this new client system. For each transaction, we needed to define the wording to print on the client statement. We prepared a customized scribe form to capture this information. A filled-in sample of this form is shown in Figure 22.1. We selected a scribe from the business area who was an expert on the various policy administration transactions.

The session was certainly not the most inspirational endeavor. Can you imagine going through 80 separate transactions, filling out the same scribe

TRANSACTION DESCRIPTION FORM

Transaction	1
Transaction code	2002
Transaction type	Historical
System source	CFO
How generated	External
Description	Premium Payment
Other parameters	Agency 13
Variables in the wording	V1- Time Period (1-12 months)
	V2- Premium due date
Wording of the client statement	Premium for (V1) months due by (V2). This amount is paid by the company.
Amount description	Gross modal premium

Figure 22.1 Scribe form for the Transactions JAD.

form for each one? Nevertheless, the people in the business area felt it was worthwhile and the programmers got all the information they needed to program the system.

JAD 3: Cornucopia of Calculations

We have defined calculations in several of our JADs. One such project involved the business area and IS people defining how various insurance pieces (such as premiums and dividends) would be calculated for a new product. These general calculations did not include actual formulas. Figure 22.2 shows a sample from the Policy Administration session. Although the

To calculate . . .	*Use these rules . . .*
Death Benefits	When calculating death benefits: • For death within 31 days following any unpaid premium, charge the pro rata part of the full modal premium up to the death date. • Allow scheduled increases up to the death date and charge the appropriate premium to the death date.
Modal Premiums	Given az due date and mode, the calculation determines a modal premium based on: • Rate data • Historical event data • Scheduled increase data
Bonus Dividends	Inside and outside additions reserves are combined for bonus dividend calculations. • When dump-ins occur during the policy year, use weighted gross funds based on the number of whole months between the effective date of the dump-in and the anniversary. • When dump-ins occur after the dividend has been calculated, pay no bonus dividend on the dump-in for that policy year.

Figure 22.2 Summary calculation definitions.

To calculate . . .	Use this formula . . .
Depreciation	Depreciation = system date (month/year) *LESS* purchase date (month/year) *TIMES* ((purchase price *LESS* salvage value) *DIVIDED BY* depreciation period))
Monthly Depreciation	Monthly Depreciation = (purchase price *LESS* salvage value) *DIVIDED BY* depreciation period

Figure 22.3 Detailed calculation definitions.

terminology may not be entirely clear (it is insurance-specific), you can get an idea of the kind of information that was captured.

In another project for a Fixed Assets system, we defined calculations in such detail that they were documented as formulas. We did not bog down the session by defining these formulas in the presence of all 18 participants. Instead, people from the business area prepared proposed formulas before-hand. In the session, the group reviewed them for accuracy and complete-ness. Figure 22.3 shows a portion of these calculations.

JAD 4: Endless Edits

One JAD project involved enhancing the underwriting process to support both individual and variable life products. This required expanding exist-ing data element definitions to accept variable life data and creating new data elements. To document this, we built a chart listing the data elements and their corresponding values. Figure 22.4 shows a portion of this chart.

Data Element	Values
Dividend Option	C = Pay in cash P = Reduce premium U = Unscheduled premium
Dump-in Separate Account	1 thru 8

Figure 22.4 Edits for data elements.

Edit No.	Warning Message
0050	Aviation questionnaire form needed
0051	Hazardous sports questionnaire needed
0052	HO specimen needed for this amount
0053	Electrocardiogram needed for this amount
0054	Chest X-ray needed for this amount
0055	Need blood profile, urinalysis, cocaine screen

Figure 22.5 Edits and their warning messages.

Another project involved defining the edits required for some new underwriting screens. Warning messages would display on these screens when certain conditions for policy approval were not met. For example, if a user entered a face amount for a new policy that exceeded a certain limit and no chest x-ray was included with the application, the system would display a warning: "Chest x-ray needed for this amount." Figure 22.5 shows a sample of these messages.

Processing requirements such as these may best be handled in separate, smaller meetings between the business area people and IS. But if many people are involved in the decisions, then a facilitated session will do fine.

The Pilot Project

Setting JAD Criteria

Training the Facilitator

Facilitator User Groups

Measuring JAD Success

Charging Back Your Services

Internal Consulting

JAD Contracts

JAD Evolution

TWENTY THREE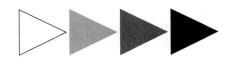

ASSURING
JAD SUCCESS

You now have the information you need to run a JAD project. But what do you do to actually bring JAD into your organization and make it successful? You can't just pick up a felt-tip pen and start making flip charts. You need to select a pilot project, set JAD criteria, train other facilitators who will assist you, determine ways to measure the success of the JAD process, and decide how much your services are worth.

THE PILOT PROJECT

It is especially important that your first JAD project be successful. To help ensure that this pilot project accomplishes your goals, select one that is:

- A small- to medium-sized project
- Moderately complex
- Unlikely to fail
- Not controversial
- Supported by eager, progressive users who have a strong need for the project results
- Certain to have strong management commitment

Nothing can absolutely guarantee the outcome you want on that first project, but selecting one with these attributes will give you a good chance of success.

JAD consultant Judy August further recommends picking a project that "incorporates many user interfaces (such as screens and reports), as they are more fun and rewarding to design than extensive processing routines." (August 1991)

SETTING JAD CRITERIA

JAD has a way of catching on in the organization. Overnight, skeptical users turn into strong JAD proponents. People will want to use JAD for anything that seems "jadable." This sounds good, but it can lead to problems due to limited resources. (And who has unlimited resources?) For example, you might have to turn down the following projects:

- An IS project manager and user are having trouble working together and you are called in solely to buffer a personality conflict between IS and the user department.
- The actuaries can't seem to find time to sit down and crunch out those detailed calculations, so a JAD is proposed solely to force a time commitment to the project.
- The business area would like to enhance a couple of printed reports that you originally designed in a JAD session.

Certainly you *could* use JAD for any of these situations. Nevertheless, to assure JAD is used effectively, you should set criteria for its use. For example, the criteria might say, JAD should be used for projects that:

- Have high business priority
- Have aggressive target dates
- Involve complex requirements
- Impact more than one department

To communicate these criteria to your company, you can produce a brief document or brochure that explains JAD and when to use it. Send this "manifesto" to business area and IS managers.

Properly used, JAD can save money. But it should not be used when less time-consuming management techniques would suffice. If you are not sure whether or not to use JAD on a project, ask yourself: How important is the project? How many departments are affected? Would the project benefit from an impartial facilitator? Could the request be handled directly between the programmers and the users? How complex are the requirements? And, most important, is the project worth the concentrated effort of 12 participants for three to five days? Measure your answers against the criteria you have defined to decide if the JAD process is appropriate and cost effective for that project.

TRAINING FACILITATORS

JAD success requires a trained facilitator. Once you have run a few JAD projects, you will need a way to get additional facilitators up to speed. Relying on one facilitator makes you vulnerable. For example, your one facilitator might get the flu and you'll need someone else to step in immediately. You also need backup for when people move on to other jobs. If you prefer outside training, there are many companies offering services relating to JAD and facilitation.

Some colleges and universities offer these courses as well. For example, The University of Southern Maine offers a certificate program in conflict management, which includes courses on facilitating groups.

Figure 23.1 lists some companies offering courses in facilitation. It focuses on courses relating directly to facilitation. For example, many of these companies also offer courses in data modeling, Information Engineering, and CASE as well.

Some companies actually certify facilitators who have had appropriate training and experience (like an "advanced degree"). As IBM describes:

> We have an aggressive training program and we provide an opportunity for the JAD leaders to be certified once they have had extensive experience and a long history of client success.

When considering companies that offer training, find out what the training session covers. The facilitator needs training in people skills as well as technical skills. JAD facilitators should be trained in:

- JAD process
- Communication skills
- Group dynamics and behavioral psychology
- Negotiation skills
- Methodology (for example, Information Engineering)
- CASE tools
- Meetingware
- Project management

JAD training courses are always beneficial. We feel, however, that on-the-job training is the best way to learn. Training a facilitator can be done in three steps:

Company	*Training Courses Offered*
American Management Association (AMA) P.O. Box 319 Saranac Lake, NY 12983 (800) 262-9699	• JAD: The Key to Rapid Development of Quality Systems
APLAN Information Services, Inc. 4020 Birch Street, Suite 107 Newport Beach, CA 92660 (714) 975-1307	• Odyssey® technique and software tool
ATLIS Performance Resources, Inc. 6011 Executive Boulevard Rockville, MD 20852 (301) 770-3000	• JAD Overview Seminar • Method Leader Training • Facilitation Skills and Techniques • Advanced Facilitator Seminar
Business Reengineering Resources, Inc. 6805 Canal Bridge Court Potomac, MD 20854 (800) 618-5699	• Facilitation Skills for Business Reengineers • The JAD Institute: JAD Facilitator Training • Facilitation Skills for Information Systems Managers
Computer Sciences Corporation (CSC) Consulting 1 University Park Waltham, MA 02154 (617) 647-0116	• Facilitating Business Solutions: Basic Skills
The DBA Group 4020 Birch Street, Suite 107 Newport Beach, CA 92660 (714) 263-9111	• Modern JAD Facilitation Training • Downsizing Through Reengineering using Modern JAD Facilitation • JAD Certification Program
EDGE Productivity Group 436 Roberts Avenue Suite 201 Syracuse, NY 13207 (315) 471-2810	• Joint Application Development Training
Ernst & Young Suite 2800 2001 Ross Avenue Dallas, TX 75201 (214) 979-1700	• Facilitated Session Leader Training for Information Technology

Figure 23.1 Companies offering facilitation training

Company	*Training Courses Offered*
Facilitated Services International, Inc. 401 Spruce Brook Road Berlin, CT 06037 (203) 828-6640	• Facilitation: A Practical Approach • Team Building

Gould-Kreutzer Associates, Inc.
River Court, 10 Rogers Street
Suite 120, Box 3
Cambridge, MA 02142
(617) 577-1430
	• Facilitation Tools for Building a
	  Learning Organization
	• Advanced Facilitation Skills: A
	  Systems Thinking Approach

IBM Skill Dynamics (800) 426-8322 Contact: local IBM representative	• Introduction to Joint Application Design • JAD Specialist Workshop
Interaction Associates 600 Townsend St., Suite 550 San Fransisco, CA 94103 (415) 241-8000	• Mastering Meetings • The Complete Facilitator • Facilitative Leadership
JAD Masters 38 Waller Avenue Toronto, Canada M6S1B9 (416) 769-9829	• JAD for Business Process Reengineering

JRH Associates, Inc.
5107 Leesburg Pike, Suite 2602
Falls Church, VA 22041
(703) 931-0930
	• Stragetic Planning Facilitation Skills
	  Training
	• Transition from Traditional to
	  Electronic Meeting Software
	  (EMS) Facilitation
	• Basic Facilitation Skills With
	  Traditional Tools

Leadership Strategies Institute 550 Pharr Road, Suite 850 Atlanta, GA 30305 (404) 233-1630	• Principles of Systems Facilitation • The Effective Facilitator • Advanced Facilitation Techniques
MCK Associates 7313 Hidden Creek Dallas, TX 75252 (214) 380-5719	• JAD Overview • JAD Facilitation and Group Dynamics • Group Dynamics and Team Building

Continued on next page

Figure 23.1 *(Continued)*

Company	Training Courses Offered
MG Rush Systems, Inc. P.O. Box 3186 Barrington, IL 60010 (708) 304-1464	• FAST Session Leader Training • Advanced Session Leader Workshop
Organizational Dynamics, Inc. (ODI) 25 Mall Road Burlington, MA 01803–4176 (800) ODI-INFO	• The Effective Facilitator • Advanced Team Facilitation • High-Performing Teams • Quality Action Teams/Problem Solving Techniques
Pierson Applications Development, Inc. 71 Michael Road Stamford, CT 06903 (203) 322-1606	• Facilitation Principles and Techniques Workshop • Advanced Facilitation Techniques
Process Improvement Institute Anthony Crawford and Associates 461 Lakeshore Road West Oakville, Ontario L6K1G4 (800) 4NEWJAD	• Business Engineering with Design in Mind
QED Information Sciences, Inc. P.O. Box 812070 Wellesley, MA 02181 (800) 343-4848	• Joint Application Design
Riva Training Institute 4800 Montgomery Lane, Suite 1000 Bethesda, MD 20814 (301) 652-3632	• Focus Group Moderator Training School
The Saunders Consulting Group, Inc. 1210 Sheppard Avenue East Suite 300 Postal Box 36 Toronto, Ontario M2K1E3 (416) 499-9944	• Facilitation 201 • Facilitation 301
Source 1 Training 4 East Sixth Street Hinsdale, IL 60521 (708) 920-9278	• JADs, RADs and ASAPs: Higher Quality in Less Time • JAD Facilitation and Facilitator Training • Introduction to SDLC Using JAD

Figure 23.1 *(Continued)*

Company	*Training Courses Offered*
Vanguard Information Architects 6223 108th Avenue NE Kirkland, WA 98033 (206) 889-8422	• Facilitation Training Course
Villard Lindsay & Company 45 Eager Court Marlborough, MA 01752 (508) 481-0211	• Facilitating and Building Self-Managing Teams • Facilitation Techniques for Building Group and Team Effectiveness

Figure 23.1 *(Continued)*

- In the first JAD project, the trainee works as an apprentice with an experienced facilitator. He observes all phases of the project. He attends the interviews, assists in preparing the documents and visual aids, and may even scribe the session.

- In the second JAD project, he co-leads with an experienced facilitator. Under this supervised live practice, the apprentice builds skills and confidence.

- In the third JAD project, the new facilitator is on his own. This person handles all the preparation work and leads the session.

The Organization for Professional Facilitation

Another source for information is the Organization for Professional Facilitation (OPF) This organization was created in September 1993 by a group of facilitators, vendors, and academicians who had an interest in developing a central resource for facilitators.

Among their endeavors, they produce a newsletter called *The Facilitator*, which covers facilitator training, conference notes, book reviews, automated tools, and other hot topics in facilitation. For more information contact:

The Facilitator
P.O. Box 670705
Dallas, TX 75367

FACILITATOR USER GROUPS

There's nothing like a room full of facilitators to invigorate your session-leading propensities. Accustomed as we are to a world fairly balanced between introverts and extroverts, and between leaders and followers, it's quite an experience to be surrounded by outgoing, vivacious, consensus-building, agenda-following facilitators, all of whom are used to running the show. Hearing about how other people are struggling through the same challenges as yours is always comforting and the information exchanged is invaluable. Furthermore you develop excellent contacts.

Here are some user groups active in this country and one from abroad. Hopefully you can join the group nearest you. If there's not one in close proximity, perhaps you could start one.

- Facilitators' Network (Hartford, Connecticut)
- Facilitators RoundTable (Boston, Massachusetts)
- Midwest Facilitators' User Group (Chicago, Illinois)
- Southwest JAD Users Group—SWJUG (Dallas/Fort Worth, Texas)
- Southeast/Atlanta Facilitator's Forum (Atlanta, Georgia)
- European JAD User Group (based in London, England as of this publication)

Many of the groups have a charter which officially describes their purpose. For example:

> Facilitators RoundTable exists to promote and improve facilitated interactive techniques among individual members and the community at large. The group shall share experiences and knowledge as well as investigate methodologies, tools, and techniques. Areas of interest may include training, marketing, implementation, and use of facilitation for system design and development and non-system related activities. (Facilitators RoundTable 1991)

Some user groups meet bimonthly (others meet quarterly) from October to June. Friday seems to be the most popular meeting day. Companies rotate the role of the sponsor, who provides the room and facilitator for the meetings. For example, last year Stone and Webster sponsored the Facilitators RoundTable. After one year of meetings at their site, they passed the baton to Blue Cross/Blue Shield of Massachusetts.

Usually, membership is limited to those actually doing facilitation. Vendor memberships are permitted with certain restrictions. As the European JAD user group so ably states:

> It is suggested that the group retains the right to exclude vendors of JAD techniques if information and experience is not given freely and/or the group becomes the target of a sales pitch. (European JAD User Group 1991)

What Happens at These Facilitator Fan Clubs?

These user groups discuss all the latest and greatest facilitator subjects. Each user group has its own meeting format. Some groups bring in outside speakers, others keep it more informal. The Facilitators RoundTable prefers a structured presentation in the morning and a roundtable discussion in the afternoon. The European JAD User group includes a "Pracniques" agenda item at each meeting where members share techniques or hot tips from their personal experiences.

Meeting topics vary. For example, here is a list of past meeting topics from the Midwest Facilitators' User Group:

- Brochure Basics: Putting Your Best Foot Forward (how to make your JAD marketing brochure effective)
- Honing Your Group Interaction Skills (how to get the best contribution from everyone in the group)
- Facilitator Profile: Tailoring the Personality to the Process (how to apply your strengths to improve your performance as a facilitator)
- Information Engineering: Getting your foot in the door and keeping it there (how to optimize user participation in JAD/IE workshops)
- Tips and Tricks (how to make your JADs successful)
- Creative BAAs or How Not to Create a Herd of Sheep (how to make creative use of workshops)
- VisionQuest Demonstration (a mock demo of a meetingware tool)
- Creativity Panel (techniques for helping people think creatively)

HOW DO YOU MEASURE JAD SUCCESS?

In a 1992 CSC/Index survey, "implementing measurement for systems development" made the top 10 list of critical issues for IS managers. (Rubin 1993) This burgeoning interest in measuring software productivity and quality can be attributed to such industry movements as SEI's process maturity model and the Baldrige Quality Award. However, the problem in measuring software productivity is this: unlike nuts, bolts, widgets, or automobiles rolling off an assembly line, there's nothing clear-cut you can count.

A Brief History of Metrics

The software industry is only about 50 years old (if you start counting from the ENIAC computer in 1943). Consequently the youth of the industry has served as an excellent excuse for not having to measure itself. But now, well into middle age, we find competition with foreign countries compelling us to pay closer attention to quality and productivity.

So what should we measure? For systems development projects, some companies still rely on counting lines of code (LOC). But what does LOC mean?

> Does [counting lines of code] mean all the lines a programmer coded during the development of a program (i.e., including throw away code, if any, and the code that was added, changed, or deleted because of specification changes), or just the lines in the final product? Does it include data definitions and comments, or just the executable statements? Unless LOC is precisely defined, the productivity measurements do not make much sense and the productivity comparisons are misleading. (Parikh 1982)

It was later shown that the LOC method was useless across multiple programming languages:

> Since there are now well over 400 programming languages in the world, usage of lines of code for productivity purposes is rapidly declining. (Jones 1993)

Indeed, Capers Jones has proposed that "LOC metrics be considered *professional malpractice* starting in 1995."

In 1979, function point metrics revolutionized software productivity measurement. This particular metric quantifies the total amount of function provided by the system by counting external inputs, outputs, interfaces, inquiries, and logical files of an application. In this way, you can track the development cost per function point, function points per person month, number of defects per function point, and so on. Function points are still the most popular metric in use today. In fact, there's even a user group called IFPUG (International Function Point Users' Group) dedicated to spreading the word on function points.

However, in a 1991 survey of IS organizations,

> . . . fewer than 1 in 5 had any measures in place beyond time reporting, and fewer than 1 in 100 had any operable productivity or quality measures . . . . Since 1980, more than 400 [IS] organizations have tried to put measurement in place; unfortunately, few (estimated at fewer than 80) have been successful. (Rubin 1993)

Can You Really Measure JAD Success?

While researching a report on Cobol preprocessors, Girish Parikh (programming metrics expert) asked several professionals for information on increasing productivity. One reply was:

The improvement in programmer productivity has not been measured statistically. Most shops do not measure productivity at all—they just have a gut feeling about it . . . .(Parikh 1982)

More than a decade later, most companies still rely on that "gut feeling." Practical quantitative methods have proved elusive. Thus, the key measure is still customer satisfaction. Quality means that the user requirements were met at the time the system went into production.

Why is measuring JAD productivity such a difficult task? The problem is, as they say in the world of science, there's no "control group" to compare results with. There's no second set of similar users and programmers who are given the same design challenge but instead of jadding it, do it the traditional way. In today's climate of budget cuts and downsizing, can you imagine proposing such an experiment to management? ("Well, boss, it's like this: We want to do the same exact development project *twice* with two separate teams, which will require an extra $150,000." The response might be less than pleasing.)

Believe it or not, someone actually did this test. In 1983, CNA Insurance Company in Chicago (one of the first organizations to use JAD) conducted a study on the productivity of JAD.

A control project that did not use JAD was compared with [a pilot JAD project]. The control averaged 5.2 hours per function point during the requirements and external design phases of development. The [JAD] pilot, on the other hand, averaged 2.5 hours per point, which equates to more than a 50% increase in productivity. (Gill 1987)

The Real Test

We feel that JAD success cannot be determined through counting lines of code or function points. The real evaluation comes down to this:

- *Work product.* Based on the final JAD Document, can the people on the project team easily continue with the next step in the project?

- *Commitment.* Does the project team endorse the decisions made in the JAD session and will they continue to be involved in the project? Do they want the project to succeed?

- *Enthusiasm.* Do the people in the business area feel the design will help them perform their jobs more effectively than before? Do they want to use JAD again?

There may be other criteria for measuring success. Some companies capture stats on the size of the system, key project characteristics, and the actual time and people required to complete the JAD project. Based on this

---

JAD User Satisfaction Survey

1. Do you feel that requirements/specifications that resulted
    from the session more accurately reflected those of the
    user than if they had been prepared in the more traditional
    manner?

				Much more accurate
Not at all				
1	2	3	4	5
			74%	26%

2. Do you feel any improvement in communications resulted
    from the session?

				Much improved
Not at all				
1	2	3	4	5
	11%	16%	42%	31%

3. Do you feel that the requirements/specifications were
    completed in less elasped time than they would have
    been using traditional methods?

				Much sooner
Not at all				
1	2	3	4	5
			53%	47%

Figure 23.2 JAD user satisfaction survey.

project history, they can estimate what resources will be needed for new projects. Other companies measure JAD success by counting the number of change requests received from users after the system is in production. For example, they might track requests for the first eight weeks.

Finally, there's the survey approach. The Royal Bank of Canada measured JAD success strictly on user satisfaction. (Brown 1987) Figure 23.2 shows the results.

CHARGING BACK YOUR SERVICES

Some feel that having to pay for facilitated services discourages management from using the process. For example, because of the expense, they might not bring in quality facilitators or they might abbreviate the session length. This is sometimes the case:

> [The company] had been constrained by resource control structures (ISD budgets and chargeback policies) from using facilitation staff in the prescribed way. Instead, they shortened workshop schedules to min-

imize facilitators' time (and thus the charge) or used facilitators already in their budget, even where such facilitators were actually *developers* assigned to the project. (Davidson 1993)

Similarly, in another company:

Workshops tended to be shorter as the ISD organizations came under financial pressure. Five day workshops were rare. Even two or three day sessions were sometimes squeezed into one day to reduce chargeback costs. (Davidson 1993)

Others feel that charging back *encourages* people to use the services. In fact, some recommend charging back a hefty amount, equivalent to consulting fees. This is based on the same psychology that governs the pricing of luxury cars and high-priced lawyers: If something costs a lot, people will perceive it as valuable.

In a survey to several facilitator user groups, we asked, "Do you charge back for your facilitation services? If so, how do you charge?" People responded:

17%   Chargeback by the hour

48%   Chargeback by the day

 7%   Chargeback by the project

28%   Don't chargeback

We chargeback for our services by the hour. These services have value; people know it and they are willing to pay for them.

INTERNAL CONSULTING

Another option is to set up an internal consulting group. This approach is similar to charging back for services, except the people charging back their time are much more accountable for bringing in business. The profit (or loss) doesn't necessarily affect their salaries directly, but the viability of the job position rests largely on the ability to cover expenses.

Consequently, these internal consulting positions include much more than just facilitating. Marketing and contract negotiation take on stronger roles. Internal consultants have to find their own internal clients. As Andrea Tannenbaum (of ITT Hartford in Hartford, Connecticut) says, "You have to cover the cost of not only your salary, but also your benefits, education, allocated overhead, and your bench time, too!" While some people are not as comfortable with the pressure this arrangement brings, others prefer it. As Andrea says, "I view this as *intra*preneuring. I am motivated by it. It's like running your own business."

How Much To Charge

As an internal consultant, how do you figure how much to charge your customers? As in any business, much of it is based on what the market will bear. For example, internal consultants in one New England company charge mostly by the actual session day. They do *not* charge additional fees for the preparation or documentation time. They figure that amount into the rates for the session days. Their charges generally run as follows:

- For half-day sessions, $500 per session day
- For full-day sessions, $1000 per session day
- For longer sessions (for example, three days or more), $800 per session day
- For extended projects, $500 per day (or sometimes they charge by the hour)

These are just guidelines. During slow times, this company might charge less. For example, at the end of the year when costs have already been covered, they offer a year-end special, charging only $500 per *full* session day. Charges are negotiated by the project and written into the contract.

JAD CONTRACTS

Some companies use contracts to formalize agreements between the facilitator and the person requesting services (the facilitatee). One facilitator passed along a list of the following contract components that she uses:

- *Project purpose.* This describes the intent of the JAD project. What is to be accomplished? For example, solving a problem, gathering requirements, or making recommendations.
- *Background.* This covers a brief history of how the project request came about. For example, a department wants to make a process more efficient, or meet schedules that have fallen behind, or improve the quality of a product.
- *Project Scope.* This defines the boundaries of the project. It includes the constraints, project schedule, people involved, and critical success factors. For example, "this is a three-month JAD effort, involving a two-day strategic planning session followed by a five-day data modeling workshop. The participants include five people from Accounting, three from Purchasing, and two from IS." (The contract would list the actual dates and people involved.)
- *Project Resources.* This describes who does what including who facilitates, sets up the meeting room, documents the session, as well as who makes the decisions.

- *Deliverables.* This lists the expected deliverables from the JAD effort. For example, a proposal, strategic plan, document, or recommendation.

- *Measurements of success.* This explains how you will measure your success. For example, are the users satisfied with the design? Can the programmers code from the specs?

- *Change of Scope Process.* This defines the process for handling scope changes. For example, will you require a new specification document or additional sign offs?

- *Project acceptance.* This identifies who needs to approve the deliverables. It includes signatures and the date of approval.

Figure 23.3 shows a typical JAD contract.

THE EVOLUTION OF JAD

This section covers the evolution of JAD. No, not the history of JAD (we already covered that), and not the phases of JAD through a project (we covered that, too). Rather, it describes how JAD (or any facilitated process) can change over time, once you bring it into your organization.

We are not going to reinvent the wheel on this, because Michael J. Cavaliere (of F.S.I., Inc. in Berlin, Connecticut) has already come up with an excellent analysis of how JAD can evolve in an organization. The following describes the five stages Michael has defined, the characteristics of each stage, and how you can handle the hazards that each stage offers.

Stage 1 (Implementation)

As in the implementation phase of anything (whether it be a software package, the JAD process, or a marriage), expectations are high. Most people involved expect full fruition of all promises made and have little inkling of the problems in store.

In this stage, the facilitator has probably had some training in running sessions or maybe even some limited experience. This freshman condition naturally induces the facilitator to operate "by the book." Sessions seem to take too long to prepare for. And the nervous facilitator tends to offer a high level of structure and control over the session. The spectrum of deliverables is narrow, because time has not yet allowed for creative uses of JAD. Success, however, breeds requests for broader use.

Furthermore, each session is well publicized (we go all out in the beginning to guarantee success) and morale is high as well.

In this stage, remember that preparation will take longer since you are

PROJECT CONTRACT
Production Line JAD Project
November 30, 1995

PROJECT PURPOSE
The Production Line JAD project will determine how to relieve the increased load on the production line during the summer season.

BACKGROUND
Over the last three summers, the increase in the production line load has caused us to miss deadlines in the late summer and early fall. This results in dissatisfied customers. (We lost customers on two occasions.) With customer retention being our number one focus for the upcoming year, the marketing area endorses this project as a way to improve its procedures.

PROJECT SCOPE
This project includes a three-month analysis and design effort. We will produce a list of possible solutions for handling the increased business in the summer season. After production management reviews the list, we will pilot the highest priority solutions (in the spring).

The list of possible solutions will address the production line only, from cutting to finishing. Suggestions for improving the supporting departments will be routed to those departments, such as Packing.

PROJECT RESOURCES

Executive Sponsor:	Elizabeth Taransky
Role:	Review and approve project contract.
	Provide resources, staffing, and facilities.
Facilitator:	Terry Silver
Role:	Prepare project contract.
	Arrange and schedule analysis and design sessions.
	Perform all JAD tasks.
JAD Team:	Barbara Dash (Training)
	Chris Hellman (Production Manager)
	Bruce Lee (First Shift Production)
	Phil Mugler (General Manager)
	Gail Trachtenberg (Engineering)
Role:	Analyze the problem.
	Design solutions.
Technical Support:	R & D Associates
Role:	Provide measurement study support

DELIVERABLES
List of recommended improvements
Implementation plan for the pilot project
Follow-up analysis of the pilot
Recommendations for full implementation

Figure 23.3 JAD contract.

MEASUREMENTS OF SUCCESS

Follow up analysis will be performed during the summer production schedule. Success will be indicated by no late deliveries with no increased operating expense.

CHANGE OF SCOPE PROCESS

Any change in scope will require a re-specification of the effort and signoff by the executive sponsor and production manager.

PROJECT ACCEPTANCE

Executive Sponsor: _____Date: _____

Production Manager: _____Date: _____

Figure 23.3 JAD contract. *(Continued)*

new to the JAD process. It's a bit like a first-time teacher preparing an initial curriculum and standing up in front of 20 kids.

Stage 2 (Maturing)

In this most productive stage, expectations become more realistic, the use of JAD expands, and the range of deliverables broadens. The focus of the JAD staff is more on the customers.

In this stage, beware of the mesmerizing effects of success. Don't become complacent and lose your edge. Keep management involved and aware of the value of JAD. If you do all these things, hopefully you can avoid the next stage.

Stage 3 (Ailing)

When JAD ails, facilitators become burned out, preparation is short-changed, and the term "JAD" tends to become applied to meetings that have nothing to do with JAD principles. All these characteristics are pathways to the danger zones of the next stage.

If you want JAD to continue, take action to reengineer the process. Make sure your approach aligns with company needs. This requires constant analysis, since the company is undergoing the stages of its own evolution.

Stage 4 (Expiring)

Ah, that fateful stage when facilitators transfer out to new assignments, users exclaim "Oh no, not another JAD!", and IS project managers say,

"Well we have some magnetics and flip charts, let's have our own JAD!" It doesn't get any worse than this.

At this stage, funding of JAD resources gets tough. And once you reach this stage, it's difficult to rejustify the funds. The best way to deal with this dilemma is to avoid this stage entirely by following the precautions described in stages 2 and 3. But if you find yourself caught in this difficult place, the next stage describes how to regain your footing and get back to the "good ol' JAD days."

Stage 5 (Renewal)

In time, people miss JAD's availability. Some will request the resources that are no longer there. And people may be somewhat confused about when to use JAD.

At this stage you have several challenges. One is marketing. You need to tune your product, work the old customer network, and do some fresh marketing. Then as JAD requests begin to rekindle, you need to justify funding. If you have trouble justifying new facilitator positions, you can bring in consultants to run several sessions to get the process rolling again.

Figure 23.4 summarizes these five JAD stages as they are likely to evolve in the organization. This is based on a similar chart prepared by Michael Cavaliere.

CONCLUSION

We have described for you the JAD process—its phases, psychology, tools, and techniques. You have read many JAD war stories and know that no two JADs are alike. You understand the importance of impartiality on the part of the facilitator, of having the right people in the session, and of following a structured agenda.

Now the question is this: Can you do it? Can you stand in front of 15 people for three days and guide them through the agenda for developing a strategic plan, deciding between two alternatives, or defining requirements for a new business process? Once you have management support, the only person left to persuade is yourself. The only thing standing between you and a stream of successful sessions is your own uncertainty. You can get through that only by jumping in and doing it. Then, after a couple of successful projects, your management and your users will understand what the process can accomplish. They will see JAD as an efficient way to get consensus in a group and produce a quality product in a shorter time. They will see the power of JAD.

Stage	Characteristics	What to Do
Implementation	• High expectations • High direction and structure in sessions • Narrow spectrum of deliverables • Sessions are highly publicized • Morale is high	• Understand that you are new to the process • Success breeds requests for more deliverables
Maturing	• Realistic expectations • Broader use of JAD • Increased focus on customers	• Don't be complacent • Keep management involved
Ailing	• Facilitators burn out • Preparation is short-changed • Other meetings are called "JADs" • No new customers	• Reengineer the JAD process • Realign with the company's changing needs
Expiring	• Declining use of JAD • Facilitators transfer out • Project leaders try to hold their own JADs • Funding of JAD resources declines	• Avoid this stage by following advice in stages 2 and 3 • Or take renewal steps in stage 5
Renewal	• Customers miss JAD's availability but are confused about its benefits and use	• Tune your product • Work the old customer network • Do fresh marketing • Justify funding

Figure 23.4 The evolution of JAD.

APPENDIX A:
SCRIBE FORMS
FOR THE
MANAGEMENT
DEFINITION GUIDE

This appendix shows the scribe forms used to capture information for the Management Definition Guide. In Phase 1 of a JAD project, the facilitator can give these forms to the key managers in the business area. These people research the requirements and complete the forms. The resulting information is compiled into the Management Definition Guide.

PURPOSE OF THE PROJECT

Figure A.1

SCOPE OF THE PROJECT

Impacted business areas:

_____
_____
_____
_____
_____
_____
_____

Expected growth of business:

_____
_____
_____
_____
_____
_____
_____

Impacted systems:

_____
_____
_____
_____
_____
_____
_____

Figure A.2

MANAGEMENT OBJECTIVES

1. _____
   _____
2. _____
   _____
3. _____
   _____
4. _____
   _____
5. _____
   _____
6. _____
   _____
7. _____
   _____
8. _____
   _____
9. _____
   _____
10. _____
    _____

Figure A.3

BUSINESS PROCESSES

1. _____

   _____

2. _____

   _____

3. _____

   _____

4. _____

   _____

5. _____

   _____

6. _____

   _____

7. _____

   _____

8. _____

   _____

9. _____

   _____

10. _____

    _____

Figure A.4

CONSTRAINTS

1. _____
   _____
   _____

2. _____
   _____
   _____

3. _____
   _____
   _____

4. _____
   _____
   _____

5. _____
   _____
   _____

6. _____
   _____
   _____
   _____
   _____

Figure A.5

RESOURCE REQUIREMENTS

PEOPLE
_____
_____
_____
_____
_____

PHYSICAL SPACE
_____
_____
_____
_____

HARDWARE
_____
_____
_____
_____
_____

OTHER
_____
_____
_____
_____
_____
_____

Figure A.6

ASSUMPTION

SUBJECT _____

DESCRIPTION _____

_____

_____

_____

_____

_____

_____

_____

_____

_____

_____

_____

_____

_____

_____

_____

_____

_____

_____

Figure A.7

OPEN ISSUE

ISSUE NO. _____

ISSUE NAME _____

ASSIGNED TO _____

_____

_____

RESOLVE BY (Date) _____

DESCRIPTION _____

_____

_____

_____

_____

_____

_____

_____

_____

_____

_____

_____

_____

Figure A.8

SESSION PARTICIPANTS

Who	Department	Mail Code	Role

Figure A.9

APPENDIX B:
SCRIBE FORMS
FOR THE
JAD SESSION

This appendix shows five sample scribe forms you could use to document decisions made in the JAD session. These particular forms apply to the Design phase of a systems development project. You can design your own forms based on the kind of JAD project you are facilitating.

DATA ELEMENT DESCRIPTION

DATA ELEMENT _____

LENGTH _____

FORMAT _____

DESCRIPTION _____

_____

_____

_____

_____

_____

_____

_____

_____

_____

_____

_____

_____

_____

_____

_____

_____

Figure B.1

FIELDS BY SCREEN

Screen Name _____

B=Bright N=Normal	I=Inquiry U=Update				
Screen Field Name	*B/N*	*I/U*	*Source*	*Target*	*Screen Field Values*

Figure B.2

SCREEN ACCESS BY JOB FUNCTION

Screen Name – – – – – – >

Job Function

I = Inquiry
U = Update

Figure B.3

SCREEN MESSAGE

SCREEN NAME _____

MESSAGE TYPE

Confirmation _____   Error _____   Other_____

CONDITIONS (When does this message display?)

_____

_____

_____

_____

_____

MESSAGE TEXT _____

_____

_____

_____

_____

_____

_____

_____

_____

_____

_____

_____

Figure B.4

REPORT DESCRIPTION

REPORT NAME _____

DESCRIPTION _____

_____

_____

_____

_____

FREQUENCY _____

COPIES _____

DISTRIBUTION _____

SORT BY _____

DATA ELEMENTS

_____   _____

_____   _____

_____   _____

_____   _____

_____   _____

_____   _____

Figure B.5

REFERENCES

Abuls, Tia, and Sue Leonard. 1993. "Creativity—Panel Discussion." *Midwest JAD Facilitators' User Group—January 19, 1993 Meeting.* April 28: 97–99, 101.

Adams, James L. 1974. *Conceptual Blockbusting: A Guide to Better Ideas.* New York: Addison-Wesley.

Aiosa, Frank J. 1989. "The Marriage of Sales and Technology." *Best's Review* (May):111.

Andrews, Dorine C. 1991. "JAD: A Crucial Dimension For Rapid Applications Development." *Journal of Systems Management* (March): 23, 26.

Andrews, Dorine C., and Naomi S. Leventhal. 1993. *Fusion: Integrating IE, CASE, and JAD.* Englewood Cliffs, N.J.: Prentice Hall, 6, 8, 69, 78, 192, 224.

Anthes, Gary H. 1992. "User Role Gains CIO Backing." *Computerworld* (February 24): 63.

August, Judy. 1991. *Joint Application Design.* Englewood Cliffs, N.J.: Prentice Hall, 97, 137, 138, 140.

Baum, David. 1992. "Go Totally RAD and Build Apps Faster." *Datamation* (September 15):80.

Borovits, Israel, Shmuel Ellis, and Orly Yeheskel. 1990. "Group Processes and the Development of Information Systems." *Information & Management,* (September):67.

Bozman, Jean S. 1992. "Fidelity's Development Plan Leans on JAD and Prototyping." *Computerworld* (September 21):74.

British Telecom of the United Kingdom. 1993. *Rapid Application Development (RAD) Workshop Guide* (March):39.

Brochu, Earl. 1992. "Making JAD Workshops Work." *Direct Access* (July 17):6.

_____. 1993. "New JAD Approach Taking Shape." *Computing Canada* (July 19):21–22.

_____. 1994. "High-Tech, Low-Tech and No-Tech in Teamwork." Correspondence from the author.

Brown, Darlene. 1987. "Everyone's Talking about JAD." *GUIDE 69* (Atlanta, GA). Session no. MP5471A (November 2):1–33.

Carey, Jean. 1991. "Quality Management and Performance Measurement in Information Services." *Carey Project Organization,* Ardmore, PA, 25.

Carmel, Erran, Joey F. George, and Jay F. Nunamaker, Jr. 1992. "Supporting Joint Application Design (JAD) with Electronic Meeting Systems: A Field Study." *Proceedings of the International Conference on Information Systems,* 223–232.

_____. 1992. "Supporting Joint Application Development (JAD) and Electronic Meeting Systems: Moving the CASE Concept into New Areas of Software Development." *Proceedings of the Hawaii International Conference on System Sciences* (January):331–340.

Carmel, Erran, Randall Whitaker, and Joey F. George. 1992. "Participatory Design versus Joint Application Design: Trans-Atlantic Differences in Systems Development." *Proceedings of the Participatory Design Conference* (November 6–7):115–123.

Carroll, Lewis. 1872. Reprint 1967. *Through the Looking Glass.* New York: Collier Books.

Chamberlain, Wilt, and David Shaw. 1973. *Wilt.* New York: Macmillan, 134–137.

Classe, Alison. 1993. "Don't Tinker with It: BPR It!" *Accountancy* (July):64.

Collins, Paul. 1993. "VisionQuest Demonstration." *Midwest JAD Facilitators' User Group—January 19, 1993 Meeting.* April 28, 73–84.

Corbin, Darrell S. 1991. "Team Requirements Definition: Looking for a Mouse and Finding an Elephant." *Journal of Systems Management* (May):28–30.

Crawford, Anthony. 1994. *Advancing Business Concepts in a JAD Workshop Setting.* Englewood Cliffs, N.J.: Prentice Hall, 75.

Crinnion, John. 1992. "Methodologies for Rapid Application Development." *Rapid Application Development.* England: Xephon plc., 1–7.

CSC PEP. 1993. "Rapid Applications Development." *Index PEP Paper 25* (August):28.

Currid, Cheryl. 1993. "A Case Against CASE: It's Expensive and Often Unsuccessful." *InfoWorld* (August 2):68.

Davidson, Elizabeth J. 1993. "An Exploratory Study of Joint Application Design (JAD) in Information Systems Delivery." *Proceedings of the Fourteenth International Conference on Information Systems* (December 5–8):271–278.

Doyle, Michael, and David Straus. 1993. *How to Make Meetings Work.* New York: Berkley Publishing Group, 3–4, 232–234, 237.

Dunlop, Stuart. 1992. "Practical Experience with RAD." *Rapid Applications Development.* England: Xephon plc., 19–25.

Eckerson, Wayne. 1992. "Users Enthused about Electronic Meetings." *Network World* (June 15):1.

Edwards, Pat, Gary Rush, and Miriam Wyrick. 1993. "Strategic Planning/BAA Workshop—Panel Discussion." *Midwest JAD Facilitators' User Group—January 19, 1993 Meeting* (April 28):55, 56, 59, 63, 64, 66.

Employee Benefit News. 1992. "Product Intended to Facilitate Bias-free Corporate Decision Making, Idea Generation." vol. 6, no. 9 (September):1.

European JAD User Group. 1991. *Constitution* (June 13).

Facilitators RoundTable. 1991. *Charter* (December 11).

Foss, W. Burry. 1993. "Fast, Faster, Fastest Development," *Computerworld* (May 31):81, 83.

Freedman, David. 1991. "What Do Users Really Want?" *CIO* (September 1):24, 26, 27.

Galitz, Wilbert O. 1993. *User-Interface Screen Design,* New York: Wiley.

Gardner, Martin. 1978. *aha! Insight.* New York: Scientific American.

Gill, Allen. 1987. "Setting Up Your Own Group Design Session." *Datamation* (November 15):88, 90.

Guide International Corp. 1989. *JAD Across the Life Cycle Project (MP-1417)* (July 1987—November 1989):1–87.

Hamilton, Rosemary. 1992. "Electronic Meetings: No More zzz's." *Computerworld* (September 14).

Hosier, Jeffrey. 1992. "User Survey—Development Methods and the Application Backlog." *Rapid Application Development*. England: Xephon plc:91.

Hsu, Jeffrey, and Tony Lockwood. 1993. "Collaborative Computing." *Byte* (March):113, 120.

Jiwani, Rif A., and Gary Coles. 1993. "Achieving Goals through Systems Technology and Teamwork." *LIMRA's MarketFacts* (March/April):36–38.

Johnson, Maryfran. 1990. "Drowning in a Sea of Code." *Computerworld* (December 25, 1989—January 1, 1990):10.

Jones, Capers. 1993. "Software Measurement: Why, What, When and Who." *American Programmer* (February):5, 19.

Kashdan, Norman R. 1991. "CASE and Distributed Computing Environments." *American Programmer* (July):32.

Kerr, James. 1989. "Systems Design: Users in the Hot Seat." *Computerworld* (February 27):87–94.

Kerr, James, and Richard Hunter. 1994. *Inside RAD*. New York: McGraw-Hill, 3, 14, 69.

Kettelhut, Michael C. 1993. "JAD Methodology and Group Dynamics." *Information Systems Management* (Winter):46–53.

_____. 1993. "Joint Application Development and Group Empowerment in MIS Organizations." *Strategic Systems*. vol. 6, no. 5 (May): 16–18.

Kirkpatrick, David. 1992. "Here Comes the Payoff from PCs." *Fortune* (March 23):93–97.

LaPlante, Alice. 1993. "Brainstorming." *Forbes ASAP* (October):48, 54.

Larsen, Gail. 1993. "Improving Outpatient Registration with TQM." *Healthcare Financial Management* (August):77, 79–80.

Lederer, Albert L., and Jayesh Prasad. 1993. "Systems Development and Cost Estimating." *Information Systems Management* (Fall):37–41.

Leonard, Sue. 1993. "Marketing Your Services." *Midwest JAD Facilitators' User Group—January 19, 1993 Meeting* (April 28):23–50.

MacKay, Charles. 1980. *Extraordinary Popular Delusions and the Madness of Crowds*. New York: Crown.

Malone, M., and W. Davidow. 1992. "Virtual Corporation." *Forbes ASAP* (December 7):104–107.

Martin, James. 1984. *Information Systems Manifesto*. Englewood Cliffs, N.J.: Prentice Hall.

_____. 1990. "Improving Application Development Productivity." *I/S Analyzer* (March):2–6.

_____. 1990. "JAD Workshops Help Capture Design Specifications." *PC Week* (February 19):58.

_____. 1990. "Success of JAD Workshops Depends Largely on Leaders." *PC Week* (February 26):51.

Mills, Michael. 1992. "RAD and I-Case." *Rapid Application Development*. England: Xephon plc; 35.

Mimno, Pieter R. 1991. "What is RAD?" *American Programmer* (January):28–37.

Minasi, Mark. 1994. *Secrets of Effective GUI Design*. Alameda, CA: SYBEX.

Nykamp, Susan, and Joseph Maglitta. 1991. "Software Speeder-Uppers." *Computerworld* (August 26):51–53.

O'Leary, Meghan. 1993. "The Reluctant Ally." *CIO* (March):50, 52, 58.

Parikh, Girish. 1982. *How to Measure Programmer Productivity*. Wellesley, MA: Q.E.D. Information Sciences; 10–12.

Phillips, Lawrence D., and Maryann C. Phillips. 1993. "Facilitated Work Groups: Theory and Practice." *Journal of Operational Research Society*. vol. 44, no. 6; 534, 535, 540, 547.

Post, Brad Quinn. 1992. "Building the Business Case for Group Support Technology." *1992 Proceedings of the 25th Hawaii International Conference on System Sciences, Vol. IV, Information Systems: Collaborative Technology Organizational Systems and Technology*, pp. 34–44.

Rubin, Howard. 1993. "Debunking Metric Myths." *American Programmer* (February):25.

Rush, Gary. 1985. "A Fast Way to Define System Requirements." *Computerworld* (October 7):11–12

———. 1990. *Interactive Design User Seminar;* p. 10.

Saunders, Paul R. 1991. "Effective Interviewing Tips for Information Systems Professionals." *Journal of Systems Management* (March):28–31.

Schrage, Michael. 1993. "Trying Groupware on for (Down)size." *Computerworld* (August 30):33.

Shelby, J. B. 1994. "How Can I Tell If I Have High or Low Metabolism?" *University of California at Berkeley Newsletter* (March):8.

Spates, John, and Bev Grou. 1993. "Groupware—Panel Discussion." *Midwest JAD Facilitators' User Group—January 19, 1993 Meeting* (April 28):87–91.

Strunk Jr., William, and E. B. White. 1979. *The Elements of Style,* New York: Macmillan.

Systemation. 1986. *Fast Start In Systems Analysis*. FS 5–3, 1–2.

Tozer, Jane. 1992. "True RAD—The End of the Application As We Know It." *Rapid Application Development*. England: Xephon plc, 45, 46.

Weinberg, Randy S. 1991. "Prototyping and the Systems Development Life Cycle." *Journal of Information Systems Management* (Spring):50.

Wetherbe, James C. 1991. "Executive Information Requirements: Getting it Right." *MIS Quarterly* (March):51–53, 57, 62, 64.

Williamson, Mickey. 1989. "Joint Application Design—Getting It Right the First Time." *CASE Strategies*. vol. 1, no. 7 (December):1.

———. 1991. "Beyond Rube Goldberg." *CIO* (March):54, 55.

Yourdon, Ed. 1992. "Whither or Wither?" *American Programmer* (November):20.

———. 1993. "Editor's Comments." *American Programmer* (June):1.

———. 1994. "What Ever Happened to 1993?" *Guerilla Programmer* (January):8.

Zahniser, Richard A. 1993. "Storyboarding Techniques." *American Programmer* (September):9.

INDEX

A

Abilene paradox, 178–179, 259
Acronym alert exercise, 220
Administrative items, reviewing in JAD
　　session, 118–119
Affinity analysis technique, 211
Agenda for JAD session:
　　how to prepare, 91–93
　　putting on flip chart, 101–103
　　reviewing in session, 119
　　samples, 91–92
　　straying from, 183–184, 345–346
　　in Working Document, 97
AJAD, 240
Alternatives, deciding between, 227–233
Approval form, 160
Approving the JAD Document, 160
Assumptions:
　　description of, 52–53
　　gathering during interviews, 55
　　in JAD session, 121
　　in Management Definition Guide,
　　　66–67
　　scribe form for, 382
　　in Working Document, 97
Audio visual aids, see Visual aids

B

Beat it to death exercise, 220
Benefits of facilitated sessions, 336–339
　　accelerating systems design, 336–337
　　compared to traditional systems design,
　　　4–6
　　improving project estimates, 337–338
　　improving user relations, 338–339
　　increasing quality of final product, 337
　　summary of, 6–7
Brainstorming, 207–210
Brochure for marketing your services,
　　331–332
Business Process Reengineering, 19–20
Business processes:
　　creating data flow diagrams, 78–89
　　in the Management Definition Guide,
　　　65
　　scribe form for, 379
　　in the session, 123–126

C

Calculations in JAD session, 351–352
CASE, 238–251
　　code generation, 239–240
　　graphics, 239
　　in JAD, 240–245
　　problems with, 169
　　prototyping, 239
　　quality assurance, 240
　　in RAD, 317
　　repository, 240
　　success in, 249–250
Changing hats exercise, 205
Changing seats exercise, 219–220
Charging back your services, 366–367
Checklists:
　　for JAD supplies, 113–115
　　for JAD tasks, 113
Closing JAD session, 144, 146

Code and test validation life cycle phase, 292
Code generation with CASE, 239–240
Commitment, see Management commitment
Commitment errors in groups, 178
Companies using JAD, 16–17, 23–26
Computer Assisted Software Engineering, see CASE
Computer screen projection, 106
Conflict:
  between users and IS, 188–189
  deciding between alternatives, 227–233
  how to handle, 186–189
Consensus, 32–33
Constraints:
  defining, 66
  scribe form for, 380
Consulting:
  charges for, 368
  setting up internal group, 368
Context diagram, how to create, 83–84, 85
Contracts for JAD projects, 368–369
Creativity in the session, 201–225
Criteria for holding JADs, 356–357

D

Data elements:
  in JAD session, 122–123, 349–350
  sample descriptions, 122
  scribe form for, 386
Data flow diagrams, 78–79
  balancing, 88
  context diagram, 83–84, 85
  data flows, 80
  data stores, 80
  external entities, 80
  how to create, 78–89
  processes, 80
  samples, 79–80, 84, 85, 86, 87, 125
Data modeling, 77–78, 122, 240–245, 287–288
Data stores in data flow diagram, 80
Decomposition diagrams, 89
Digressions, how to handle, 183–184
Distribution:
  for JAD Document, 144, 146, 171–172
  for Working Document, 97–98, 99
Dominators:
  how to handle, 189–190
  in meetingware sessions, 260
Downsizing a department, 305–307
Dysfunction in groups, see Group dysfunction

E

Edits in JAD session, 352–353
E-JAD, 282. See also Meetingware
Electronic Meeting Systems, 256. See also Meetingware
Electronic white boards, 106
Empowered groups:
  benefits, 324
  compared to facilitated sessions, 324–325
  description of, 323–324
EMS, 256. See also Meetingware
Entity-relationship diagrams, see Data modeling
Error message location on screens, 134
Estimates, improving project, 337–338
Estimating JADs, 288
Evaluation form, 145
Evolution of JAD, 370–373
Executive sponsor:
  description of role, 38–39
  in resolving conflict, 188
External design life cycle phase, 290–291
External entities in data flow diagram, 81

F

Facilitator:
  authority of, 168–169, 195–196
  characteristics of, 40–41, 51, 193–198
  description of role, 39–42
  in meetingware sessions, 262, 267–270
  psychology of, 198
  reporting structure, 39–40
  training, 168, 357, 361
Field prompts for screens, 135
Fields by Screen scribe form, 387
Fields for screens, 129–130
Fill in the blank exercise, 205
Final Document phase, see also JAD Document
  description:
    detailed, 149–161
    summary, 10–11
  for large projects, 279
  list of tasks, 114
  time required, 69
Flexible target dates, 72
Flip charts:
  how to prepare, 101–103
  setting up in meeting room, 109
Floor plan exercise, 205–206
Focus groups, 330–331
Force field analysis technique, 213

Forms, see also Scribe forms
  Approval, 160–161
  Evaluation, 145
  for JAD session, 385–390
  for Management Definition Guide, 375–384
  JAD Supplies checklist, 115
  JAD Tasks checklist, 113–114
Full-time participants, 45–47. See also Participants in the JAD

G

Goal-setting problems, 178
Graphics with CASE, 239
Ground rules for session, 119–120
Group dynamics in JAD:
  advantages of groups, 176
  building group identity, 179–181
  conflict, how to handle, 186–189
  digressions, 184
  dominators, how to handle, 189–190
  dysfunction of groups, 175–179, 180
  having right people in the room, 167–168, 181–183
  humor, use of, 223–225
  indecision, how to handle, 227–233
  scope creep, how to prevent, 183–184
  shy users, how to encourage, 190
  side-bar conversations, 190–191
  starting on time, 186
  staying flexible, 184–185
  when facilitator should interrupt, 185–186
Group dysfunction, 175–179, 180
Groupthink, 176–177
Groupware, 255–256. See also Meeting-ware
GUI screen design, 136–138
GUIDE study, 287–293

H

Headings in screen design, 136
Highlighting in screens, 135–136
History of JAD, 4
Human factors in screen design, 133–136
  error message location, 134
  field prompts, 135
  highlighting, 135–136
  indents, 135
  uppercase vs. lowercase letters, 134
Humor in JAD sessions, 223–225

I

I-CASE, see CASE
Icosahedron technique, 281–282
Indecision, how to handle, 227–233
Indents in screens, 135
Information Mapping, 153–155, 156
Internal design life cycle phase, 291–292
Interviews, see also Meetings
  for marketing your services, 329–330
  questions to ask, 54–55, 58
  tips for success, 56–61
  using forms, 55
  with business area people, 76
  with IS, 76
Issues, see Open issues

J

JAD (Joint Application Development):
  across the life cycle, 285–301
  benefits, see Benefits of facilitated sessions
  criteria, see Criteria for holding JADs
  definition, 3
  measuring success in, 363–366
  misuses, 343–345
  origin, 4
  participants, see Participants in the JAD
  phases, see JAD Phases
    in RAD, 317, 322
  scheduling, see Scheduling the JAD
    for specific purposes, see Types of JAD
  team, see Participants in the JAD
  ten commandments, 172–173
  terminology, 29–34
  topics for, 285–286
  training, see Training
  types of, see Types of JAD
  use in companies, 16–17
  user groups, 361–363
JAD Approval form, 161
JAD Document:
  approving the document, 160
  assembling the document, 156–158
  changes after release, 160–161
  converting from the Working Document, 150–151
  for defining corporate policy, 309–311
  distribution, 144, 146, 147
  editing the document, 155–156
  with Information Mapping, 153–155
  memo for, 160
  organizing the source documents, 152

JAD leader, see Facilitator
JAD overview, 167–168
JAD phases:
    chart of resulting output, 10
    Final Document phase, 9–10,
      117–146
    JAD Project Definition phase, 8–9,
      51–73
    Preparation phase, 9, 95–115
    Research phase, 9, 75–93
    Session phase, 9, 117–146
    summary of, 7–10
JAD Project Definition phase:
    description:
      detailed, 51–73
      summary, 8–9
    for large projects, 277–278
    list of tasks, 114
    time required for, 69
JAD Supplies checklist, 113–115
JAD support person, 42
JAD Tasks checklist, 113, 114
Jargon (technical), minimizing in session,
    170–171
Joint Requirements Planning, 318
JRP, see Joint Requirements Planning

K

Kepner-Tregoe method:
    description of, 227–233
    for platform decisions, 299, 301
    for software package evaluation, 299,
      300

L

Large projects, 275–282
Leader, see Facilitator
Life cycle:
    breaking out of, 303–312
    methodologies, 295
    phases of:
      code and test validation, 292
      external design, 290–291
      internal design, 291–292
      maintenance, 293–294
      post implementation evaluation,
        292–293
      project definition, 287, 296
      requirements, 287–288, 296–297
      software package evaluation,
        288–290, 298–301, 329–332

M

Magnetics
    for data elements, 123, 124
    how to prepare, 103
    sample shapes, 104
    for screen flow, 127–128
    where to buy, 103
Maintenance life cycle phase, 293–294
Management commitment, 166
Management Definition Guide:
    producing the document, 61–67, 68
    reviewing in the JAD session, 120–121
Management objectives:
    defining, 64–65
    described in the session, 119
    flip chart for, 102
    scribe form for, 378
Mandated target dates, 73
Marketing your services:
    focus groups, 330–331
    identifying your customers, 327–328
    interviewing your customers, 329–330
    packaging your services, 334–336
    techniques for spreading the word,
      331–334
Measuring JAD success, 363–366
Meeting room:
    how to find, 71–72
    illustration of, 110, 111
    offsite, 71
    requirements for, 71–72
    setting up, 109–111
Meetings, see also Interviews
    with IS, 76
    with management, 53–55
    with people in business area, 76
    pre-session, 107–108
    review meeting, 158–160
    with scribe, 100
    statistics on, 7
Meetingware:
    benefits, 257–260
    definition, 255–256
    description, 256–257, 264–266
    history, 257
    justifying, 272–273
    productivity gains, 271–272
    shortcomings, 260–263
    study of, 262–263
    tips, 266–270
    training, 269–270
    uses, 270–271
    vendors, 257

Memos:
  for distributing working document, 99
  for final document, 160
  for JAD session, 73
  for review meeting, 158
Metrics, brief history of, 363–364

N

Newsletter for facilitators, 361
Nominal group technique with Post-it
  notes, 214–219

O

Objectives, see Management objectives
Observers, 48–49, 220–221
On-call participants, 48
Open issues parking lot technique,
  211–212
Opening the JAD session, 118–121
  reviewing administrative items, 118–119
  reviewing agenda for session, 119
  reviewing ground rules, 119–120
  reviewing Management Definition
    Guide, 120–121
  reviewing session objectives, 119
Open issues:
  in defining corporate policy, 309–311
  description of, 52–53
  on flip chart, 102–103
  gathering during interviews, 55
  in handling conflict, 187
  in JAD session, 141–143
  in Management Definition Guide, 61
  scribe form for, 383
  for voice response project, 348
  in Working Document, 98
Out of the box thinking, 206–207
Overhead projection:
  how to use, 103–106
  setting up meeting room, 110–111
Overview of JAD, see JAD overview

P

Package evaluation, see Software package
  evaluation
Participants in the JAD:
  description of roles, 37–49
  executive sponsor, 38–39
  facilitator, 39–42
  full-time participants, 45–47
  importance of, 166–167

JAD support person, 42
  listed in Management Definition Guide,
    67–68
  listed in Working Document, 97–98
  number of people, 183
  observers, 48–49, 220–221
  on-call participants, 48
  sample participation list, 47
  scribe, 42–45
  scribe form for, 384
  selecting the right people, 181–183
Participants in PD session, 322–323
Participation List scribe form, 384
Participatory Design, 322–323
Pass the cube exercise, 204
Pavlovian rewards exercise, 206
PD, see Participatory Design
Phases:
  of JAD, see JAD phases
  of life cycle, see Life cycle phases
  of RAD, see RAD phases
Pilot project, 355–356
Planning JADs, 280–281
Playscripts, 309, 310
Post implementation life cycle phase,
  292–293
Preface:
  for JAD Document, 151
  for Management Definition Guide,
    62
  for Working Document, 96
Preparation phase:
  description:
    detailed, 95–115
    summary, 9
  for large projects, 278
  list of tasks, 114
  time required for, 69
Pre-session meeting, 107–108
Prioritizing projects, 311–312
Processes in data flow diagram, 80
Project Definition life cycle phase:
  in periodic payments project, 296–298
  using JAD for, 287
Projection panels for computer screens,
  106
Prototyping:
  in CASE, 239
  description of, 251–253
  in PD session, 323
  in RAD, 317
Purpose of the project:
  defining, 63
  scribe form for, 376

Q

QDP exercise, 203–204
Quality assurance with CASE, 240
Quality in final product, 18, 337

R

RAD:
    description, 315–318
    history of, 315–316
    integrating CASE tools, 317
    and JAD, 317, 322
    measuring success, 319–320
    phases of, 318–319
    rapid prototyping, 317
    roles, 319
    SWAT teams, 317
    timeboxing, 317
    training, 321
    when to use, 318
    why not being used, 320–321
Rapid prototyping, see Prototyping
Report Description scribe form, 390
Reports:
    defining new, 140
    gathering preliminary information for,
        89–90
    in JAD session, 138–140, 141
    preparing descriptions of, 138–139
    sample design, 141
    sample list of, 139
    scribe form for, 390
Repository with CASE, 239
Requirements life cycle phase:
    in periodic payments project,
        296–298
    using JAD in, 288
Research phase:
    description:
        detailed, 75–93
        summary, 9
    for large projects, 278
    list of tasks, 114
    time required for, 69
Resource requirements
    defining, 66
    scribe form for, 381
Review meeting
    description, 158–159
    memo for, 158
RIPP (Rapid Iterative Production Proto-
    typing), 316
Risky-shift behavior, 177

S

Scheduling the JAD, 67–71
    finding a room for session, 71–72
    flexible target dates, 72
    half-day or full-day sessions, 70–71
    length of session, 68
    mandated target dates, 73
    off-site sessions, 71
    time required for each phase, 69
Scope creep, 183–184
Scope of the project:
    defining, 64
    scribe form for, 377
Screen Access by Job Function scribe form,
    388
Screen Message scribe form, 389
Screens:
    creating prototypes of new, 251–253
    defining field prompts, 130–131
    defining fields, 131
    defining screen flow, 126–128
    defining screen messages, 131, 132
    designing in External Design life cycle
        phase, 290–291
    gathering preliminary information,
        89–90
    GUI design, 136–138
    how to design, 128–138
    human factors in, 133–136
    in JAD session, 126–138
    menu design, 126–128
    preparing descriptions of, 128
    scribe forms:
        Fields by Screen, 387
        Screen Access by Job Function, 388
        Screen Message, 389
    security requirements, 132–133
Scribe:
    characteristics, 43
    how to select, 43–45
    promoting the role, 100–101
    role:
        in JAD, 42–45
        in RAD, 319
    taking notes in session, 143
    training, 99–101
Scribe forms:
    for JAD session, 385–390
    list of:
        Assumption, 382
        Business Processes, 379
        Constraints, 380
        Data Element Description, 386

Fields by Screen, 387
Management Objectives, 378
Open Issue, 383
Purpose of the Project, 376
Report Description, 390
Resource Requirements, 381
Scope of the Project, 377
Screen Access by Job Function, 388
Screen Message, 389
Session Participants, 384
for Management Definition Guide, 55,
375–384
using forms, 238
sample of Transaction Description
form, 350
Security requirements for screens,
132–133
Selecting the JAD team, see Participants in
the JAD
Session objectives, reviewing in JAD session, 119
Session phase:
description:
detailed, 117–146
summary, 9
group dynamics, see Group dynamics
for large projects, 278–279
number of people in session, 183
over preparing for, 171
scribe forms, 385–390
time required, 69, 167
when scribe takes notes, 143
Working Document in, 118
Software package evaluation:
in periodic payments project, 298–301
using JAD in, 288–290
Starting from scratch exercise, 202
Stick figure technique, 213
Storyboarding, 211–212
Strategic planning, 304–305
Stress test exercise, 221
Stretch break exercise, 221
Survey:
activities done in sessions, 285–286
chargeback for services, 367
description, 13
Joint Application Design or Development, 29–30
non life cycle topics in sessions,
303–304
tools used, 236
where facilitators report, 40
Survey, on JAD user satisfaction, 366
SWAT teams, 317, 319

T

Table arrangement for meeting room, 109,
110
Table of contents:
for JAD Document, 152
for Management Definition Guide, 63
Tabs for JAD Document, 157–158
Tape recorders in the session, 106
Target dates, 72–73
Templates for word processing, 237–238
Ten commandments of JAD, 172–173
Test plans in External Design life cycle
phase, 291
Title page:
for JAD Document, 151
for Management Definition Guide, 62
for Working Document, 96
Traditional systems design, 4–6
Training:
companies offering, 358–361
for data modeling, 244–245
of facilitator, 357, 361
of meetingware facilitators, 269–270
of scribe, 99–101
Transactions in JAD session, 350–351
Transparencies, see Overhead projection
Trends toward JAD, 17–23
Truth and lie exercise, 202
Types of JAD for
code and test validation, 292
defining calculations, 351–352
defining corporate policy, 307–311
defining data elements, 349–350
defining edits, 352–353
defining transactions, 350–351
defining voice response script,
346–349
downsizing a department, 305–307
estimating, 288
external design, 290–291
internal design, 291–292
large projects, 275–282
maintenance, 293–294
periodic payments project, 295–301
planning, 280–281
post implementation evaluation,
292–293
prioritizing projects, 311–312
project definition, 287, 296
requirements gathering, 287–288, 296
software package evaluation, 288–290,
298–299
strategic planning, 304–305

U

Uppercase vs. lowercase letters on screens, 134
User groups for facilitators, 361–363
User relations, 338–339
User review board in RAD, 319

V

Visual aids:
    computer screen projection units, 106
    electronic white boards, 106
    flip charts, 101–103
    how to prepare, 101–107
    magnetics, 103
    overhead projection, 103–106
    in PD session, 322–323
Voice response JAD, 346–349

W

Word processing, 237–238
Working Document:
    converting to final document, 150–152
    distribution, 97, 99–100
    how to prepare, 95–99
    memo for, 99
    preface for, 96
    using in JAD session, 118